LOVERS FOR LIFE

Strengthening and Preserving
Your Marriage

LOVERS
for life

KENNETH C. MUSKO, COMPILER
JANET M. DIXON, EDITOR

CHRISTIAN PUBLICATIONS, INC.
CAMP HILL, PENNSYLVANIA

CHRISTIAN PUBLICATIONS, INC.

3825 Hartzdale Drive, Camp Hill, PA 17011
www.christianpublications.com

Faithful, biblical publishing since 1883

ISBN: 0-87509-994-7

© 2004 by Kenneth C. Musko

*Note: Italicized words in Scripture quotations
are the emphasis of the authors.*

Contents

Preface

by Ken Musko

The institution of marriage has today become distorted and perverted from God's original plan. It is my belief that if marriage continues on this destructive course, in the next ten to twenty years, very few people will choose to marry. Today over fifty percent of marriages end in divorce, and that now includes a high percentage of Christians.

We live in an imperfect world, and people seem to think that a good marriage is when two perfect people come together. It isn't! It's when two *im*perfect people come together and learn to enjoy their differences. We need to enjoy filling each other's emotional tanks with words of affirmation, affection and a servant attitude. We need quality time together and to learn to be kind to one another.

Couples who play and pray together stay together. The simple act of praying together reduces that horrible Christian divorce rate to 1 in 1,000. One reason the percentages plummet so dramatically is that praying together brings a couple closer to God. Your relationship to your spouse is directly proportional to your relationship with God: As you draw closer to God, you will grow closer to each other.

When we use words that uplift, edify, praise and encourage each other, our emotional tanks stay filled. We also need many hugs and kisses each day just to maintain our emotional levels. If you're not doing this, you're already at risk. As we spend quality time together with acts of servanthood and kindness, we begin planting seeds of encouragement that will help our marriages and families grow. When our communications begin to deteriorate, so do our relationships.

Guarding our words is also important. Once you say something hurtful, you can't take it back. I often ask couples to place a dab of toothpaste on a small piece of paper. Then I ask them to try to return the toothpaste back into the tube. It's impossible! I encourage them to tape the paper on the bathroom mirror to remind them that once you say something hurtful, you can't take it back. It's also a reminder to use holy and acceptable words that uplift, edify and encourage one another.

Many influences in today's culture (TV, Internet, movies, etc.) sow seeds destructive to Christian marriages and the family. Because of "sowing of the flesh," one of the major dangers facing couples today is adultery. With such busy schedules and so many outside influences, couples are falling into the arms of anyone who romances them (and fills their emotional tanks). Scripture tells us that whatever you sow, you will also reap. Too often, we are sacrificing our marriages on the altar of materialism. We still come up empty and unsatisfied.

In marriage, the grass sometimes seems to look greener on the other side of the fence. That's because it's Astroturf. If we would just water our own brown grass, it would get green again. Marriages are like our bodies: If we don't feed them with experiences and opportunities to grow, they die. Many couples fail to nurture their marriages until it's (almost) too late. Our pride often gets in the way and we fail to see any personal need to deal with problems threatening our lives as a couple. It is said that pride comes before a fall.

As we take opportunities to grow through our experiences, we gain tools needed to keep our love alive for a lifetime. Try some of the suggestions in this book with your heart and mind open to what God might be saying to you about your marriage. We *must* strive for marriage renewal in a world that has all but lost hope for marriages to survive—even in the Christian home.

Introduction

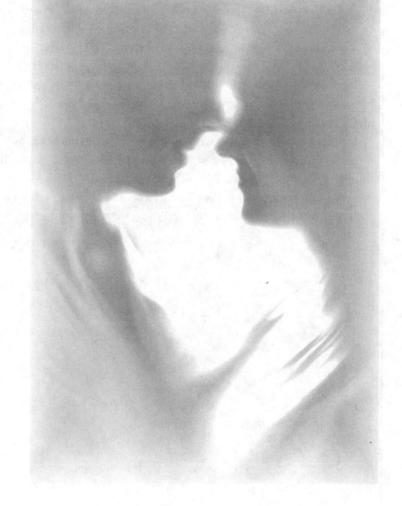

*T*he Lord has placed a call on Randy Ietto's life to teach and preach His Word. The Father is not looking for gifted people, but for ones whom He can gift through their willingness to do what He has called them to do. "The very fact that I am included in this book," Ietto says, "is a statement of what the Lord can do. I have no seminary background, and I am not involved in full-time ministry, yet as part of the Body of Christ, He has something to say through me."

Ietto has just recently felt the Lord's call to the pastorate. In response to this call, at the start of 2003, he returned to college to seek a master's degree in biblical studies.

It is Ietto's hope that you will be blessed through this book, as it was a blessing for him to be involved with Ken Musko's family-strengthening ministry. He believes that when the family crumbles, the society is not far behind, and it is his prayer that by the power of Almighty God, we will return to values that protect and nourish the family unit.

God's Plan for Marriage

Randy Ietto

> For this reason a man will leave his father and mother and be united to his wife, and they will become one flesh. (Genesis 2:24)

Today marriage is under attack in our culture and in most cultures around the world. Why? Because marriage is at the core of what God wants to do on this earth, and the devil is opposed to any plan of God's!

Marriage Was God's Idea

In the book of Genesis, or the Book of Beginnings, Scripture says,

> So God created man in his own image,
>   in the image of God he created him;
>   male and female he created them.
>
> God blessed them and said to them, "Be fruitful and increase in number; fill the earth and subdue it. Rule over the fish of the sea and the birds of the air and over every living creature that moves on the ground." (Genesis 1:27-28)

The concept of marriage did not come from man, nor did it come from any form of government. Rather, marriage was the first institution established by our Father. "For this reason a man will leave his father and mother and be united to his wife, and they will become one flesh. The man and his wife were both naked, and they felt no shame" (2:24-25). These verses, which contain the elements of separation, permanence, unity and intimacy, truly define marriage.

To find a proper concept of marriage, we must go back before humans sinned to see how the man and woman interacted before the consequences of the Fall affected their relationship. The first family before the Fall were not competitors but covenant partners, each the perfect match for the other. When mankind fell into sin, we became incapable of godly love and began to pit ourselves against our spouses.

What is this "godly love"? When God speaks of His love for us, in the Old Covenant He uses the Hebrew word *chesed*, which is translated as "lovingkindness," and in the New Covenant He uses the Greek word *agape*. God's *chesed* or *agape* love says to us, "No matter what you do to Me, I only want the best for you." This type of love is not self-centered—it is selfless. Without the life of Christ within us, fallen, sinful people cannot give the kind of *chesed* and *agape* covenant love that God can.

Satan Brought Marriage Down to His Level

Satan is not ignorant of the importance of this institution called marriage. The Enemy is not wasting any time in his attempt to usurp the plan and purpose of God by attacking the family.

In Genesis 1:27-28, we see that God gave man dominion over this earth and all that was in it. Satan, who himself fell because he desired to be worshiped as God is worshiped, also wanted this anointing (or empowerment) that God gave to Adam. He set out to steal it from Adam. The consequence was the fall of man into the same fallen state as Satan.

Redemption for Us—and for Marriage

When Jesus, the Son of God, came to earth, He changed the fallen state of man and marriage. Those who believe in Him and receive Him are given, at the very instant of their salvation, all the Fruit of the Spirit of Christ (the Holy Spirit).

> But the fruit of the Spirit is love, joy, peace, patience, kindness, goodness, faithfulness, gentleness and self-control. Against such things there is no law. Those who belong to Christ Jesus have crucified the sinful nature with its passions and desires. (Galatians 5:22-24)

The first fruit named is love, and this is the primary ingredient of the marriage covenant. Love is not only an emotion that we can feel, but it is also a powerful spiritual action and attitude.

Our families were designed to be havens of safety, not battlefields over our rights. Marriage is a covenant relationship, and a covenant relationship is not concerned about rights. Instead, *agape* love says, "No matter what you do to me, I only want the best for you."

In biblical times, a covenant carried a severe penalty—usually death—if either party broke it. This is not to suggest that death should be the penalty for a failed marriage, but it does point out our society's error in viewing divorce as merely a legal matter when it is really a spiritual matter. In fact, the Lord said, "I hate divorce" (Malachi 2:16). Please note, however, that God hates the *behavior* of divorce; He does not hate the divorced person.

The Apostle Paul gives us God's perspective on what a marriage should be using the analogy of Christ and His Church as the model:

> Submit to one another out of reverence for Christ. Wives, submit to your husbands as to the Lord. For the husband is the head of the wife as Christ is the head of the church, his body, of which he is the Savior. Now as the church submits to Christ, so also wives should submit to their husbands in everything.
>
> Husbands, love your wives, just as Christ loved the church and gave himself up for her to make her holy, cleansing her by the washing with water through the word, and to present her to himself as a radiant church, without stain or wrinkle or any other blemish, but holy and blameless. In this same way, husbands ought to love their wives as their own bodies. He who loves his wife loves himself. After all, no one ever hated his own body, but he feeds and cares for it, just as Christ does the church—for we are members of his body. "For this reason a man will leave his father and mother and be united to his wife, and the two will become one flesh." (Ephesians 5:21-31)

Paul is stating in the New Covenant the very same words that the Father used in Genesis 2:24.

There has been more than a fair amount of misconception and misunderstanding about the biblical teaching regarding a woman's submission and a man's headship in a marriage. If any husband loves his wife as Christ loved the Church, this means that he would give himself for her, to the point of giving his own life. Is there any woman who would not submit to a man's headship in a marriage if she were convinced that he would give his life for her benefit? Revelation 1:6 says that Jesus Christ "loves us and has freed us from our sins by his blood." This is a picture of Christ loving His Church more than Himself and is the picture used to demonstrate how a husband's love should be for his wife.

"Submit to one another out of reverence for Christ." The first word is *submit*, not "demand our rights," and this is to be done out of obedience to Christ. The word *Christ* is an untranslated Greek word that means "the anointed one." Jesus of Nazareth was *the* Anointed One, and His ministry took off with power when He was baptized by John and received that anointing from God. After His death, burial and resurrection, He ascended into heaven. On the day of Pentecost, the Holy Spirit was sent to the earth to fill believers with the same anointing that was on Jesus.

Choose to Follow the Spirit of Christ in Your Marriage

A paraphrase of Ephesians 5:21 might read, "Submit to one another out of reverence for the Anointed One, and for His anointing within us." In the time before our salvation, we had only one nature, and that resisted God. But when we were saved, we received all of Christ through His Spirit. Now we must choose which nature we are going to follow. If we are unforgiving toward our spouses, we are cutting ourselves off from the anointing of Christ. When we are cut off from the anointing of the Holy Spirit, we have only our own thoughts and old natures to live by.

If confusion and arguments are the primary effects of a marriage, that couple is hooked up not to the Spirit of Christ, but to the spiritual forces of Satan. "For where you have envy and selfish ambition, there you find disorder and every evil practice" (James 3:16). Confusion and evil practice come only from the kingdom of darkness.

Which nature will we follow? As creatures made in the image of God, we are given the capacity to form our own thoughts and words and to call upon either the kingdom of light or the kingdom of darkness.

God, as a gentleman, will not force us to join His side. Satan, however, is no gentleman, and he will attempt to pressure us. But he has no capacity to make us do anything. We, the Body of Christ, are no longer in Satan's camp, and we have already been translated into the heavenly kingdom. "For he has rescued us from the dominion of darkness and brought us into the kingdom of the Son he loves" (Colossians 1:13). We need to make a decision to choose the light instead of darkness, because if we do, Satan must flee. James 4:7-8 says, "Submit yourselves, then, to God. Resist the devil, and he will flee from you. Come near to God and he will come near to you. Wash your hands, you sinners, and purify your hearts, you double-minded."

In our marriages we must choose to put the needs of our spouses before our own. If we will do that, the Holy Spirit who dwells within us will do the work of love. "But if we walk in the light, as he is in the light, we have fellowship with one another, and the blood of Jesus, his Son, purifies us from all sin" (1 John 1:7). If we walk in the light, then we can love our spouses with His covenant love flowing unimpeded through us.

Part One
Growing Together

*Enjoy the girl you married
when you were young.
(Proverbs 5:18, GOD'S WORD)*

Zig Ziglar is a talented author and speaker whose international appeal has transcended every color, culture and career. Recognized by his peers as the quintessential motivational genius of our times, Ziglar's unique delivery style and powerful messages have earned him many honors. Having shared the stage with Presidents Ford, Reagan and Bush, Generals Norman Schwarzkopf and Colin Powell, Paul Harvey and Dr. Robert Schuller, he is one of the most sought-after personal development trainers in the world. As a patriot he has been recognized three times in the Congressional Record of the United States for his work with youth in the drug war and for his dedication to America and the free enterprise system.

From humble beginnings in Yazoo, Mississippi, to the Hall of Fame in Sales and Marketing, Ziglar's career has been one of consistent accomplishments. Most recently, the National Speakers Association honored Ziglar with its highest award, "The Cavett."

Since 1970, individuals and institutions have utilized an extensive collection of Ziglar audio resources, videos, books and training curricula. The client list of Ziglar Training Systems reads like a who's who in American and global business. Nine of his twenty-one books have been on the best-seller lists, and his titles have been translated into more than thirty-eight languages and dialects. Having been featured in such publications as the *New York Times*, the *Washington Post*, the *Dallas Morning News*, *Fortune* and *Time* and *Esquire* magazines, to name a few, Ziglar has also appeared on the *Today* show, ABC's *20/20*, CBS's *60 Minutes* and *Hour of Power*.

Books
Confessions of a Grieving Christian
Courtship After Marriage
Life Lifters
Raising Positive Kids in a Negative World
See You at the Top
Success for Dummies
Top Performance
Zig (his autobiography)

Seminars
Born to Win
 and many others

Web
www.zigziglar.com

Six Steps to a Good Marriage

Zig Ziglar

> Any closed system, left to itself,
> tends toward breakdown.

That principle includes marriage! Relationships tend to disintegrate unless we put time and energy into sustaining them.

Strange, isn't it, how you initially planned everything to the "T," how you connived to get your girlfriend off by herself, how you figured every way possible to hold her hand, put your arm around her, what you were going to say, and how you were going to say it, *and then one day you got married*. Most marriages do not end in a blowout. They gradually die because of a lot of slow leaks that take away the joy, excitement and enthusiasm that man and wife really can enjoy. A major reason for this loss is that we become so accustomed to having each other around, assuming we have now learned everything about each other, we make little or no serious effort to cement the relationship we worked so hard to bring about, and we start taking a lot of things for granted.

I'm really talking about an attitude. Starting over to build a successful, loving marriage depends on having the right "marriage attitude." You must understand that marriage is not a fence to hem you in; it's a guardrail to protect what's inside. Several years ago, the Redhead and I were driving through the beautiful Colorado mountains. From time to time, we would see a sign that said "mountain overlook." On many occasions we stopped, and there was a guardrail that enabled us to walk right up to the edge and look at the magnificent scenery. We felt much more secure having that guardrail and were able to enjoy the spectacular view because of it.

That's really the way marriage should be. The security of knowing that you have someone to love, to trust, to encourage, to laugh with, grow with and enjoy life with and that he or she is yours—and yours alone—makes marriage so incredible! Marriage is not designed to place restrictions on you; marriage is for the purpose of completing you, thus enabling each member of the "team" to be more than you could be as individuals. Marriage is designed to enable you to grow to your maximum because of the support, love and encouragement of your mate.

We see the "expanding-to-the-maximum" concept demonstrated on school grounds. In the inner-city schools, if there are no fences, the kids congregate and play primarily toward the center of the yard. If there is a fence, however, they play right up to the very edge of the street and, I might add, in safety. A good marriage affords the excitement of utilizing all our abilities and yet provides the safety of protecting the one we love.

Any marriage, almost regardless of how good it is, will ultimately go bad unless both husband and wife make a conscious decision to work on making the marriage even better—and then take the steps to do exactly that. At that same time, any marriage, regardless of how bad it is, has an excellent chance of not only surviving, but flourishing, if both husband and wife take the positive approach *and* start taking the steps necessary to make the relationship work.

Survey after survey indicates that the number-one source of satisfaction in our lives is a good marriage, rating above fame, fortune, good jobs or even good help. Over and over, happily married couples and marriage professionals acknowledge that a good marriage is viewed by most not as a means to some other end but as an end in itself. That's the kind of marriage attitude that will make "starting over" for you a happy and loving success. Now let's dig deeper and carefully explore "starting over" in depth.

Step One: Respect Your Mate

This respect factor certainly stood out in a story that hit all the newspapers concerning Nolan Ryan, the tremendous pitcher for the Texas Rangers. The year 1989 was incredibly successful for Nolan. He had been signed as a free agent by the Texas Rangers from the Houston Astros, and at age forty-two, he had recorded well over two hundred strikeouts and had an excellent won-lost record. Everyone just knew that since he was pitching with a one-year contract with an option for another year, he would automatically sign for that one-year contract extension, especially since he had made baseball history by recording his five thousandth career strikeout during the course of the season. I might add that he would also make more than $1 million for the coming season. However, before Nolan Ryan agreed to accept the Rangers' offer for the next year, he had a long discussion with his wife concerning all the pros and cons. The bottom line is, her input was the determining factor in Nolan's decision.

There's a tremendous lesson for every husband who reads these words. In the procedure that Nolan Ryan followed, he showed his wife the ultimate respect by the length and depth of their discussion and the fact that he valued her input so much. You can bet they are friends and their relationship is a special one.

Later in 1989, many people were encouraging Nolan to run for political office as Texas Commissioner of Agriculture. They felt he had an excellent chance to be elected because of his public profile, his extraordinary public acceptance and his unique qualifications for the job. However, Ryan again took the same approach. He consulted with his wife, and together the decision was made that the timing was inappropriate. Any CEO worth his salt will certainly consult his executive vice president on decisions concerning their relationship and their happiness. He will also keep her informed . . . by talking with her about the "little things" that happen on a daily basis.

Step Two: Make Friends with Your Mate

One of the most important components to make yours a super, harmonious, working-together marriage is to become each other's best friend. Psychologists point out that in the happiest and strongest marriages, the spouses play not only the roles of lovers and partners, but best friends as well. In fact, as a marriage progresses over time, the friendship will deepen, and the marriage partners may become even more like each other. In a study of 125 couples, researchers found that many of the spouses became more similar in intelligence, perception, and motor skills as the years went by.

In addition, all of us have noticed that some couples, over a period of time, literally begin to look like each other.

Deep and lasting friendships take time—lots of time. That time invested with your mate brings many rewards. You can truly form a deep and lasting friendship and become "best friends." In my opinion the two most negative words ever put together are the words *quality time*. The words contradict each other and have wrecked many marriages and caused emotional damage to many children.

Step Three: Build a Few Sand Castles

Many divorces could be prevented and more fun could be had if husbands and wives took time to plan more activities with each other and with the entire family. And friendships within the entire family would grow.

For example, in the summer of '89 we experienced a rare, magnificent vacation in Myrtle Beach, South Carolina. Our entire family, including our three daughters and their husbands, our son and his wife, and the grandchildren, was there. The circumstances were truly marvelous. However, it was the unanimous opinion of everyone there that the sand castle experience was the highlight of the entire trip.

Our son-in-love, Jim Norman, took the initiative and decided he was going to build a sand castle. The sand castle (and it truly was a "castle") was about six feet long, four and a half feet wide, and about three feet tall; it was complete with a moat, drawbridges, gates, towers, stairways, storage rooms, sleeping quarters—the whole bit.

There we were, anywhere from thirteen to twenty-five hundred miles away from home spending significant parts of two days hovering around a sand castle and having a marvelous time in the process.

The point I'm making is simply that families of long-term duration who are friends and have love and concern for one another can have a grand time doing simple things. Needless to say, you don't have to go to Myrtle Beach or anywhere else to have this kind of experience.

Step Four: Make the Commitment

When your commitment is total and the inevitable problems arise, you will look for a solution to those problems. If your commitment is weak—or nonexistent—you will look for an escape from the problems.

The importance *and* the effectiveness of commitment were best demonstrated in the answers we received from the survey we conducted on couples who have been married twenty-five years or more *and* who would marry the same person again. We believed quite strongly that most of these couples would feel that marriage was a lifetime commitment, but we were pleasantly surprised to discover that 100 percent of the couples felt that when they said, "I do," they literally meant for better and for worse as well as for life.

I once heard a counselor say, "You can't scrub the deck of a sinking ship." He was making the point that some marriages are too far gone to save. In some cases, serious and irreparable damage has been done, but let me encourage you to get off the deck and get into the engine room. Locate the source of the excess water your ship is taking on and do everything possible to stem the flood. If you will look for reasons to stay married, instead of reasons to part, you will find them. Where do you start looking? Well, I'm glad you asked!

Step Five: Rebuild the Foundation

I'm convinced that if the basic commitment and the character foundation are there to build upon, as in the case of my two friends who had the courage to "keep on keeping on," every marriage can be an enduring one. Most can be a pleasant experience, and many can be truly beautiful, romantic, and exciting. I emphasize the character foundation, though, because as the Blackfoot Indians say, "You can't carve rotten wood."

On November 29, 1983, I participated in a most unusual ceremony in Lubbock, Texas. My long-term friends, James and Juanell Teague, were celebrating their twenty-fifth wedding anniversary, and they wanted to exchange their vows again. They asked me to "officially" perform the "unofficial" ceremony. Because it was unofficial (I'm not licensed to perform weddings) and because of our friendship, I agreed. In the process of planning and preparing for the occasion, the concept of a covenant occurred to me. A *covenant* according to the dictionary is a "solemn agreement; compact, the Promises of God as recorded in the Bible." Because marriage is so sacred and the restating of those vows so important, I took my assignment very seriously. Here is the covenant:

Covenant
ONE LOVE SHARED BY TWO

Because we, _____ and _____, have chosen to become "one," we quite naturally want our marriage to be successful, happy, and permanent.

To accomplish this objective, we individually and jointly pledge to respect, encourage, and support each other as individuals. We further agree to ensure the success, happiness, and permanence of our marriage by keeping the promises stated in our marriage vows and in this sacred covenant.

Understanding that marriage is under attack and the family is in trouble, we promise to demonstrate to the world that a truly committed husband and wife, with God's help, can have a beautiful marriage and grow in love for one another in the process.

Accepting the fact that God is the Author of success in marriage, and believing the best way to stay in His will is to stay in His Word, we agree to seek His will and direction every day by reading the Bible and humbling ourselves before Him in prayer.

Because God specifically promises, "For them that honor me will I honor," we solemnly promise to honor God in every phase of our individual lives as well as in our life together.

Knowing that the fellowship of believers gives encouragement to individuals and support to the family structure, we agree to make a maximum effort to attend worship services together each week.

Believing that marriage is ordained and blessed by God, we pledge our love and faithfulness to Him and to each other. Being aware of the frailties of man and recognizing the probability of falling short of this lofty objective, we further pledge to love, honor, and forgive one another even as God, for Christ's sake, has loved, honored, and forgiven us.

We thank God for bringing us together and ask Him in His Providence to keep His hand on our marriage, and to heal any hurts we inflict upon one another. Because we now more completely commit this marriage to Jesus Christ, our faith assures us that under His watchcare, "The best is yet to be." We reverently enter this sacred covenant because we know these pledges and procedures will completely assure greater happiness and permanence of our "one love shared by two."

Step Six: Become Partners for Life

The story about Sir Edmund Hillary and his historic climb of Mount Everest gives us a classic example about a partnership and friendship attitude that will build a great marriage. While becoming the first man in history to reach that mountain peak, Sir Edmund was accompanied by his trusted native guide, Tenzing Norgay. After scaling the mountain, Sir Edmund lost his footing on the way down, but Tenzing held the line taut and kept them both from falling to their deaths by digging his axe into the ice.

When questioned later, Tenzing refused any special credit for saving Sir Edmund's life. He considered it a routine part of the job and expressed his feeling simply, but eloquently, when he said, "Mountain climbers always help each other."

What a fantastic philosophy for marriage partners to adopt! They should always help each other. After all, it really is true that you can have everything in life you want if you will just help enough other people get what they want. When you get close enough and stay close enough to help your mate, you really will be making that fresh start. Based on observation and personal experience, I can tell you that "starting over" can be fun and exciting.

Reprinted by permission of Thomas Nelson Publishers from the book entitled Courtship after Marriage, *Copyright © 1990 by Zig Ziglar.*

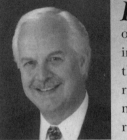

*D*r. Willard Harley is a licensed clinical psychologist and marriage counselor who has been helping couples build stronger marriages for over thirty years. His popular Web site, www.marriagebuilders.com, logs over 15 million hits per month. He has been called "America's top marriage counselor" by *Women's World* magazine.

After earning his Ph.D. in psychology from the University of California at Santa Barbara in 1967, Harley taught psychology at the graduate and undergraduate levels for ten years. During that time, he was a part-time marriage counselor, making steady improvement in his theory and technique. When his success rate climbed to over ninety percent, he left academia to counsel full-time. His solo practice grew into 32 clinics with over 200 counselors, all of whom were trained by Harley.

Harley now devotes his time to writing books and articles, conducting research in marriage counseling methods and leading seminars for counselors and couples. He has appeared on thousands of radio and television programs.

The Harleys live in White Bear Lake, Minnesota. They have two grown children and four grandchildren.

Books
Buyers, Renters, and Freeloaders (also CD)
Fall in Love, Stay in Love (also CD)
Five Steps to Romantic Love
His Needs, Her Needs (also audio and CD)
His Needs, Her Needs: For Parents
Love Busters
Marriage Insurance
Surviving an Affair

Media
In Focus with Joyce Harley (AM 980, Minneapolis, MN) Mon. and Thurs., 1-2 p.m. CT

Seminars
Church management and mobilization
Diagnosis and treatment of emotional disorders
Evangelistic methods
Marriage (presently limited to Marriage Builders weekends)
Use and interpretation of the Minnesota Multiphasic Personality Inventory (MMPI)

Web
www.marriagebuilders.com

The First Thing She Can't Do Without

2

——— *Willard Harley*

Affection Is the Cement of a Relationship

To most women affection symbolizes security, protection, comfort, and approval, vitally important commodities in their eyes. When a husband shows his wife affection, he sends the following messages:

- I'll take care of you and protect you. You are important to me, and I don't want anything to happen to you.
- I'm concerned about the problems you face, and I am with you.
- I think you've done a good job, and I'm so proud of you.

A hug can say any and all of the above. Men need to understand how strongly women need these affirmations. For the typical wife, there can hardly be enough of them.

I've mentioned hugging often because I believe it is a skill most men need to develop to show their wives affection. It is also a simple but effective way to build their accounts in a wife's Love Bank. . . .

Obviously a man can display affection in other ways that can be equally important to a woman. A greeting card or a note expressing love and care can simply but effectively communicate the same emotions. Don't forget that all-time favorite—a bouquet of flowers. Women, almost universally, love to receive flowers. Occasionally I meet a man who likes to receive them, but most do not. For most women, however, flowers send a powerful message of love and concern.

An invitation to dinner also signals affection. It is a way of saying to one's wife, "You don't need to do what you ordinarily do for me. I'll treat you instead. You are special to me, and I want to show you how much I love and care for you."

Jokes abound on how, almost immediately after the wedding, a wife has to find her own way in and out of cars, houses, restaurants, and so on. But a sensitive husband will open the door for her at every opportunity—another way to tell her, "I love you and care about you."

Holding hands is a time-honored and effective sign of affection. Walks after dinner, backrubs, phone calls and conversations with thoughtful and loving expressions all add units to the Love Bank. As more than one song has said, "There are a thousand ways to say I love you."

From a woman's point of view, affection is the essential cement of her relationship with a man. Without it, a woman probably feels alienated from her mate. With it she becomes tightly bonded to him while he adds units to his Love Bank account.

But She Knows I'm Not the Affectionate Type

Men must get through their heads this vital idea: Women find affection important in its own right. They love the feeling that accompanies both the bestowal and the reception of affection, but it has nothing to do with sex. Most of the affection they give and receive is not intended to be sexual. You might better compare it to the emotion they exchange with their children or pets.

All of this confuses the typical male. He sees showing affection as part of sexual foreplay, and he is normally aroused in a flash. In other cases men simply want to skip the affection business; they are aroused already. . . .

Although they shouldn't have a hard time understanding this simple logic, men lose track of Harley's First Law of Marriage:

Any Man Can Learn to Be Affectionate

Affection is so important for women that they become confused when their husbands don't respond in kind. For example, a wife may call her husband at work, just to talk. She would love to receive such a call and is sure he feels the same. She often feels disappointed when he cuts it short because, "I've got all this stuff to finish by five o'clock." It doesn't mean the husband doesn't love her; he simply has different priorities because of a different set of basic needs. . . .

Almost all men need some instruction in how to become more affectionate, and those who have developed such loving habits have usually learned how to do so from good coaches—perhaps former girlfriends. In most marriages, a man's wife can become his best teacher, if he approaches her for help in the right way.

First, you need to explain to her that you love her very much, but often fail to express your deep love and care for her appropriately. Then you should ask her to help you learn to express this affection, which you already feel, in ways she will appreciate.

Initially she will probably feel puzzled by such a request. "When you love someone, affection comes naturally!" she may reply. She may not realize that affection comes more naturally for her than it does for you.

She may think that you have sex on your mind and have devised some new angle to improve your sexual relationship.

"I don't think I let you know how much I really care for you," you may answer. "I just assume you know, because I go to work, take you out, and help you around the house. I should be doing more to tell you how much I care about you."

"Sounds great! When do we start?"

She can help you by making a list of those signs of care that mean the most to her. Women usually express a need for physical closeness, such as hugging, hand holding and sitting close together. Kissing is very important to most women, as are token gifts and cards that express your emotional attachment and commitment. Women love to have their husbands take them out to dinner, and usually a wife regards any effort her husband makes to join her in shopping for food and clothing as a sign of affection. . . .

Once your wife has helped you identify habits that will meet her need for affection, create a plan that sees to it that you'll learn those habits. To repeat a point I make throughout this book [*His Needs, Her Needs*], knowing what your spouse needs does not meet the need. You must learn new habits that transform that knowledge into action. Then and only then is that need met. Don't build up your wife's hopes with your good intentions. Go one step further: Learn the habits of affection. If you know your wife's needs and then fail to deliver, your relationship will be worse than it was before you gained understanding. At least then you could plead ignorance!

Your plan to learn habits of affection should be carefully written down so that you'll be more likely to stay on course. Clients I counsel use a form, Strategy to Meet the Need of Affection, to describe their plan. The form simply requires couples to identify the habits they wish to learn and describe how they plan to learn them.

Habits usually take time to develop—sometimes weeks, sometimes months. Your plan should include the time you expect to be "in training." The easiest habits to learn are those that you enjoy performing, the most difficult are the ones you tend to find uncomfortable. . . .

Sex Begins with Affection

Over the years I have seen nothing more devastating to a marriage than an affair. Sadly enough, most affairs start because of a lack of affection (for the wife) and lack of sex (for the husband). It's quite a vicious cycle. She doesn't get enough attention, so she shuts him off sexually. He doesn't get enough sex, so the last thing he feels like being is affectionate.

The solution to this tragic cycle is for someone to break it. I made my reputation as a marriage counselor convincing wives that if they met their husbands' sexual need, their husbands would be willing to meet their need for affection in return, and any other needs, for that matter. It worked so well that I built a thriving practice overnight, so to speak.

But it can be done the other way around, having a husband meet his wife's need for affection first. I've discovered that when her need is met, she's usually much more willing to meet his need for sex. Since I begin with the wife's need for affection, I recommend that if your need for sex is not being fulfilled, take the initiative by learning to meet your wife's need for affection first.

Affection is the environment of the marriage while sex is an *event*. Affection is a way of life, a canopy that covers and protects a marriage. It's a direct and convincing expression of love that gives the event of sex a more appropriate context. Most women need affection before sex means much to them.

Because men tend to translate affection into sex so readily, I put emphasis on learning sexless affection. I try to teach a husband to make affection a nonsexual way of relating to his spouse. He learns not to just turn it on and off to get some sex. Whenever he and his spouse come together, a big hug and kiss should be routine. In fact, almost every interaction between them should include affectionate words and gestures. I believe every marriage should have an atmosphere that says, "I really love you and I know you love me."

When I talk about sexless affection, many men become confused. What is he supposed to do with his natural feeling of sexual arousal, which can be triggered by almost any act of affection? He wants to know if he has to "take cold showers" to keep cool. I point out to him that when he was dating, he was just as sexually aroused as he is now, even more so! But he showed plenty of affection and attention that did not include groping and grabbing. He treated the young lady with respect and tenderness.

Many husbands remember the passionate encounters of their courting days and want to know, "Why doesn't she get turned on the way she did before we were married?"

I patiently explain that he isn't treating her the way he did back then. After marriage he thought he could do away with the preliminaries and get right to the main event. But it turns out that the "preliminaries" are not only required for a fulfilling sexual relationship, they're also needed in their own right. In many cases what he thinks are preliminaries are her "main event."

In most cases, a woman needs to feel a oneness with her husband before she has sex with him. A couple achieves this feeling through the exchange of affection and undivided attention.

Her need for this one-spirit unity helps us understand how affairs develop. In the typical affair, a woman has sex with a man after he has demonstrated his love for her by showering her with affection. Because her lover has expressed such care for her, the physical union is usually characterized by a degree of ecstacy otherwise unknown to her in marriage. She concludes that her lover is right for her because she doesn't feel the same way when she makes love to her husband.

In truth, any marriage can have the sizzle of an affair if it has that strong one-spirit bond. It's a tragic misconception for her to think that her husband is not right for her based on a comparison of feelings at a moment of time. If he were to lay the groundwork with affection, their bond would be restored and the affair would be seen for what it really is: a misguided effort to have an important emotional need met.

When your marriage is struggling sexually, look for the missing elements of affection. Without the environment, the sexual event is contrived and unnatural for many women. All too often she reluctantly agrees to have sex with her husband, even though she knows she won't enjoy it. In an affair, the conditions that guarantee fulfilling sex—the bonding that comes with affection—are met. Her lover has taken time and action to create the right environment for sex. Consequently, she feels sexually aroused at the very thought of him.

Most of the women I've counseled crave affection. I try to help their husbands understand the pleasure women feel when this need is met. Although [it's] not the same as [that] experienced during sex, [it] form[s] a vital part of a romantic relationship. Without it, a woman's sexual experience is incomplete.

Many husbands have this all backwards. For them, sexual arousal makes them feel more affectionate. They try to explain to their wives the importance of having sex more often so that they'll feel like being affectionate. But that argument usually falls on deaf ears. Some women will have sex with their husbands just for the affection they receive while making love, but it tends to leave them resentful and bitter. As soon as sex is over, their husbands go back to their unaffectionate ways, leaving their wives feeling unloved. They feel that all their husbands want is sex, and they don't really care about them in any other way. That attitude destroys their feeling of intimacy and the bond of unity. But that attitude can change if their husbands learn to create an environment of affection by learning habits that produce a steady stream of love and care.

Just as men want their wives' sexual response to be spontaneous, women prefer their husbands' affection to be spontaneous. There is a certain spontaneity to our behavior once it's well learned, but when we try to develop new behavior it seems contrived and unnatural. At first, efforts to be affectionate may not be very convincing and, as a result, may not have the effect of spontaneous affection. But with practice, the affectionate behavior eventually conveys accurately the feeling of care that husbands have for their wives. That, in turn, creates the environment necessary for a more spontaneous sexual response in a woman.

A woman's need for affection is probably her deepest emotional need. But all that I've said here will prove of little value if a wife fails to understand that her husband has an equally deep need for sex. To the typical man, sex is like air or water. He can't do without it very well.

If a wife fails to understand the power of the male sex appetite, she will wind up having a husband who's tense and frustrated at best. At worst, someone else may step forward to meet his need and, tragically enough, that happens all too often in our society. But it can all be avoided if husbands learn to be more affectionate and wives respond with more eagerness to make love. As Harley's First Law of Marriage says:

> When it comes to sex and affection,
> you can't have one without the other.

Taken from His Needs, Her Needs *by Willard F. Harley, Jr., Copyright ©
2001 by Willard F. Harley, Jr. Published by Fleming H. Revell, a division of
Baker Book House. Used by permission.*

*L*ouise Mandrell's talent, personality and boundless energy have already won her a legion of fans who were thrilled to hear that she would be the first woman to own her own theater in Pigeon Forge, Tennessee, and perform there full-time as well. The 1,400-seat Louise Mandrell Theater opened its doors in September of 1997 with a multimillion-dollar production that includes over thirty costume and set changes and over a dozen dancers and musicians. Mandrell's ability to relate to and reach her audience is one of her greatest attributes. When she walks out on stage, she literally owns it! She plays thirteen instruments, including the fiddle and an eight-foot piano (from the movie *Big* starring Tom Hanks), and her high-energy choreography continues to astound audiences. By any standards, Louise Mandrell is one of the hottest tickets in entertainment.

Born in Corpus Christi, Texas, on July 13, Mandrell was a junior in high school when she became the full-time bass player for her sister, Barbara, as one of the original "Do-Rite" band members. Before her sixteenth birthday, she had performed in every major city in the United States and Canada, in addition to clubs and military bases throughout Europe. She has enjoyed success in the recording industry with six albums with RCA that generated such hits as "Some of My Best Friends Are Old Songs," "Save Me," "Too Hot to Sleep," "Maybe My Baby," "I'm Not Through Loving You Yet" and "I Wanna Say Yes."

Recordings
Anthology
The Best of Louise Mandrell
Winter Wonderland

Video
Louise Mandrell Show

Web
www.louisemandrell.com

Singer, Pray-er, Wife—Louise Mandrell

interview with Ken Musko, December 27, 2002

On Growing Up in the Mandrell Family

All three of the Mandrell girls were born in Texas. Daddy still jokingly teases that Texas gave him three girls when he wanted boys!

Daddy managed all of our careers and made our family very successful. He always said, "Get your priorities straight," which for us became God, country and then family. It was especially nice when we could combine all three into one thing, and that, of course, happened when we were working together.

My parents always told us that there was nothing we couldn't accomplish if we worked hard enough. When I was a teenager, I told Dad that I wanted to go into gospel music, and he said, "Well, let's look into it." We went to a couple of friends who were in the gospel music industry, and they asked me point-blank, "Why do you want to sing gospel music?"

I said, "Because I love the Lord."

"Well, that's just not good enough," they said. "You could be preaching to more people and reaching more people if you were known for country music. If you do what you are supposed to do, you can sing gospel music where it's not normally heard." And that's what I've done. It's a dream come true.

My parents are both Christians. They met in church. My mom's job was to entertain and take care of the visiting musicians who came to the church to sing. My dad sang in a gospel trio with his brother, who was a minister, my Uncle Arlie and his wife Marjorie. That's how my dad and mom met. They hit it off and got married.

My dad never hid his love for my mom. If they had an argument, that was hidden; growing up, I never saw them argue. But they were always very affectionate. There was never a night when Daddy didn't walk into the kitchen when my mom was cooking and talk about how beautiful she was and tease her or hug her or try to kiss her neck in front of us kids while she tried to brush him off. It was just like the old movies. My parents taught us that it was OK to be affectionate. As a matter of fact, every time my daddy would come home from work or leave the house, we would play a game. He would say, "Where do you want to be kissed?" and we would point all over our faces.

These days I'm usually the one who calls my parents, because they don't like to bother their children. They think it's very important to make a marriage work, and therefore, now that we girls are married, they keep a distance unless we need them. For example, we don't celebrate Christmas with our parents on Christmas Day. They won't celebrate it with us then. They say, "We got you all married, and it's your job to stay that way. Go make the in-laws happy." If our in-laws aren't coming to town, they might stop by on Christmas Day so we can open gifts, but they will not have our big family celebration on Christmas Eve or Christmas Day. They say, "That gives you two days—one for your family at home and the other one for the in-laws." They pick a day during December that becomes December 25 for us, and we celebrate it with our parents, giving us a three-day Christmas!

On Prayer

My sister Barbara is my prayer partner. She got that title because we talk almost every day, and every time we talk we pray together. We all can get so busy, but if we have prayer partners, it helps us not go too far away from Christ. We sometimes think, *God knows my heart. I'm too busy to pray. I'm moving on.* But when you have a prayer partner and they have a need for prayer, it stops you.

You can pray anywhere. You should. Our family doesn't let much stop us from praying. For example, if we're out to eat somewhere, we still pray. We don't make a big scene, but we pray. But I also believe that a family needs a place to go to pray where it's quiet. Maybe on certain nights of the week before they go to the dinner table, they can go into that place and have prayer as a family. They need a room, a quiet place, someplace to turn off the phones, where they can sit down to pray.

We have our own special places to pray. For example, my husband put a cross, forty feet tall, up on a hill on our farm. He says that it's a reminder to people in the area to keep their hearts and minds where they should be. Of course, I tease him and tell him that since I'm never home, it's a good reminder for him to keep his heart and mind where it should be. (You have to have a sense of humor to survive a marriage.) We go up to the cross and pray at least every Christmas. It's a special place to go, and it's a special time.

I have the most precious memory of praying at Christmas. The year before last, we went up to the cross to pray. I was tired and frustrated and I had a bunch of wrapping to do, and my husband wanted me to go deliver presents. I said, "Look, do you want me to go deliver presents or get to go to bed tonight?" I guess that's the difference between a man and a woman. For me, it was all or nothing, and I couldn't see the light at the end of the tunnel.

He said, "Why don't we just go deliver the ones that need to be there and then come home and compromise?" That's why he's a negotiator for a living, I guess! So I went and delivered a couple of packages and got in the Christmas spirit and agreed to go to the cross. We went up to the cross and prayed. It was night, and it was freezing cold. When we turned to leave, the lights we had shining on the cross threw a shadow up onto the low clouds and made three crosses on the clouds.

We just stopped there and looked. As busy as Christmas was, as tired as we were, as much as I had forgotten what Christmas was about, that scene just made Christmas for me that year. I couldn't wait to get home and wrap the gifts I had for my family and share the story with everybody. It changed everything.

On Being Married

I don't think that any couple should get married until they get some Christian counseling. I wish it was a law. We [my husband

and I] didn't do that, but we did go to one day of counseling with the minister, and we learned that counseling brings out things that you never even know you should ask your spouse.

The minister asked my husband, "You've been single for so many years—why would you marry now?" I expected to hear, "Oh, I think my wife's beautiful, and she's sweeter than everybody else"—you know, all the things you might think that your husband-to-be would be thinking. Instead, I heard the truth, which I never would have been able to appreciate otherwise. He said, "Louise is independent enough that she doesn't need me all the time." My husband didn't want to get married to somebody who just needed him and hung on to him.

A lot of women, when they're first married, change because they want to please their husbands. I have to be a crowd-pleaser. I want everyone to be happy, and I want to be whatever other people need. Well, you know what? They want me to be me. And on stage I had to be me to start having successful shows. In life and in marriage, you've got to be yourself. Your spouse doesn't want you to change. And he doesn't want to change, either.

I'm divorced, and I don't want to fail again. From my first marriage I learned something that I wish all women would learn: We think we can change whomever we marry—*and we can't*. Women tend to make a dream situation in their minds of how marriage is going to be. They think everything has to be perfect. It doesn't. It'll be perfect only when we die and go to heaven. Get over it. Love each other the way you loved each other when you dated.

Because of our careers, John and I are apart a lot. From January through March I am in Nashville, and for the rest of the year, I live here and travel back and forth. When I'm too tired to drive home and John's too busy to get all the way to east Tennessee, we meet on the road. We have to make an effort to make our marriage work. We have to make an effort just to see each other.

It seems that all we do is work. You might be thinking, *How can you make it work when you're apart so much?* To me it's like, how can it fail? It's almost like we're still dating. If he's not happy with me this weekend, wait until next weekend! He's either happy to see me come or happy to see me go, but either way he's happy.

In fact, my husband usually is happy if everybody else is happy. And as long as I come home and I'm not moaning about what's been going on, he's happy. I don't think I'm a complainer, although I would certainly save it for my husband if I were going to complain. I also feel very, very strongly that my poor husband should get every side of me—the best side *and* the worst side. For example, I'm very strong at funerals. I can sing at a close friend's funeral. But then I leave there with my husband and I cry hysterically.

I really believe that the home cannot be successful if the wife does not let the husband be the spiritual leader. Now, that doesn't mean he has to lead at every single thing you do—husbands are too busy and they don't want that kind of responsibility. But a close friend of mine, knowing how much I love the Lord and how I am, told me, "Shut up when you're at home and let him be the spiritual leader." It was really hard for me to be quiet, especially since my husband is very quiet and reserved.

I've been married for almost ten years, and I find it's best to pick your battles. Not every argument is important. Years ago, when I had only been married for a short time, if we had a disagreement, John would always give me facts. He'd go down a list of why he was right and I was wrong. I said to John, "You always win because you negotiate for a living. Quit giving me facts and ask me how I feel about it." And to this day he listens and he doesn't give me facts until I want to discuss it. Sometimes men should let their wives win, and sometimes wives should hush and let their husbands win!

*H*olly Wagner is anything but ordinary. She is an actress, speaker, writer, wife, mother and co-founder, with her husband Phillip, of a multi-cultural, nondenominational church located between Beverly Hills and Hollywood, California.

The church has hosted a number of notable guests, including Martin Luther King, Jr.'s daughter. Though many entertainers and producers for shows such as *The Tonight Show with Jay Leno* and *The Oprah Winfrey Show* attend her church, Wagner says that the church's focus is to reach believers and nonbelievers in a nontraditional church setting.

In the last year and a half, Wagner has been featured on parenting shows for Fox Family Channel and appeared on CNN and in *USA Today* for the church's "Walk of Faith," their version of Hollywood's famous "Walk of Fame." Each year Wagner speaks to thousands of women throughout the United States, Canada, Australia, England and several other countries. She says that her mission is to be this generation's example of "today's Christian woman" and that she wants to give women permission to be who they are.

Books
Dumb Things She Does, Dumb Things He Does
God Chicks

Web
www.hollywagner.com

Doing What It Takes

Holly Wagner

Marriages are crumbling at an alarming rate all over the country and the world. The breakdown of marriages is affecting millions of people in many ways. Not only does divorce affect us emotionally, but it also is the number one cause of financial ruin. And so, it is imperative that we do what we can to preserve our marriages and make them strong unions. What I have noticed is that rarely does a marriage fall apart because some outside force has attacked. Even in the case when one spouse leaves the other for another man or woman, that is usually the result of damage that has been done in the marriage months or years earlier. Just as it takes years for a marriage to grow strong and solid, it also takes time for a marriage to fall apart.

Many times in counseling sessions, one spouse will complain that he or she just doesn't love the other spouse anymore. I would like to suggest that love is not merely a feeling; it is not just a place we fall into; it is not just something we're in—it is something we *do*, regardless of how we feel. Feelings come and go. We can't base our marriages on feelings.

Loving Your Wife

Leading your family is an active position. In fact, I believe that passivity is one of the top reasons marriages collapse. Don't ever let it settle in you. Be passionate about your wife and your home! Work hard at communicating with her so that the two of you stay connected. Don't adopt a "whatever will be" fatalistic attitude. Be brave enough to have a "whatever it takes" attitude.

[H]usband, I believe you need to be the example setter in your home. If you don't like the results you see in your family, quit blaming and change your actions.

The number one need of most women is to feel loved. We func-
tion at our best when we are well and truly loved, and we feel that
love. It is your job to demonstrate that love (and it *is* more than
sex, although that is definitely a part of it!). Loving your wife
means you are as concerned about her future as your own. Loving
your wife means you *do* things that show it. Ask her what you can
do that will help her feel loved.

Loving means doing. Look for ways to demonstrate the love you
feel. Don't keep it hidden in your heart. If there are times when
you aren't feeling a whole lot of love in your heart, just the actions
of doing loving things will bring the feelings back.

Plenty of men joke, saying, "Women—who can understand
them?!" Well, you don't have to understand *women*—just one
woman, the one you are building an amazing relationship with. It
takes work, like all good endeavors that are worth anything, but
you can do it!

Remember, your wife is not you. She will do most things quite
differently—but that doesn't make her wrong.

When a woman is feeling stressed or hurt by a situation, usually
she wants your compassion and your understanding. She doesn't
necessarily need you to fix it, so put the tool belt down.

One time, my feelings were really hurt by a friend's betrayal. I
was devastated. As I sat next to Philip on the couch, he began to
give me reasons why I shouldn't feel that way because this person
hadn't been a good friend anyway. He said that she had been flaky
and unfair to me, saying cruel things about me: Wasn't it good we
weren't friends anymore? Now, while all that was true, did his
comments help me deal with my hurt heart? No! What I needed
was for him to hold me and let me talk about it. I needed him to
say, "I'm sorry you're hurting. What happened was terrible." I
needed an ear, someone to talk to, not a list of what I should feel
and why. Nowadays when I'm hurt or stressed, Philip just holds
me and listens and listens. What a guy!

Ask young couples whether there is anything about their
spouses they would change, and most will respond with a loud *yes*!
However, I have asked couples who have been married forty years

or more what changes they would make in their spouses, and they can't think of one. What happened? I believe they learned to love the differences and be truly glad about them.

Romancing Your Wife

We women have gotten hip to the fact that you men are conquerors. Most of you feel that after you have put all the time and effort to capture us (marry us), you can kick back and relax. Often your passion for romance dwindles a bit. The problem with this is that *our* desire for romance and our need to feel cherished don't disappear after the honeymoon. The husband who switches from overdrive romance before the wedding to cruise control after marriage is asking for trouble.

Romance is important to your wife, and rather than resent it, just accept it. The occasional gesture, such as a flower, phone call, date, gentle touch or kind word, goes a long way toward creating a happy home. (By occasional, I mean daily!) Try something . . . anything. Be creative. Find out what she likes.

Your wife is the most important woman in your life; let her know it. I have had a few conversations with some men over the years who were having extramarital affairs. They were spending time, energy and money trying to conquer the new woman. If each man had taken that time and that energy and courted his wife, he would have the marriage he wanted. Don't look outside your home for fulfillment.

I have also known women who weren't feeling loved (our number one need) by their husbands, and so when some smooth-talking men appeared, those women were seduced. Should the women have said no? Absolutely! But your job is to keep the walls of your marriage secure; don't leave the door open for trouble to get in. Find out what makes your wife feel loved, and then do it! Do what it takes to have a great marriage!

The Freedom of Forgiving

Forgiveness isn't just a nice thing to do. I believe it is a life-and-death issue.

Forgiveness can be difficult for us because it pulls against our concept of justice. We want revenge for offenses suffered. (Oh, sometimes we won't admit it, but we do.) We want God to bless them with a lightning bolt! You may ask, "Why should I let them off the hook?" That's the problem: you're hooked. Or you may say, "You don't understand how much they hurt me!" But don't you see? They are still hurting you. You are still living the betrayal, the offense, whatever the crime. You don't forgive someone for his or her sake; you do it for *your* sake so that you can be free.

Forgiveness is pardoning someone else. It is letting go of the resentment. Forgiveness is not necessarily forgetting. Forgetting may be the result of forgiveness, but it is never the means. Forgiveness is a choice, a decision of your will. Don't wait until you feel like forgiving to begin the process; you'll never get there. Feelings take time to heal after the choice to forgive has been made. When we hold on to grudges, letting bitterness grow, we begin to withdraw from each other and withhold affection, which will ultimately destroy the relationship. Marriages are about forgiving . . . daily.

Let's be people who freely give the forgiveness we all need. In the marriage relationship, each has specific roles to fill. Husband, your job is not an easy one—so, wife, give him a break. He is not going to get it right all the time. Forgive the failures. Cheer the attempts. And husband, your wife, too, has a difficult job. There will be times when she blows it, when she isn't respectful or hasn't yielded. Please be quick to forgive, and encourage her to try again. Demonstrate forgiveness and love anyway. Each spouse will make mistakes. Give your spouse the forgiveness that you yourself will need—if not now, then the next time you blow it!

We always has to be more important than *me* if a marriage is going to weather the storms of life.

Are You Ready for Love?

Sex is a unifying bond between husband and wife. It solidifies the union. When the rest of the world might seem crazy, it is wonderful to feel connected with your spouse. Perhaps you have had a really tough day at work, your boss yelled at you, someone cut you off in traffic and pointed a finger at you (and I'm not talking about the index finger!), and you had a flat tire. However, if you can come home and later that evening have sex with your spouse, your world can perhaps be righted again because someone is on your side. A purpose of sex is to produce unity between the husband and the wife, which is why premarital sex can really mess you up because you become bedmates before you become soul mates.

To create the right atmosphere and make that woman of yours eager for love—men, pay attention—here's all you have to do: caress, praise, pamper, relish, savor, massage, make plans, empathize, serenade, compliment, support, tantalize, humor, purr, hug, cuddle, excite, pacify, stroke, protect, phone, correspond, anticipate, nuzzle, smooch, Jiffy Lube, forgive, sacrifice for, entertain, charm, show equality for, trust, grovel, brag about, help, acknowledge, polish, embrace, upgrade, accept, butter up, hear, understand, beg, bleed, nourish, resuscitate, respect, kill for, dream of, promise, deliver, tease, flirt, commit, snuggle, snooze, elevate, enervate, serve, love, bite, taste, nibble, gratify, take her places, swing, slip-slide, slather, squeeze, moisturize, lather, tingle, slicken, gelatinize, indulge, wow!, dazzle, amaze, idolize, and then go back, Jack, and do it all again!

That's how you make a woman ready for love, which might seem overwhelming, especially when you realize that to get a man eager for love, all you have to do is show up naked (smile)! And remember, great sex starts hours before intercourse. A loving touch, an "I love you" phone call, a note, or a soft kiss goes a long way in creating the atmosphere you both want.

Because men are visual creatures, they like us to go to bed in something other than that Laura Ashley flannel gown we got when we went away to college. It's not that you can't ever wear that thing—just not often! Splurge on some new lingerie, really! Find out what he thinks looks good and get some. (Throw out that underwear you have had for five years!) I have some pieces of lingerie that are certainly not my favorite, but I am not wearing them for me! *He* likes them, so on they go. (And the truth is, they aren't on that long anyway.) And you know what, you feel sexier when you are in pretty lingerie.

Most of us women would probably be shocked at how important sex is to our husbands. (On the other hand, maybe you wouldn't be!)

Do your part in keeping it from becoming routine, and keep him satisfied at home.

Each of you men, equally important to your wife's attempting to be sexy and playful for you is your verbally romancing her. Don't let her be tempted by some suave Don Juan she might work with. No woman will leave a man who is effectively communicating love and passion to her. In your times in bed communicate to her that you find her very sexy and that she is indeed the most important part of your life.

Never Stop Learning

One of the most important things to do in a marriage is to continue learning how to be a better spouse. (I tell singles that the number one question to ask yourself about a potential mate is, *Is that person a learner?* A person who is a learner will learn to be a great wife or a great husband . . . a great parent . . . a great employee at a job . . . whatever.) Each of us must continue to grow in the role of husband or wife because it is one we will have for a lifetime.

As part of a couple, we need to continually learn about building relationships. Many great books, tapes and videos out there are designed to strengthen you as a couple. I have shelves of them. I figure that being a wife is one role I will have for the rest of my life, and I want to continually improve.

Oftentimes people will come to me for some help in their marriage. I am always amazed when I find out that neither spouse has read a book or listened to a tape on relationships. If they wanted to know how to build a car, they would study and read books on how to do it. Yet most people want to build a great marriage and aren't taking advantage of the wonderful products available. There are conferences, seminars and retreats available for you to attend. They will provide not only great information, but also a boost that all relationships will enjoy. Please read books, listen to tapes or go to a seminar. Expending this effort will definitely be beneficial.

Reprinted by permission of Thomas Nelson Publishers from the book entitled Dumb Things She Does, Dumb Things He Does, *Copyright © 2002 by Holly Wagner.*

Part Two
Common Pitfalls

*Many a man claims to have unfailing love,
but a faithful man who can find?
(Proverbs 20:6)*

*Better to live on a corner of the roof
than to share a home with a quarreling
wife. (Proverbs 21:9, GOD'S WORD)*

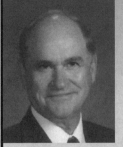

*D*r. David Ludwig is a pastor, professor and family counselor with over thirty-five years of professional experience. He holds a doctorate in psychology from Washington University in St. Louis, Missouri, and has written numerous articles, books and video-based courses. He and his wife Kathy present marriage and family workshops in the United States, Canada and Australia, offering scriptural understanding and day-to-day practical applications. Their Web site, www.thinkwenotme.com, is connected to The Power of WE: Center for Family and Community Relationships, a research and education facility housed at Lenoir-Rhyne College, Hickory, North Carolina.

Books

The Power of We (also leader's guide and video curriculum kits)
Renewing the Family Spirit

Web

www.thinkwenotme.com

Think We, Not 5 Me

David J. Ludwig

The Mystery of the Mood

"I can't wait to go to church this Sunday!" Joscelyn confided as she walked back from lunch with Tonya. "Adam and I met with the pastor last night, and we have our wedding all planned out."

Tonya replied with excitement, "I bet you will have a lot of people to talk to at church!"

Sunday morning came quickly. Joscelyn took her time getting dressed for church and was in a super mood as she waited for Adam to come pick her up. She planned to get to church early. She had quite a list of people to tell.

She waited, first wondering if something happened, then getting upset that Adam was not considerate enough to show up on time. It was almost time for church to start when he finally came to the door. "Where have you been?" Joscelyn asked with an annoyed edge in her voice.

Adam felt that sinking feeling that he got whenever he felt criticized, and he immediately got defensive. "Tom needed help loading a new program on his computer," he began.

Joscelyn broke in. "Couldn't that have waited?"

Adam sighed, feeling his good mood slipping away. "I thought it would only take me a minute or two . . . but we ran into a snag."

With that, Joscelyn looked away, the old, familiar hurt growing in her stomach. "I would like to be more important just once in my life," she said in a wistful, hurt voice.

Adam only heard more criticism and sighed again. "So I messed up again," he said with a touch of resigned anger in his voice.

They walked out of the door in silence. The mood had changed. They did not look at each other or touch, but got into the car like robots and drove to church.

Isn't this scene all too familiar? You look forward to doing something together only to have the mood shift, and you end up feeling

41

upset and confused. What happened to change the mood? What caused the turbulence and confusion in the atmosphere?

The answer lies in the spiritual dimension of your relationship. The word *spirit* literally means "wind" or "air." When the atmosphere changes mysteriously between the two of you, spiritual forces are at work. These forces are invisible, yet they control the mood or attitudes you have toward each other.

Do a Quick Check

Think of two people in your life. The first should be a good friend. The second should be someone you would rather never see again. Imagine being face-to-face with your friend. Check the atmosphere. Isn't it warm, friendly and uplifting? Now go to the second person. Imagine being face-to-face with him or her. Check the atmosphere. It's dramatically different, isn't it? It's cold, tense and upsetting.

There is a *spiritual* problem in the situation with the second person. You have a bad attitude toward each other that shows up in the mood you feel when you are in each other's presence. And you do not control the mood! Just try to produce the same atmosphere as you had with your friend. It is impossible. The mood is controlled by the "spirit," the attitude you hold toward each other.

Moods Happen When the "We" Breaks Apart

Think of the last time the mood shifted between the two of you. Perhaps it was last night when Mother called, or when you talked about money. Let me guess who you blamed for your frustration and internal upset. It wasn't yourself, so you blamed the only other person you could see, right?

Well, you made a critical error! Neither of you controls the mood of your relationship. The "we" controls the atmosphere! When the two of you are allies and your spirits are united, the *mood is uplifting* and friendly. But when the "we" breaks down and you are at odds with each other, the *mood shifts to turbulent* and upsetting. When you harbor resentment toward each other, a *bad mood* settles into the relationship.

No wonder St. Paul advises, "Make every effort to keep the *unity of the Spirit* through the bond of peace" (Ephesians 4:3). He uses even stronger language in Philippians 2:1-2:

> If you have any encouragement from being united with Christ, if any comfort from his love, if any fellowship with the Spirit, if any tenderness and compassion, then make my joy complete by being like-minded, having the same love, being *one in spirit* and purpose.

When you are "one in spirit," you have a safe place with each other. The mood is friendly, and you are allies. You are a "we" and are working together. It is safe to share your thoughts and feelings with each other. You can be "soul mates."

But when the "we" breaks down, it is no longer safe! You have to be defensive and guarded. The relationship splits into "you" and "me." There is no one in charge, and the atmosphere becomes uncertain and confusing. Both of you get your feelings hurt and end up upset and angry with each other. Since you cannot see the "we," you blame each other for the hurt and frustration. You think, *If only he/she would not react that way*. Then you spend your energy trying to change the other person.

Time for a Spiritual Reality Check

But the other person is not to blame! You cannot see the "we," but it does control the spirit (mood) of the relationship. When this "one another" breaks down, the mood shifts. So blame the relationship, blame "we," blame the "one another." No wonder St. Paul uses the words *one another* so often: "Submit to *one another* out of reverence for Christ" (Ephesians 5:21). The "one another" is the "we." The deep spiritual meaning of this passage is to make the "we" more important than the "me." When your feelings are hurt and you are upset, it is natural to nurse the hurt feelings and to seek to get even. Both of these actions put the "me" as more important than the "we."

You Can Control the Mood . . . with God's Help

So how do you do the "unnatural" and put the "we" above your own hurt and upset? The answer is in the aforementioned verse:

"out of reverence for Christ." The Holy Spirit can change your attitude at this critical moment. Christ's presence has the power to change your heart and mind to make this shift from "me" to "we."

As you pray, "Lord, help my spirit; help change my attitude," His Spirit will be at work in your heart to change reality. Call this a "reality check." Right in the midst of your desire to nurse your hurt feelings, Christ will remind you of His love and of your love for one another. This will help to put the relationship in its proper place—the "we" will become more important than the "me."

Private Strategies Never Work to Form a "We"

As they drove to church in tense silence, Adam's mind was filled with thoughts of how to make the mood better next time. I'll make sure never to be late again, *he resolved.* Then she won't get upset with me.

Adam had used this strategy many times before—a private way of working on the mood by keeping Joscelyn from getting upset. But it was energy wasted. He tried and tried to do the right thing, but she still would get upset. So as he struggled to make the relationship better, he was building some resentment over the fact that his efforts were never enough. He still could not please her. He often had the angry thought, Nothing I do is right.

As they drove in tense silence, Joscelyn's mind was filled with thoughts of how to make the mood better. Why did I let it bother me? *she fussed at herself.* Why can't I just let things like that go?

Joscelyn had used this strategy many times before—a private way of working on the mood by stopping her natural reactions to things. She tried and tried not to get upset, but it did not seem to help. Adam still did not seem to care about what she felt, no matter how she tried to express it. But as she shut down more and more, she also held some anger against Adam for not responding to her feelings. She often thought, I guess he really doesn't care about what I feel.

So How Do You Make Sure You Stay a "We"?

They were back in the car, driving out of the church parking lot, when Joscelyn made the first move. "I think we have a problem. Neither of us wanted the mood to shift this morning, but it did anyway."

Adam was shocked. He expected to hear that he had ruined the day by being late and had his defenses ready. But when he heard Joscelyn blame the "we," he felt a bit more open and responded with an "ally" signal. "I don't blame you for being upset. I just think we missed each other," Adam said with more energy in his voice.

Soon they were in a much different conversation. They were using the word we *every other sentence and were searching out what each had felt when the mood shifted. In fact, the mood shifted back the moment the first "we" was said. Now they could be allies, working against the common problem of miscommunication.*

Steps to Reconnecting

The next time the mood shifts and you are left confused, hurt and upset, try the following steps:

1. Become aware that the "we" just broke down.
2. Stop blaming the other person.
3. Assume that there has been a misunderstanding.
4. Offer a prayer to get your attitude right.
5. Approach the other person in the right spirit.
6. Begin by saying, "*We* have a problem. Let's talk."

Don't think this is easy! It is highly unnatural. It is more natural to assume that the other person is to blame. This is what puts the "me" above the "we." So don't overlook the importance of bringing Christ into the equation. His love changes reality. His presence can make the "we" more important than the "me."

Put the following on your refrigerator door or bathroom mirror: *Submit to one another out of reverence for Christ.*

Why Does Misunderstanding Occur?*

	Painter	**Pointer**
Perception	Notices everything	Notices task at hand
Consciousness	Keeps many things in mind	Focuses on one thing
Defense of Self	Vigilant, so no surprises	Puts things in perspective
Communication	Paints a picture	Sticks to the point

*Note: There are many helpful typologies that describe differences in personality, such as the Myers-Briggs (Myers, 1962). The typology presented here is designed to explain differences in communication style and give insight into the breakdown in communication between two people.

How does a pointer misunderstand a painter? The pointer focuses on the first thing said and assumes that this is the point when it is in actuality only the first brushstroke. Also, the pointer is confused when the painter jumps around, because the pointer thinks sequentially.

How does a painter misunderstand a pointer? The painter is looking for detail and misses the summarization that the pointer starts with. Also, the painter is frustrated and starts digging for details by asking specific questions, which forces the pointer to jump from point to point.

How do you spot the cause of misunderstanding? Both must take a different look at reality!

Since the Pointer:

    a. does not notice

    b. does not react emotionally

    c. wants to withdraw when there is tension

    d. shifts focus and gets involved in something else immediately

    e. rolls over and goes to sleep

    f. seldom brings thing up

the Painter assumes that the Pointer does not care. This is not reality! The Pointer cares just as much as the Painter, but handles things differently!

Since the Painter:

    a. brings things up again and again

    b. goes on and on about something

    c. seems to overstate things for effect

    d. will not let something go

    e. gets emotionally upset over things

    f. starts with an attack on the Pointer

the Pointer assumes that the Painter is trying to make him/her feel guilty. This is not reality! The Painter is not blaming, but trying to connect!

Where Do Bad Moods Come From?

Look closely at the spiritual wisdom in Ephesians 4:26-27: "In your anger do not sin: Do not let the sun go down while you are still angry, and do not give the devil a foothold."

So what should you do with your anger? It is clear that you should not deal with it on the inside, for then the devil gets a foothold. So every time you swallow your anger and let something go, you run the risk of building resentment.

> *Marcie remembered the very first time money came up. They were on their first date. When it was time to pay the bill, Greg put on a show of generosity and picked up the check. That was fine with Marcie, but when he put down a thirty percent tip, she was puzzled and quizzed, "That much?"*
>
> *Greg's eyes met hers, and with a touch of annoyance he said, "Sure. The service was excellent."*
>
> *The mood shifted for about three seconds as both were puzzled and upset by the other's reaction. Then Marcie mumbled, "OK," and they went on chatting about their mutual friend.*

Mood Particles Build Up!

Greg and Marcie did not talk about their anger with each other, and the same situation occurred again and again. She felt he was too generous and careless with money, and he thought she was trying to control him. Each time this happened, remnants of the unresolved mood stayed stuck in the atmosphere. Let's call these "Freeze-Dried Mood Particles." As these particles accumulated, attitudes started to change. Three hundred and twenty-seven times later, the anger had turned into resentment (sin):

> *"What did you charge this time?" Marcie asked as she looked at a half-hidden charge slip. "Why didn't you tell me what you bought?" she continued with hurt in her voice.*
>
> *Greg felt the resentment growing in his stomach as he clenched his teeth and responded sarcastically, "What are you doing snooping around? And who made you the stupid dictator?"*

This time it was not just a three-second mood shift. The "we" broke apart with a spiritual explosion equivalent to the detonation of a thousand pounds of dynamite as they glared at each other with bitterness smoldering in their eyes. The bad mood would stay around all night and still be there to affect the mood for the next week. Wow, this is spiritual power!

*Before y*our anger builds up inside, it can be described as "upset" or "frustration." *After* the mood particles build up, it becomes "bitterness" or "disgust." The change is in the attitude of your heart. You start believing that things are not fair, gradually building resentment.

Resentment is always "justified." It always carries a big list of things that caused you to feel that way. And it is the resentment at work in your heart that changes your spirit. Such a bad attitude is a spiritual problem for your relationship! When the resentment builds to a critical point, then you can justify a deliberately hurtful comment or a hateful comment filled with disrespect. When you cross this line, you damage the relationship. It is hard to forget such disrespect. In fact, it can be remembered for ten or twenty years!

So How Do You Fight Such Damage?

The "we" can heal past damage! The process is called "confession and forgiveness." This can restore the spirit.

But how do you start the process when you don't want to?

Confession

When you have crossed the line and damaged the relationship, what can you do?

1. Realize that you feel justified in what you did.
2. Admit to yourself and to God that you do not want to apologize.
3. Spend time in prayer, asking God to change your hardened heart.
4. Meditate on Psalm 51:10: "Create in me a clean heart, O God; and renew a right spirit within me" (KJV).
5. Approach the other person "in the right spirit" and say, "Please forgive me."

Greg stomped out of the room and slammed the door. He was tired of Marcie's control. He felt like he was a little boy again, asking permission from his mother for everything he did. The anger and bitterness burned in his stomach. She has to make every decision, he thought with growing resentment. Why does she have to criticize everything I want to do? He flipped on the TV and tried to bury himself in the program, but his thoughts went back to Marcie. Deep in his heart he did not want to feel this way. He bowed his head and prayed, "God, help me. I don't want to give up my bitterness."

The rest is mysterious. Sometime within the next twenty minutes as Greg thought back over the situation for the twentieth time, he pictured Marcie's hurt over his sarcasm. He felt a tug at his heart and had a tear in his eye as he thought of her. With a prayer for strength, he went to find her and tell her, "Please forgive me."

Forgiveness

How do you give the other person his or her rights back when you don't think he/she deserves it?

1. Realize you feel justified in holding things against the other person.
2. Admit to yourself and to God that you do not want to forgive.
3. In prayer, ask God to help you forgive.
4. Meditate on Ephesians 4:32: "[Forgive] each other, just as in Christ God forgave you."
5. Look at the other person in the right spirit and say, "I forgive you."

Marcie heard Greg's apology and thought, Too little, too late. *She looked away for a moment. She was not about to let him off the hook that easily. As she prayed, she struggled in her heart. If she gave up her mood, it felt like she was letting him get by with something! But when she looked back, she saw the genuineness in his eyes and her face softened. "I forgive you," she said.*

This began a two-hour heart-to-heart talk about money. Greg gradually developed a deeper understanding of Marcie's concern. At the end, he could say, "Thanks for looking out for our future."

Marcie gradually developed a deeper understanding of Greg's frustration. "Let's work on this together," she said, "so that money does not split us apart again."

How to Make Your Home a "Grace Place"

Since the "we" controls the atmosphere in your relationship, the best strategy you can develop for your marriage is to *make sure that you stay a "we."*

Pray Together

Establish a place in your home where you will pray together each day. Call it a "grace place." As you pray, the Holy Spirit will help you strengthen the "we."

For he himself is our peace, who has made the two one. (Ephesians 2:14)

And in him you too are being built together to become a dwelling in which God lives by his Spirit. (2:22)

"For this reason a man will leave his father and mother and be united to his wife, and the two will become one flesh." This is a profound mystery—but I am talking about Christ and the church. (5:31-32)

Steps to praying together:

1. Come together and pray silently, putting the other person in your heart.
2. Then tell the other person what you prayed for.
3. Then have one person end by praying for the relationship.
4. Work toward praying aloud for each other and for the relationship.

Each time you pray together, you strengthen the "we." It is harder to stay at odds with each other when you both acknowledge Christ's presence among you. Then, after you establish this "grace place," you have a place to go when you have split into "you" and "me" and are controlled by the upset mood. Let God help restore the "we" as you come to Him in prayer.

All this is from God, who reconciled us to himself through Christ and gave us the ministry of reconciliation. (2 Corinthians 5:18)

Don't Blame the Other Person for Your Upset Feeling

Blame the relationship. Realize that the mood happened because the "we" broke apart and that both of you are feeling hurt and upset at the same time.

Recognize that you formed your half of the relationship.

Why do you look at the speck of sawdust in your brother's eye and pay no attention to the plank in your own eye? . . . You hypocrite, first take the plank out of your own eye, and then you will see clearly to remove the speck from your brother's eye. (Matthew 7:3, 5)

On your knees, first seek to clean up your half of the relationship so that you can approach the other person in the right spirit.

Don't Hide Things from One Another

Stop the temptation to keep the other person from getting upset. Tell the truth, but do it to help clear the air.

> Instead, speaking the truth in love, we will in all things grow up into him who is the Head, that is, Christ. (Ephesians 4:15)

Remember that God can heal the truth, but He can never heal a lie!

Have Heart-to-Heart Talks

Stop your private strategies to get the mood back. Stop wasting your energy and running the risk of building resentment. Don't try to deal with your anger privately.

> Therefore, if you are offering your gift at the altar and there remember that your brother has something against you, leave your gift there in front of the altar. First go and be reconciled. (Matthew 5:23-24)

Whenever the mood gets bad, always seek to ally! Remember that you are only five seconds away from changing the mood back by becoming a "we" again. The moment that you look at each other and say, "*We* have a problem," you are allies again.

Always See Your Spouse as a Gift of God

Remember that you are human and that there will be conflict. But see your differences as gifts! Instead of trying to change the other person, seek to put the relationship together so that your gifts complement each other.

In other words, affirm your spouse as he/she needs affirmation. And thank God daily for the gift you have in him/her. Try doing it out loud when you are praying at your "grace place."

Utilize the Support of the Christian Community

Christian friends help your mood when you share things with them. A Bible study group made up of those you trust as a couple is a wonderful place to talk over family struggles. This is a place to go for additional help with the spiritual dimension of your marriage.

If you do not have a church community, look for one that will offer you spiritual support. Do not miss this source of personal and marital strength.

And remember—think we, not me!

A pastor and counselor for thirty-six years, Wayne Coggins brings a broad understanding of life, relationships and Christian living to his ministry. His seminars, workshops, retreats, counseling and church ministry are filled with practical illustrations that enable participants to put biblical principles into practice in their daily lives.

Coggins is married and has three grown children and six grandchildren. He and his wife Marveen divide their time between Anchorage, Alaska, and Steamboat Springs, Colorado.

Seminars
  Anger Management
  Authentic Manhood
  Blended Families
  Divorce Recovery
  Marriage Enrichment
  Parent-Teen Communication
  Single Parenting
  Simplifying Your Life

Web
    www.cornerstonefamilyministries.com

The Doctor Is In 6

Wayne Coggins

I have always enjoyed Valentine's Day—a day to celebrate love
and romance. But on a recent Valentine's Day I was a little nervous when I was introduced as the speaker at a large multichurch
Valentine's banquet being held at the elegant officers' club at
Elmendorf Air Force Base in Anchorage, Alaska. Having been a
pastor in Alaska for over thirty years and having performed nearly
300 weddings, I recognized in the audience many couples—and
the children of couples!—whom I had joined in marriage. I'd spent
thousands of hours with these folks doing premarital counseling,
and then marriage counseling down the road when they'd hit
snags and felt help was needed. Some I had walked with through
the dark valleys of divorce or the death of a mate. But, although I
knew many of these people, I was not prepared for the expectations that were running high that night after the churches had
been told that "the Love Doctor" would be speaking on diagnosing
and treating marriages. I'd been called a number of things in my
years of ministry, but never "the Love Doctor."

After the introductions and a few attempts to be funny and
break the ice, I stood for a moment and studied my audience. For
the most part, they were a festive bunch, but in the eyes of some I
sensed a look of quiet desperation that said to me that all was not
well on the home front. I could tell that some were hoping beyond
hope that I would say something, anything, that night that would
help to relight the pilot lights in the furnaces of marriages that had
long ago flickered and gone out. In others I could sense a marital
bankruptcy that nice suits and evening gowns could not disguise. I
became acutely aware that some of the things I was going to say
that night needed to be aimed and timed for maximum impact or

that might be the last Valentine's Day banquet for some of those present.

I began with, "Well, the Love Doctor is in session. And though I am not a real doctor, my ministry as a pastor and therapist does bring me into contact many times each week with folks who are in need of healing. Many of the people I see register very low in the hope factor when it comes to their marriages ever getting any better. I am aware that there are some here tonight who feel exactly like that, so please let me say this to you: *I have lots of hope! I am a merchant of hope, and if your hope tank is a few quarts low tonight, use some of mine for a while and let's go to work!* God can help you and bring life to every part of your marriage. Resurrection power is His stock in trade, and He still is able to bring life out of the throes of death."

I then pulled out my "doctor's bag" that I'd picked up at a toy store and began to explain the diagnostic tools used to check the status of a marriage. In the bag I had the following:

- A stethoscope for listening below the surface for the issues of the heart.

- An otoscope (the little instrument for looking in a patient's ear) to discover any communication blockages.

- A thermometer to check the temperature of the relationship to see if it is hot, cold or lukewarm.

- A blood pressure device to check for buildup of anger or stress.

- A tongue depressor for helping us to "open up" and share how things really are.

- A hypodermic needle in case a relationship is in need of an injection of romance or creativity.

- A reflex hammer to check out responsiveness to one another's needs.

- Scales to see how much heavy baggage was brought into the marriage and how much is still being carried around.

- Band-Aids to protect surface nicks and hurts from becoming infected.

- An eye chart to check for blind spots that can sneak up on any of us.

We had some fun with some of those applications, but the conversation got very serious when I began to talk about five common marriage maladies.

1. Marital Anemia

I am convinced that more marriages are in danger of anemia (tired blood) than of getting blasted apart by a surprise affair or deception. Drifting apart a little each day can leave a couple vulnerable to all kinds of problems. For a marriage to stay fresh and vibrant, it needs frequent doses of fun and *re-creation*. I am not advocating being irresponsible, but I am saying that all responsibility with no breaks for fun and frolic is a sure ticket to burnout and boredom. I often ask couples whose responsibility it is to find or make the time available for investing in their marriages. God's? Should we requisition God for an extra day of the week right after Sunday and call it Funday? While that may be a nice fantasy, the truth is that if we value our marriage relationships, we simply *must* take the time to keep them alive and exciting. Now, if a marriage has degenerated to the excitement level akin to that of watching paint dry, this may be a bit of a challenge, but believe me, there are more exciting things to do as a couple than sitting in your matching recliners arguing over how often the husband goes channel-surfing during the commercials.

I love the scene at the beginning of the movie *Never Cry Wolf* where Tyler (a New England geek) is being flown in a small rattle-trap airplane out into the wilderness to study wolves by a wacky bush pilot named Rosie. In the middle of a mountain range, the plane's engine stops. Before climbing out of the plane to fix a frozen fuel line, Rosie, waving a crescent wrench in Tyler's face, pauses to philosophize for a moment that the problem with many folks sitting in their living rooms, glued to the television set, is *boredom*. As he opens the door of the rapidly descending plane, Rosie quips, "Do you know the cure for boredom, Tyler? Adventure! It's adventure, Tyler!" Well, I don't want to leave you hanging in suspense—the plane engine does finally restart, and in a tense scene that only someone with experience flying in a small plane can fully appreciate, they gain enough altitude to narrowly clear a craggy mountain ridge.

A couple of years ago my wife and I had a wonderful *adventure* during which we had many incredible moments of closeness and excitement. We took a break from our busy lives and ministries and spent a full year at 8,000 feet in the Rocky Mountains near Steamboat Springs, Colorado, living in an old miner/trapper's cabin with no running water and a big, ancient fireplace for heat. This had been my wife's dream since she was a child, and with some health problems threatening her, we decided we'd just go for it. We worked and played and explored and enjoyed what solitude and simplicity brought our way for a year, and today we wouldn't trade the experience for any amount of money or position we could have obtained during those twelve months.

I remember the first November night when the temperature dropped down to around ten degrees and we hunkered down under a big down comforter to try to sleep for the night. We could see our breath in the moonlight, and it felt for all the world like I had frost crystals forming on my balding head. I grabbed a stocking hat out of the nightstand, and we pulled the covers up a little higher and laughed ourselves to sleep. In the morning, as we stood on the porch and counted the deer tracks in the frosty grass, we held each other close and savored a moment of genuine, real-life adventure.

While taking a year off to live in the mountains (it was a lot of work too) may not be something that your life circumstances can afford right now, there are mini-adventures that you can have every day. A surprise picnic lunch in the park or under a blanket tent in the living room can be a fun way to liven up an otherwise ordinary noon break while the kids are at school. Or try a dress-up night at the opera, pretending that you really understand what the singers are singing and that you are high-society types who do such things all the time. Simple things like creative notes in his lunchbox or a surprise $50 bill in her checkbook so she can do something special for herself can work wonders. Adventure and creativity are surefire cures for marital anemia.

2. Presumption

While attending a Marriage Encounter weekend back in the '70s, I learned that most relationships go through three distinct stages. The first is *romance*, that goofy time when we are so enamored with our newly discovered love that talking for hours is done genuinely and joyfully, and not because it is a homework assignment for your marriage class. I sometimes jokingly share that romance is the anesthetic that enables two normally very cautious people to cast fate to the wind and commit marriage.

The second relational stage is *disillusionment*. This is the time when we discover that the packages we thought we got when we married our sweethearts aren't exactly what we'd expected. It is when we become inescapably aware of the painful truth that in order for there to be disillusionment, there must have been an illusion. That girl who was so witty and funny and always had the right thing to say turns out not to have an off button on her vocal chords! And that guy who didn't always have a lot to say, but what he did say was deep, turns out to be the strong, silent type who doesn't know how to communicate at all in matters of the heart.

The third stage presents a fork in the road with one direction marked *acceptance* and the other *rejection*. It is during this stage that the "rubber meets the road," so to speak, and the real work of keeping a marriage healthy and growing is done or evaded. This is where presumption does its deadly deed by presuming that "it will all work out somehow." You see, "it," or the marriage, doesn't do the work of communicating when you are weary of forgiving each other. It is *you*, the partners in marriage, who do that work. It is you who makes the value judgment that the imperfect person you married is indeed the most valuable treasure in your life, in spite of those imperfections.

The halfhearted attitude that is symptomatic of presumption in marriage needs to be given shock therapy! As with any endeavor in life, maximum enjoyment is achieved when marriage is done with the whole heart.

When I was a kid growing up on our little farm, summertime afternoons were occasionally made special by the appearance of a big, cold watermelon on the back porch. After a day of work in the fields or the barn, we'd gather on the back porch, and, dressed in our jeans and T-shirts, the four of us kids would watch as Mom or Dad carved off big slices of the juicy, cold melon for each of us. Now, I know that today you can go to the grocery store and bring back a plastic tub of watermelon balls that you eat with a fork and never get so much as a drop of juice on your fingers. But what kind of fun is that? It is a much more exciting and memorable experience to bite with wholehearted enthusiasm into one of those big slabs of watermelon and spit the seeds out into the grass while the juice dribbles off your chin and down your forearms. Sure, the sticky juice washes off, but the memory stays. I believe the cure for the marital malady of presumption is wholeheartedness, and it doesn't cost you a penny for the treatment. Ask your therapist for "watermelon therapy" and watch him search through the manuals for that one!

3. Heart Problems

The third marital malady that can appear in a relationship is a heart condition. While there are many variations of this condition, probably none are as threatening as *unforgiveness* and *bitterness*. If allowed to remain in a marriage, these two can clog marital arteries quicker than cheeseburgers and french fries can clog your natural ones. They will cut off the life-giving love and communication that are necessary for the health and growth of the relationship. As a counselor, I am well aware that forgiveness is easier said than done. It is one thing to say, "I forgive you," and another thing to walk it out in real life.

Have you ever wondered what God does to put joy in the courts of heaven? Well, I have concluded that one thing that brings God joy is the healing of the human heart from its hurts and wounds. Psalm 147:3 says that God "heals the brokenhearted and binds up their wounds." The reason that I think God enjoys this so much is that it seems that He is the only one who can do it. For all the training and mentoring I have undergone as a pastor and counselor, in the finality of it all, in my counseling office or kneeling beside a painfully wounded person, it is that miracle moment in prayer when God touches the heart, heals it and enables forgiveness to become a reality as well as a decision, that makes the difference.

Have you ever heard the expression "nursing a grudge"? A pastor friend of mine once did an illustrated sermon on that topic. He shared that if we ignore the biblical admonition in James 5:9 not to hold grudges (KJV), we will eventually come to the place where we don't have grudges—instead, they have us. He illustrated this by cradling a doll (an ugly one named "Grudge") in his arms while feeding it a bottle. Then he graduated to a bigger and uglier doll requiring a bigger bottle to feed it. He then had a nearly life-sized gorilla draped over his shoulders while he reached back to keep feeding it from a baby bottle. Then, in the finale, someone dressed like Darth Vadar from Star Wars came striding ominously onto the platform and began shoving my pastor friend around while he tried unsuccessfully to fend the creature off with the baby bottle. I think the point is obvious. I can't count the number of married couples I have counseled who are exhausted by trying to carry a lifetime of accumulated offenses in their relationships.

May I suggest a simple procedure that can fix this problem? Try reaching over to your loved one and taking his or her hand in yours. Then, simply pray for one another, asking God to help each of you forgive the other for the hurts that have occurred in your relationship. You see, I believe that if God asks us to do something, He is faithful to provide the ability to do so. In Ephesians 4:32 we are told to be "kind to one another, tenderhearted, *forgiving one another* even as God for Christ's sake hath forgiven you" (KJV). If it feels like the walls of bitterness are too high and trust too shattered to glue back together, believe me—no, believe God—forgiveness is the miracle cure that can make healing possible.

4. Secret-Life Syndrome

In his book *Men's Secret Wars*, Patrick Means exposes a deadly virus that has begun to be an epidemic in the marriages of both unbelievers and believers alike. It is the secret-life syndrome that occurs when a secret part of our lives is allowed to grow until it suddenly springs into view with a vengeance. While this malady has been around since Adam and Eve tried to hide their secret life and sin from God, in recent years a very virile strain has been at work through the unlikely agent of the computer. While home and office computers can be wonderful tools for good, the addictive nature of Internet pornography and on-line chat rooms is taking a huge toll on marriages. I would estimate that in more than half of the marital counseling I do, the devastation created by the deception and betrayal of these addictions is a major component. It is such a shame-saturated problem in people's lives that it often grows hidden and undetected until it has done severe damage to a marriage.

The real heart-cry that I hear from couples is for true intimacy and that wonderful feeling of connectedness that a healthy marriage can bring. That which can be found in clandestine chat-room affairs or cyber fantasies is *not* the real deal. It is somewhat akin to what the prostitute offered to the young man in Proverbs 7:18 when she entrapped him with the words "Come, let us take our fill of love until the morning: let us solace ourselves with loves" (KJV). Real love can't be found in a one-night stand or a secret life apart from your spouse.

My counseling supervisor and mentor recently attended a conference on the whole cybersex addiction issue and shared with me that research is now showing that the addictive intensity of Internet pornography is close to that which snares cocaine junkies. We have all read of the famous athletes and celebrities who put their careers in a tailspin of desperation because of this kind of addiction.

Consider this for a moment: An average reader can read aloud at about 200 words per minute or silently around 600 words per minute. I read once that we can process self-talk, or have inner conversations, at a rate of at least 1,300 words per minute! Now, it has been said that "a picture paints a thousand words" (roughly two pages of writing), and a person could easily write two pages describing a sunset or a duck swimming on a pond among the lily pads. So, if a person brings up sexually charged images on his computer screen and views 1,000-word pictures every few seconds, and if those are processed with adrenaline-driven sexual fantasy at 1,300 words per minute (or more), you have sensory overload. Then, if you figure in the added spike of the allure of the forbidden and the fear of getting caught, you have very fertile ground for a serious addiction. In the chat-room arena, the bait is appealing on a different emotional level than are the visual come-ons for men, but the setup for women to get drawn into addictive fantasy relationships is just as deadly.

As a pastor and counselor, I am so grateful for the work done by groups such as Prodigals International (Pat and Marsha Means), Stonegate Resources (Harry Schaumburg), Every Man's Battle (Steve Arterburn and Fred Stoeker), the National Association for Christian Recovery and others in bringing this issue out of the closet and pointing the way to hope and healing. If this syndrome is eating away at the core of your heart and marriage and you want to use that PC for something highly beneficial, log on to the Web sites of any of those organizations. Help is only a click away.

And while there are many components of recovery in these areas, I recently attended a conference in which the speaker asserted that "the best Internet filter on the planet is your heart." A person whose heart is intimately connected with God and his or her spouse is going to experience a joy that is worth more than anything that would jeopardize it. Trust is the pearl of great price in a marriage, and it is worth everything to preserve it.

5. Obsessive Perfectionism

The fifth marital malady is often passed on from generation to generation in the form of obsessive perfectionism. I know of few marriages that can flourish under this slave-driving taskmaster. The good news is that even though a parent or grandparent may have modeled this as something you just have to live with, it can be cured with a good dose of grace and regular, honest therapy with someone you love and trust, a person who isn't afraid to let you know when you are being compulsive and obnoxious.

I know most of us can identify to some degree with one of the two characters in the *Odd Couple* comedy. We tend either to be meticulously fastidious like Felix or to find week-old hotdogs in our overcoats like Oscar. Now, both extremes can make for friction in a relationship, but I have observed that perfectionism is particularly oppressive in marriages. I believe that the underlying thing at work here is the message that acceptance and love can be based only on excellence or perfect performance in life. Perhaps you were raised with that recording playing over and over in your mind and have a sneaking suspicion that God Himself is a fussy perfectionist. The truth is that while God is perfect and the Bible sets before us what perfect behavior looks like in principle, God has chosen to relate to us redemptively and loves us unconditionally in spite of our propensity to be human and mess up.

In marriage, this plays out the same. None of us is all that lovable all the time, and being married to a demanding perfectionist can feel like boot camp. And the fact is that being a perfectionist isn't a picnic either, because being a performance cop is a hard and thankless job. So let me suggest that if you need some counseling to find the roots of the insecurity that is driving your perfectionism, don't wait another day to get with the program. I can guarantee that if you will seek the God of grace for a greater dose of it in your life, He won't disappoint you. He did, after all, promise grace to the humble.

I remember memorizing a poem years ago that I think was attributed to Ogden Nash: "To keep your marriage brimming with love in the loving cup, when you're wrong, admit it, and when you're right, shut up." Amen.

Thank You

Thanks for allowing me to wander around the landscape of marriage using this medical metaphor. Let me conclude with this truth: The Lord, who is the Great Physician, can and does heal and restore marriages in need of a miracle moment of healing. He is also more than willing to share His rich wisdom with us on this subject so that we can build healthy marriages right out of the chute. The fact is that He wrote the Book on it, and His office is never closed.

*D*r. Al Huba is a licensed clinical pastoral counselor in Butler, Pennsylvania, where he is also the pastor of a local church. After receiving a Ph.D. in counseling psychology, he practiced in Alaska for several years before relocating to his hometown.

Huba and his wife Brenda have seven children, four of whom are at home. Huba brings a wealth of clinical as well as practical experience regarding marriage—being a parent and step-parent to a bevy of children allows him to relate well to the people to whom he ministers.

The Blended Family—Chopped or Whipped?

Al Huba

The blended family, by definition, is a combination of two pre-existing families that have been broken by divorce or the death of a spouse. The remainder of the broken family then combines with another family and makes an effort toward living a happy life together.

Despite good intentions, the blended family often ends up being something far from its best design. The name "blended" is usually a misnomer in that the combined family frequently does not experience blending—becoming a homogeneous mixture of individuals—but rather becomes a chopped and diced mixture more resembling a tossed salad. Now, salads are fine for cuisine, but in a familial sense there must be more blending among the ingredients.

Conversely, there are combined families that are overblended. They more resemble a puree in which there is no separation between the ingredients; they have lost their identity or individuality. I can remember a few years back when learning to make mushroom soup. Not being inclined to use recipes, I decided to cook the mushrooms and then puree them before adding the other ingredients. Needless to say, it was a disaster. When I pureed the mushrooms, they lost much of their flavor and all of their unique texture.

In this article I will attempt to guide combined families through a series of steps to a truly blended family. Let's picture ourselves in a kitchen with God our Father, the Master Chef. As we follow His directions, we will be successful, for, remember, He does have a plan for you—in fact, a recipe.

Some of the primary ingredients in the recipe are kids, grandparents (biological or step) and ex-spouses or biological parents. But here I'd like to focus on the main ingredients tossed into the blender: husband and wife. The factor that impedes the homogeneous blending of these ingredients is not so much the man and the woman themselves but what they bring into the marriage. This is frequently referred to as "baggage." Some people bring so much baggage into their marriages that the "blended-family plane" can't get off the ground. As an airline limits the amount of baggage we can bring aboard, so it should be in the step-marriage. But how many of us ever give this a passing thought?

Here is a partial list of some of the excess baggage brought into the blended family: past abuses, prior marital and family-of-origin dysfunctions, a family or personal history of drugs and alcohol, broken trust, poor communication and conflict-resolution skills, guilt for past mistakes, unresolved anger and resentment and, last but certainly not least, unforgiveness and unrepentance. Unless this baggage is dealt with, it will affect the family in a most unpleasant way. Due to the brevity of this article, I will attempt to help with the resolution of the baggage problem only in a somewhat cursory manner.

As a psychological sage once put it, "Whatever we don't resolve we will reproduce in our children." Much of the marital baggage that needs to be resolved consists of emotional wounds. Picture for a moment a tree that has a lot of unhealthy fruit growing on it: unforgiveness, anger, guilt, distrust, anxiety, fear, compulsive behaviors, etc. We can try to treat these fruits directly or symptomatically, or we can address them at their origins and roots.

Many of these negative emotions/behaviors are rooted in pain caused by an emotional or spiritual hurt, usually in the form of rejection. Rejection in turn stems from past acts of *commission* (something that someone did to us): possibly physical, sexual, spiritual or verbal abuse. Acts of *omission* are equally rejective in nature and can be categorized as what a significant person should have done for us but didn't; this is otherwise known as a withholding of love. This could have been in the form of nonacceptance, lack of physical affection, disapproval, overcriticism or lack of praise. A person with this type of background will inevitably suffer from some or all of the following: low self-worth or self-esteem, feelings of inferiority, perfectionism, procrastination, performance orientation and hypersensitivity to certain issues. The process of healing damaged emotions is an arduous one, but it is certainly possible with the help of God.

Forgiveness and Reconciliation

The process of emotional healing starts with forgiveness and reconciliation (where possible). Forgiveness is not an option but an act of obedience to the Lord. Reconciliation, however, must involve the cooperation of both alienated members. Where that is impossible—because of the unwillingness of one member or perhaps the death of a party or the impossibility of physically locating a person—the reconciliation must take place in the heart of the person seeking reconciliation. In the case of blended families, it is imperative that husband and wife forgive their former spouses and their associated families (grandparents, aunts, uncles, etc.).

Without forgiveness it is guaranteed that the past will be revisited in the present family. The only way to ensure that the past will not "come back" is to give it a proper burial. Forgive and bury the past by forgiving the people who have hurt you. Through human means it is impossible to completely forgive. However, our responsibility is to agree with the Lord's command to forgive and allow Him to help us carry it out. Much of the anger and resentment that we carry in blended families can be assuaged through forgiveness.

Quite often the most difficult person to forgive for issues stemming from the past is ourselves. It is not unusual for people trying to start a new family to suffer from guilt regarding the past. When one forgives oneself, however, the guilt will soon disappear. People who come from abusive or otherwise dysfunctional backgrounds can often be easily manipulated by guilt or fear. Forgiveness of self often allays these negative emotions.

Conflict Resolution

In order to mix our ingredients properly, we must approach the subject of conflict resolution. The combined family will always be the proving ground for conflict. By its very nature the blended family will constantly be faced with conflict. Too often we view conflict as totally negative, with nothing but casualties. But this need not be the case. Conflict is the natural by-product of growth and change. As a tree grows and changes, it comes into conflict with its neighbors, but somehow they make room for each other. I'm sure there are times when the oak would prefer to call for the chain saw rather than give in to the growing pine tree, but that would invite a casualty. Likewise, as the family grows and changes, it must adapt to each member.

Conflict is not evil. It is necessary and eventually results in good for the family, for it is through conflict that values are more clearly defined. And clearly defined values make a healthy family. Only through conflict can we really get to know each other. If I want to really get to know someone, I play a couple of rounds of golf with him. No conflict in golf, you say? Try counting your opponent's strokes for him!

Communication

Conflict can be resolved only through good communication. Simply put, people who know how to resolve conflict communicate well. Notice I didn't say "talk a lot," but rather "communicate well." Just talking can be a monologue; communication is a two-way conversation. Looking at communication more closely, Roy Brewer, a teacher with many years of experience, relates, "Communication is the foundation of all relationships. Communication is an interesting thing. I may know what I'm going to say, but I still have no idea what you are going to hear; and communication is to love what blood is to life."

It is interesting to note that only seven percent of what we communicate is actually made up of content; thirty-eight percent is made up of tone, and the remaining fifty-five percent consists of nonverbal components such as body position, eye contact, facial expressions, etc. Those who are trying to communicate should beware of "killer words." These are words that choke off the discussion, send a message of finality and totality and often bring retaliation. How often we hear the following expressions: "You *never* listen to me." "You find fault with *everything* I do." "You *always* say that to me." "*Everyone* else is doing it." Starting the disagreement with the word *you* should also be avoided. *You* is often regarded as accusatory, somewhat like having a verbal gun pointed at you. When we perceive that we are being accused of something, the natural recourse is to defend and/or retaliate. When this happens, communication deteriorates.

The following is a topical approach to effective communication taken from the book of Proverbs:

1. The power of our words—11:9; 18:21
2. The source of our words—4:20-23; 6:12
3. Don't talk too much—10:19; 11:12-13
4. Avoid nagging—17:9; 21:9
5. Use a calm, soft answer—15:1; 25:15
6. Listen—15:31; 18:13
7. Ignore insults—19:11
8. Think before you speak—12:18; 14:29
9. Timing is everything—15:23; 25:11
10. Speak the truth—12:17, 22
11. Avoid quarrels—17:14

Sometimes when we attempt to discuss an issue, we forget that there are rules to abide by. Imagine football, basketball and hockey without rules! A great deal of the chaos we experience in communication is caused by not adhering to certain rules or guidelines. The following is a list of rules that will prove helpful.

1. We will express irritation and annoyances we have with one another in a loving, specific and positive way rather than holding them in or being negative in general.
2. We will not exaggerate or attack the other person during the course of a disagreement.
3. We will attempt to control the emotional level and intensity of the argument. No yelling, uncontrollable anger or hurtful remarks.

4. We will never "let the sun go down on our anger" or run away from each other during an argument.

5. We will all try hard not to interrupt the other person when he or she is talking. As a result of this commitment, there will be no need to keep reminding the other person of his or her responsibility, especially during an argument.

6. We will carefully listen to the other person when he or she is talking rather than spend the time thinking up a defense.

7. We will not toss in past failures of the other person in the course of a disagreement.

8. When something is important enough for one person to discuss, it should be important for the other person as well.

Assertiveness

One of the secrets to good conflict resolution is learning to be more assertive. Unfortunately, most people confuse "assertive" with "aggressive." The two are radically different, however. When we are assertive, we are cool, calm and collected; being aggressive is generally loud and "in your face." Being assertive is also being totally honest with the other person. When we are not assertive, we can sometimes be passive-aggressive, where we put up a facade or a front so that we appear to be OK, but behind the scenes we are plotting how to get even. Many people are suppressors or "stuffers." They hold things in instead of laying them on the table. Stuffing is especially dangerous because, as in stuffing a garbage bag, there is only so much you can stuff in and compress before the bag explodes.

It is good for all families, but especially blended ones, to learn to drop trivial issues and ignore the small things. Pick your battles carefully and count the cost before engaging in a potentially dangerous conflict.

The blended family is here to stay. In fact, studies indicate that they are becoming more and more the norm. By examining our ingredients and following wise directions, I believe we can find a recipe that will preclude having "chopped and whipped" families but will rather produce truly "blended" ones.

*R*on Hostetler has spent most of his life dedicated to his mission of giving this generation, and the next, a hope and a future. As an author, educator and public speaker, he has inspired thousands of people to create a more powerful and purposeful future for themselves and their families by helping them recognize and use their God-given, innate abilities in their business, civic and personal lives. His message has universal appeal to all audiences because he speaks about things of the heart as well as the home.

Hostetler earned his bachelor's and master's degrees from Penn State Univeristy. He teaches at the Milton Hershey School, a private residential school for disadvantaged children in Hershey, Pennsylvania, and has coached at all interscholastic levels. He is a former congressional candidate for the US House of Representatives of Pennsylvania's 17th District, school board president, Penn State football team co-captain and preseason All-American linebacker. After the Los Angeles Rams drafted him for the NFL, he cut short his professional career due to a debilitating knee injury. He is the brother of former NFL quarterback and Super Bowl champion Jeff Hostetler and author of *What It Takes: More Than a Champion* (Multnomah Publishing, 1997) and *There IS No Joy In Gruntsville, But There's Plenty To Learn* (Executive Books, 1996). He has been a guest on local and national radio and television talk shows and has spoken throughout the United States and abroad to conventions, associations, nonprofit groups, businesses, churches and schools. He and his wife Holly have four children and live in Hershey, Pennsylvania.

Books

There Is No Joy in Gruntsville, But
   There's Plenty to Learn
What It Takes

Seminars

Message topics available upon request by calling 717.533.8349 or by e-mailing hossusa@msn.com

Intentional Walk 8

Ron Hostetler

M om ran out the door of the house, jumped into the driver's seat of the car and turned the ignition switch. The roar of the engine matched the roar that had just come from her and Dad—another argument, another verbal slug-fest, another fast getaway.

It was enough to awaken all seven of us kids. And we followed them both out the door, watching, listening, and waiting. Hoping Dad would stop her from leaving.

Well, he didn't. The moment Dad stepped in front of the car to signal her to stay, Mom stepped on the accelerator. The car darted forward, just missing him by inches, leaving a wake of smokey exhaust, rubber and troubled children.

No, it wasn't a Kodak moment. Looked more like a Prozac one. A moment in time that seemed to signal a middle-aged, marital meltdown.

But Mom came back. She returned home to work things out and to renew and restore the covenant commitment she and Dad once made. It was a winning moment for all of us when she did. A real memory maker. One that would someday help keep her kids from taking intentional walks in their marriages too.

Yes, there have been times I intentionally walked out on Holly during an argument. Times in my marriage when I'd "hit and run" rather than give our marriage a chance to win or give her a chance to swing at my barrage of verbal fastballs I call "heaters."

But then the memory of Mom's intentional walks would return, and so would I.

I'll bet some of you have taken intentional walks too. And if you haven't walked away physically, you have emotionally. You play the old "silent treatment" ball game, leaving your spouse emotionally stranded on base rather than bringing him or her home into your arms and heart.

Yes, too many partners are revving up their internal engines so fast to escape their Prozac moments in marriage they don't even wait for the automatic garage door to finish opening. They're out the door before their spouse can open his or her mouth to respond. And like many runaway partners facing a diminished life span, waistline, or hairline, they walk away from difficulty and one another rather than working through it together. And when it happens no one wins. Everyone loses, especially the kids, because love strikes out when it walks way.

Now I'm not saying it isn't a good strategy to take a hike to cool off when things get hot at home. In fact, that's exactly what you might need to do at times. But there is a difference between cooling off and avoiding conflict. Helen Crohn, a marriage counselor in New York City, lists several ways in which partners handle stress and conflict.[1] She calls them fighting styles.

Fight-phobics go into emotional overload and withdrawal by playing **"ostrich."**

Terrified of showing anger, **"pleasers"** become apologetic for their actions.

"Blamers" hate to show weakness and are quick to find fault with everyone else.

"Stoics" are inflexible fighters fond of citing the rules and expecting others to follow suit.

And the **"deniers"** avoid eye contract and insist that they are not at all upset.

Dr. Neil Warren, counselor and author of *The Triumphant Marriage,* lumps fighting styles into three categories.

1. **Cats and Dogs.**
2. **Rational and Orderly.**
3. **Bury and Forget It.**

Couples who fight like "Cats and Dogs" get the matter resolved quickly, but it leaves both spouses bruised and battered emotionally. It's an "in your face" style that's loud and explosive. Although it gets everything out in the open and introduces every shred of evidence with intensity and passion, it can get nasty and out of hand for those who don't have a strong enough relationship to handle it.

Partners using the Rational and Orderly style "sit down together and calmly explain their opinions, examine all sides of the issue, dialogue back and forth, and then come to some sort of consensus," says Warren. It's probably the preferred style to use because it doesn't escalate into a major league brawl.

And then there are couples who simply "Bury and Forget It." Feeling the conflict is too difficult or dangerous to talk about, they silently agree to leave it alone or pretend it doesn't exist. This is a kind of "intentional walk" that will lead to destruction. "The relationship stops growing and expanding at the point that conflict is no longer processed. If a couple cannot process their differences, as they should in a 'rational and orderly' approach, they simply cannot move forward," says Warren.[2]

So what's your fighting style? How do you and your spouse resolve conflict? Is there anything you can do to change? And if so, what's the first step?

According to Crohn, "pinpointing your individual styles is an important first step in resolving difficulties, changing your fighting style, and learning to express your feelings in a positive, constructive way."

In addition, Warren lists "eight tips that will help you clear conflict from the road of love":

1. **Recognize marriage as a "we" business.** In other words, look for a "win-win" rather than an "I-win-you-lose" encounter.
2. **Process the data as quickly as possible.** Prolonged conflict is not good or healthy.
3. **Stick to the subject.** Bringing into the conflict unrelated comments we call "emotional trading stamps" stalls any effort to move toward resolution.
4. **Don't intimidate.** Warren explains: "When the heat is turned up and things get a little mean, some people become focused on self-preservation. They fear losing part of themselves in the process of hashing out a disagreement. Panic builds, and they start

throwing verbal punches. They become obsessed with winning—
or at least not losing."

5. **No name-calling.** Words hurt. And disparaging labels only depre-
ciate and demean one another. It's not going to help overcome the
problem. So make it a rule: No name-calling.

6. **Turn up your listening sensitivity.** Bad communication is at the
top of the list for creating marital discord. Someone once said,
"Seek first to understand, then to be understood."

7. **Practice give and take.** Warren adds, "Show me a marriage in
which one person has mastered the art of giving, and I'll show you
a marriage in which conflict gets resolved quickly and completely."

8. **Celebrate every victory.** Take your spouse into your arms and
heart and thank God for the gift of reconciliation. After all, gifts
are meant to be celebrated.[3]

"Be careful that your marriage doesn't become a duel instead of
a duet." —*God's Little Instruction Book*

"Let us therefore make every effort to do what leads to peace
and to mutual edification." (Romans 14:19)

Highlights

- The "intentional walk" refers to refusing to deal with a dispute in a constructive way, choosing instead to physically
or emotionally leave your opponent (a.k.a. partner).

- Taking a break to "cool off," however, can be helpful in controlling emotion—as long as the goal remains resolving the
conflict.

- Each of us reacts in our own way to conflict; some run,
some fight, some referee, and some simply deny.

- Conflict is best resolved by accepting responsibility, showing respect, watching your mouth, being willing to give, and
reconciling.

Extra Innings

- Read Acts 15 to examine two instances of serious conflicts
among believers.

1. What were some of the keys to resolving the conflict about doctrine?
2. What would have happened if the dispute had not been resolved?
3. How might personality differences explain the different perspectives of Paul and Barnabas?
4. Is conflict like this necessarily an evidence of sin? Do you think it was in this case?
5. One of the problems Paul and Barnabas faced was that both were strong leaders, and apparently neither held ultimate decision-making authority to guide their joint mission. What is the role of a leader in dealing with conflict? When a leader holds ultimate decision-making authority, what did Jesus say about how that authority is to be wielded?
6. How do you personally tend to approach conflict? What do you do that turns your conflicts into a fight? How can you and your partner avoid "pushing each other's buttons"? What helps resolve your conflicts?
7. "Therefore, I, the prisoner of the Lord, implore you to walk in a manner worthy of the calling with which you have been called, with all humility and gentleness, with patience, showing tolerance for one another in love, being diligent to preserve the unity of the Spirit in the bond of peace" (Ephesians 4:1-3, NASB). Discuss the implications of this passage regarding conflict and resolution, making personal application.

Notes

1. Helen Crohn, "Can This Marriage Be Saved?" *The Patriot News* (Harrisburg, PA), March 6, 1994, reprinted from *Ladies' Home Journal.*
2. Neil Clark Warren, "The Triumphant Marriage," *Focus on the Family* magazine, October 1995, pp. 2-4.
3. Warren, "The Triumphant Marriage."

Reprinted with permission from You Make the Call! A Parent's Guide for Covering Home, *Copyright © 1998, Ron Hostetler Publishing, Hershey, PA 17033.*

Part Three
Communicating from the Heart

*He who loves a pure heart and whose
speech is gracious
will have the king for his friend.
(Proverbs 22:11)*

 **D**r. Gary Chapman is a world-renowned speaker, author and seminar leader. He hosts a nationally syndicated radio program, "A Growing Marriage," and is the senior associate pastor and marriage counselor at Calvary Baptist Church in Winston-Salem, North Carolina. Chapman is the author of *The Five Love Languages*, which has topped the bestseller charts for years. His books, including *Loving Solutions* (a 1999 Gold Medallion Book Award recipient) and *The Five Love Languages of Teenagers* (a 2001 Gold Medallion Book Award recipient), have sold over 3 million copies.

Books
Covenant Marriage
The Five Love Languages (also video)
The Five Love Languages of Children
  (also video)
The Five Love Languages for Singles
The Five Love Languages of Teenagers
  (also video)
Five Signs of a Loving Family
Hope for the Separated
The Love Languages of God (also
  video)
Love Talks for Couples
Love Talks for Families
Loving Solutions
*The Other Side of Love: Handling
  Anger in a Godly Way*
Parenting Your Adult Child
Toward a Growing Marriage
*The World's Easiest Guide to Family
  Relationships*

Study Guide
Building Relationships

Video
Toward a Growing Marriage

Media
Host of *A Growing Marriage*, a
  nationally syndicated radio
  program

Web
www.fivelovelanguages.com

The Five Love Languages

Gary Chapman

What Happens to Love After the Wedding?

Because we give and receive love differently, keeping love alive in our marriages is hard work. If we don't understand how our spouse receives love, our marriages may dry up and we won't understand why. We need to understand each other's way of receiving love.

Keeping the Love Tank Full

Love takes a preeminent place in human behavior, yet this word has many dimensions and interpretations. The marriage relationship itself is primarily intended to foster love and intimacy. Marriage is also the primary place where that inner "love tank" can be filled.

Falling in Love

Though the "falling-in-love" experience is exciting, it is short-lived and largely self-centered. Love that truly contributes to our spouse's emotional well-being is based on reason, will and discipline. The latter alone contains the possibility of transformation and completion.

Love Language #1: Words of Affirmation

Compliments, words of encouragement and requests rather than demands all affirm the self-worth of your spouse. They create intimacy, heal wounds and bring out the full potential of your other half.

Love Language #2: Quality Time

Spending quality time together through sharing, listening and participating in joint meaningful activities communicates that we truly care for and enjoy each other.

Love Language #3: Receiving Gifts

Gifts are visual symbols of love, whether they are items you purchased or made, or are merely your own presence made available to your spouse. Gifts demonstrate that you care, and they represent the value of the relationship.

Love Language #4: Acts of Service

Criticism of your spouse's failure to do things for you may be an indication that "acts of service" is your primary love language. Acts of service should never be coerced but should be freely given and received, and completed as requested.

Love Language #5: Physical Touch

Physical touch, as a gesture of love, reaches to the depths of our being. As a love language, it is a powerful form of communication from the smallest touch on the shoulder to the most passionate kiss.

Discovering Your Primary Love Language

There are some basic but essential questions you need to ask to discover your primary love language. What do you request the most? What makes you feel the most loved? What hurts you deeply? What do you desire most of all? These provide the critical clues.

Love Is a Choice & Love Makes the Difference

Choosing to love in the language of our spouse has many benefits. It can help heal past wounds and provide a sense of security, self-worth and significance. Yet the instinctive qualities of merely falling in love differ greatly from choices of the will that meet the deep emotional needs of the spouse.

Gary Smalley is one of the country's best-known authors and speakers on family relationships. He has spent over thirty-three years learning, teaching and counseling. He has personally interviewed hundreds of singles and couples and has surveyed thousands of people at his seminars, asking two questions: What is it that strengthens your relationships? and What weakens them?

Smalley's nineteen books combined have sold over 5 million copies. Two of those won the Gold Medallion Award for excellence in literature. *The Language of Love* won the Angel Award as the best contribution to family life.

Smalley has spoken to over 2 million people in live conferences. He has been presenting his two-day workshop, Love Is a Decision, once a month for the last twenty years. He has appeared on national televisions programs such as *The Oprah Winfrey Show, Larry King Live, Extra*, the *Today* show and *Sally Jessie Raphael*, as well as numerous national radio programs.

Founder and chairman of the board for the Smalley Relationship Center, Smalley has been married to his wife Norma for thirty-six years. They live in Branson, Missouri, and are the parents of three married children and eight grandchildren.

Books
  Connecting with Your Husband
  Hidden Keys of a Loving, Lasting
    Marriage
  If Only He Knew
  Joy That Lasts
  Making Love Last Forever (also video)
  Men's Relational Toolbox
  One Flame
  Secrets to Lasting Love (also video)
  Winning Your Husband Back
  Winning Your Wife Back

Books with John Trent
  The Blessing (also video, study guide)

  The Gift of the Blessing
  The Hidden Value of a Man
  The Language of Love
  Love Is a Decision (also seminar)
  The Two Sides of Love

Video
  Homes of Honor
  Keys to Loving Relationships
  Real Love in a Real World
    (also study materials, seminar)

Web
  http://smalley.gospelcom.net

*D*r. John Trent is president of Encouraging Words and StrongFamilies.com, a team committed to strengthening marriage and family relationships worldwide. His main focus includes writing and speaking at retreats, conferences, churches and seminars across the country. He also speaks regularly to corporate America on team-building, recruiting and retaining outstanding employees. Over the past seven years alone, Trent has spoken to over 60,000 people in over 65 major cities across the United States.

In addition to speaking, he has authored and coauthored more than a dozen award-winning and best-selling books. He has been nominated for or won the Gold Medallion Award for excellence in writing fourteen times.

Trent has been a featured guest on radio and television programs such as *The Oprah Winfrey Show,* Dr. James Dobson's *Focus on the Family*, Dr. Charles Swindoll's *Insight for Living*, the Billy Graham Evangelistic Association, *The 700 Club*, *The Art of Family Living*, *The Chapel of the Air*, Drs. Meier and Minirth's *Talk to the Doctors* program, *The Chuck and Jenni Show* on FamilyNet and many, many more.

Books
Choosing to Live the Blessing
The Light of Home
Pictures Your Heart Remembers

Books with Gary Smalley
The Blessing (also video, study guide)
The Gift of the Blessing
The Hidden Value of a Man
The Language of Love
Love Is a Decision (also seminar)
The Two Sides of Love

Audio
Loving Relationships Seminar

Videos
Discovering Your Unique Personality Strengths

Life Mapping series (also book, workbook and seminar)
The Making of a Marriage (also workbook)
A Marriage for All Seasons (also workbook)

Seminars
Strong Families Build Strong Businesses
Strong Families in Stressful Times
Strong Marriages in Stressful Times

Web
www.encouragingwords.com

Communicating Your Blessing

Gary Smalley and John Trent

A thief is loose in many homes today who masquerades as "fulfill-ment," "accomplishment" and "success." Actually, this thief steals the precious gift of genuine acceptance from our children and leaves confusion and emptiness in its place. That villain's name is *overactivity*, and it can keep parents so busy that the blessing is never spoken. Even with parents who dearly love their children, as one woman we talked to said, "Who has time to stop and *tell* them?"

In many homes today, both parents are working overtime, and a "family night" makes an appearance about as often as Halley's Comet. The result is that instead of Dad and Mom taking the time to communicate a spoken blessing, a baby-sitter named *silence* is left to mold a child's self-perception. Life is so hectic that for many parents, that "just right" time to communicate a spoken blessing never quite comes around.

A father tries to corner his son to communicate "how he feels to him" before he goes away to college, but now his son is too busy to listen.

A mother tries to communicate a spoken blessing to her daugh-ter in the bride's room just before the wedding, but the photogra-pher has to take her away to get that "perfect" shot.

Spoken words of blessing should start in the delivery room and continue throughout life. Yet the "lack of time" and the thief's motto, "I'll have time to tell them tomorrow," rob children of a needed blessing today.

"Oh, it's not that big a deal," you may say. "They know I love them and that they're special *without* my having to say it." *Really?* We wish that explanation worked with many of the people we counsel. To them, their parents' silence has communicated some-thing far different from love and acceptance.

Let's look at what commonly happens in homes where spoken words of blessing are withheld. What we will see is that silence does communicate a message; and like an eloquent speech, silence too can set a course for a person's life. But it's not the path most parents would like their children to take. In fact, for many, silence affects their every relationship and leaves them wandering between workaholism and extreme withdrawal.

Both people and relationships suffer in the absence of spoken words of love, encouragement and support—words of blessing. Take a marriage, for example.

Dr. Howard Hendricks, a noted Christian educator, is fond of telling the story of a couple he counseled several years ago. This couple had been married over twenty years, but their problems had become so acute they were now considering divorce. Dr. Hendricks asked the husband, "When was the last time you told your wife you loved her?" The man glared at him, crossed his arms, and said, "I told my wife I loved her on our wedding day, and it stands until I revoke it!"

Take a guess what was destroying their marriage. When a spoken blessing is withheld in a marriage, unmet needs for security and acceptance act like sulfuric acid and eat away at a relationship.

Let's look briefly at each element of the blessing and see just how important they can be to a healthy marriage. In fact, show us a couple that is growing together, and we'll show you two people practicing these principles of blessing.

Sexual touching is important in any growing relationship; however, it should not be the only time a couple touches. Our friend, Dr. Kevin Leman, notes this in his book, *Sex Begins in the Kitchen*. He points out that genuine intimacy is developed in the small acts of touching in the kitchen, or walking through a mall together hand in hand, or sitting close together on the sofa watching television.

Meaningful touch can enrich your relationships in many ways. Studies show that regardless of gender, people who were comfortable with touching were also more talkative, cheerful, socially dominant and nonconforming; those uncomfortable with touch tended to be more emotionally unstable and socially withdrawn.

Those more comfortable with touch were less afraid and suspicious of other people's motives and intentions, and have less anxiety and tension in their everyday lives.

Yet as powerful as touch is, it is not enough to sustain, alone, a growing marriage. Researchers at the University of Illinois used three measures of intimacy to assess marital satisfaction and happiness. They found that each form of intimacy made its own important contribution. However, conflict and divorce potential were most closely linked with a lack of the next two elements of the blessing—emotional and *verbal* intimacy.

Let's combine the next two elements of the blessing into one way of making sure your spouse receives the blessing. When we decide to place high value on our spouse, and then back that up with spoken words to that effect, it can do wonders for a relationship.

A popular bumper sticker slogan reads, "Have you hugged your kids today?" Another equally important phrase that you can copy and paste to your refrigerator, bathroom mirror or forehead is: Have You Praised Your Mate Today?

An everyday dose of praise, whether in the form of a word picture or just a statement like, "Great dinner, honey" or a "You are so kind to other people" or even a "You make me so proud the way you handle the children" can do wonders in a relationship.

Spoken words that attach high value to our spouse are so powerful that they can enrich almost any marriage. Why not try a project in your home to discover just how true this statement can be?

For one month, thirty days, praise at least one thing you appreciate about your spouse each day. Be sure you point out things about his or her character (being kind, generous, thoughtful, punctual, organized, and so on) as well as what he or she accomplishes. Don't tell your husband or wife you're doing this. We give this assignment to many couples in counseling, and it in itself has caused positive changes in relationships.

While we have talked exclusively about using word pictures to praise a husband or wife, they can also be used to help discuss an important issue or avoid a heated argument. By using a word picture to convey a concern we have, instead of lashing out with damaging words, we can often motivate our mate to change and get across a message we can't seem to get across with only words.

One woman at a conference Gary was leading had a concern she had unsuccessfully tried to communicate to her husband for years. Yet by using a single word picture, she so affected him that he was willing to write her a $150,000 check right on the spot to build her dream house!

In a marriage, our mate needs to know that he or she is a special part of our future. What's more, our spouse needs to know that the way we look at him or her today leaves room for positive change and growth in the future.

Whether it is the fear of entertaining, the need to go on a diet, failing to discipline the children promptly or keeping a messy house, we do not motivate our mate to change by picturing a negative future. Our mate needs to hear words that picture a special future in the same way our children do, positive words that provide our spouse the room to become all that God can help him or her to become.

[P]roviding the individual elements of the blessing without the glue to hold them all together is not enough. That glue is our active commitment. In fact, this final element of the blessing is at the heart of "cleaving" in a marriage.

When the Scriptures tell us we are to "cleave" to our spouse (Genesis 2:24), the root words in Hebrew means "to cling, to be firmly attached." It takes a firm decision to be committed to blessing your spouse, a decision that will not remain intact if you don't make room for your mate's fallibility.

[W]hat every man or woman owes his or her spouse is the willingness to stay committed, even if the other person fumbles the ball. Amy did this, and it was the very thing her husband credits with saving his life.

Grant owned a manufacturing business that had done quite well. His business was small, but it found its niche in the marketplace and was growing by leaps and bounds. Borrowing against the property and expecting his profits to continue, Grant took out a large loan to expand the facilities. No sooner had construction begun on his new plant than a multinational manufacturing concern decided to go into competition with Grant's product.

With cash flow tight because of the huge interest payments on the loan, Grant did not have the resources to put more salesmen on the street. Neither could Grant lower the price on his product because of the profit margin needed to keep the business afloat.

In less than a year, Grant had literally gone from riches to rags. His competitor had undercut his prices drastically to get into the marketplace, and it drove Grant out of business. Saddled with unpaid employees, lawsuits from suppliers and with the bank breathing down his neck, Grant had to shut down his plant and liquidate his equipment at a fraction of its actual worth. He even lost his home that had been collateral for the note and had to move into a small apartment. Perhaps the crowning blow came when he had to explain to his children at midyear that they would have to change from the private school they loved to public school.

Grant was not a believer at the time of his business's collapse, and he was devastated as he had never been before. He even contemplated suicide, but one thing held him back:

"I didn't know the Lord at the time my business went under, and my whole world seemed to end. I would like to say it was the thought of my children that kept me from ending it all, but that wouldn't be true.

"The one thing that kept me from it was Amy and the way she constantly believed in me and blessed me with her love. Listening to her pray for me at night and having her hold me and let me cry were what pulled me through. I tell everybody she saved my life 'twice.' The first time was when the business failed; the second time was when she led me to Jesus Christ."

Grant could no longer provide for his wife and family "in the manner to which they had become accustomed," yet because of this loving wife, who based her blessing for her husband on active commitment instead of material possessions, their relationship remained strong and secure.

Every husband and wife will drop the ball and prove themselves fallible time and again. If we are to be people of blessing, our commitment will rest on our decision to love our spouse "in spite of." Our love must be the kind of love that motivated our heavenly Father to bless us with His Son, in spite of the fact we didn't deserve it and because He knew we needed that blessing so much in our lives.

Reprinted by permission of Thomas Nelson Publishers from the book entitled The Gift of the Blessing, *Copyright © 1993 by Thomas Nelson.*

*F*red and Julie Schamber attended a Marriage Encounter weekend in 1998 after being married for thirty-five years and were so impressed with the dynamic it added to their marriage that they have since become leaders in the program. Helping couples to improve their communication and to learn that they can help change the world by having their love mirror the love that Christ has for us has been their greatest joy.

The Schambers reside in the Pittsburgh, Pennsylvania, area where Fred works as a designer of electron microscopes and Julie works in a pediatrician's office. They have three children.

Rediscovering the "Possibilities" in Christian Marriage

Fred and Julie Schamber

Many marriages don't "fail"; they just misplace their "possibilities." This is pretty much what had happened to us. We were a classic example of a couple with a long-standing marriage cemented by strong bonds, but one in which much of the joy and intimacy we had once shared had somehow been misplaced during years of preoccupation with careers and child-rearing. Though the faithfulness of our union had never been an issue, we had in the course of thirty-four years of marriage developed a somewhat uneasy accommodation—two strong personalities who had largely given up on the idea of "unity" of spirit and instead settled for "getting along."

Communication was the issue—not so much from the standpoint that there were "off-limits" topics that we couldn't discuss, but rather from the standpoint that there didn't seem to be much point in trying to reopen issues where the lines had long been indelibly drawn. For us, much of the learning process of marriage had involved discovering the realistic limits to our expectations. Knowing that raising certain topics could only lead to frustration and pain, we avoided them. Or, rather, we knew that we *should* avoid them. Sometimes it seemed that our marriage was a tug-of-war in which the hopes and desires of the one could be achieved only by the concessions of the other.

Fortunately for us, there were also some strong bonds that kept us together. At the top of the list was our shared Christian faith. There was never any question about the priority of God in our lives, and even in the most strained periods of our relationship, we experienced a deep and healing bond when we sat together in worship or shared in the Lord's Table. Another was our commitment to family—though we often disagreed over the best way to exercise our responsibilities to our children, there was no question that this was an important mutual commitment. And finally, we did share a deep and unspoken trust—a trust that in the worst eventuality, the other would not let us down. Though we might have each, in our own ways, mourned the loss of closeness in our marriage, we never seriously doubted that the other would be there with us to the end—through thick or thin, wherever that might take us.

So although we sometimes found ourselves tolerating rather than celebrating our relationship, there were also these deep and largely unspoken bonds that made us a couple. By the standards of stability prevalent in today's society, ours would be judged quite a good marriage. But was "getting along" all that we could expect? Was the heady joy of our courtship and early marriage just a romantic illusion that was destined to fade? Is the natural course of a marriage like the fragile spring flower whose beauty fades as it matures and goes to seed? This seemed to be the cold reality—but we never completely reconciled ourselves to it. We wanted *more*. Though we both felt this way, we didn't have a workable model of how to achieve it.

The turning point for us came when we saw an announcement for a Marriage Encounter weekend in our church bulletin. In the course of our marriage, we had frequently agreed that we really wanted to do "something" to improve our relationship. But what? Like so many other things about our marriage, constructive changes had begun to seem like an impossible dream. Always there had been the logistics—three children and their busy schedules to worry about. Sure, it would be *nice* to attend a marriage enrichment seminar, but who would take care of the kids while we went off for a weekend? Get real! We also valued our privacy—we were not about to bare our souls and our relationship to others, particularly to strangers whose motives and agendas we might not agree with. But when we read the announcement in our church bulletin in 1998, we couldn't think of a logical reason *not* to go. Our "nest" was now empty, and this experience seemed to have the sanction of our church (and how "radical" could an event be if it was put on by Lutherans?). In retrospect, I don't think either of us had much actual enthusiasm for the prospect, but we had been talking about this for so long that neither of us was willing to go on record as opposing the idea. So we signed up.

What a difference those forty-four hours made in our lives! The following is an excerpt from something I (Fred) wrote a week after our Marriage Encounter weekend.

> Time is relative. Tonight as I sit down to write this, it has been exactly one week since we got home from our Marriage Encounter weekend. Compare that to the almost thirty-five years that Julie and I have been married. That single week represents only about 0.05 percent of our married life together—not a very significant fraction—yet in our perception of the important events in our marriage, this week has been *huge*!
>
> How did our relationship change as a consequence of last weekend? Certainly we can identify a number of areas of improvement: in communication (both expressing and listening), in sensitivity to each other's feelings and in appreciation of each other's qualities. But the most basic change in the dynamic of our relationship is also the hardest to explain. Let me call it a change in "possibilities." By this I mean that we now recognize possibilities in our relationship that we had not expected—doors we thought were permanently bolted which we now realize can still be opened, happiness that can be seized, intimacy that can be shared, joy that can be celebrated!
>
> Of course, some measure of accommodation is a necessary ingredient to a stable marriage. Part of the "decision to love" involves our choice to accept and live with those irritating little foibles that our lover brings to the relationship. A marriage where two people were constantly trying to remake each other would probably not last thirty-five weeks, much less thirty-five years. So when Julie learned to live with my distraction when I am deep in a computer program or when I tolerated her schedule for putting up and taking down the Christmas tree, we were making the kind of accommodations that an enduring marriage requires. Yet, gradually and imperceptibly, we also made ac-

commodation for things that were much deeper and more significant: hurts that went unmentioned, disappointments that
were borne silently, expectations that went unrealized, dreams
that were unshared, needs for affirmation that were unmet.

How much we had "lost" in our marriage through this process
of accommodation was something that I think neither of us appreciated until our Marriage Encounter weekend. By sharing our
feelings in dialogue, and by really listening to the other, we
learned, to our surprise, that some areas of disagreement were
neither motivated as we supposed nor were as unchangeable as
we had presumed. Julie's insistence on periodically reorganizing
my disaster-area of a desk is not just obsessive "busy-ness," but is
tied into her need for self-esteem in having an organized household. The low priority I assign to keeping my desk straightened
out isn't only a "neatness deficit," but is tied into my need for
self-esteem through the professional work I accomplish there.
This has been a source of contention in our marriage, and we
have long been living an uneasy truce on the subject.

It was at our Encounter weekend, however, that we first
understood and began to appreciate the deeper feelings that
were being played out in such seemingly trivial exchanges.
This doesn't mean, of course, that these sources of irritation
have magically gone away. Rather, understanding and accepting the feelings which lie beneath them, we now feel better
equipped to deal with (or accept) such things constructively. I
guess that you could say that we have learned that we can "give
of" rather than "give in" as we accept each other in love.

But the biggest "door" which has opened to new possibilities
in our marriage has been in the manner in which we communicate affection. I grew up in a household where my parents were
openly and verbally affectionate, and this is an expectation I
brought to our marriage—I have a need to "hear the words."
Julie grew up in a family where such verbal expressions were
rare, but the underlying love was expressed in caregiving. For
her, it is more natural to express her affection in deeds rather
than words.

During the years of our marriage, we were both conscious
that we were not communicating as fully and as naturally as
we would have liked. We both sent out "love messages" that

weren't consistently recognized and valued, and both of us at times felt the emptiness of not receiving the assurances that we needed. Though both of us knew that we shared a strong underlying bond of love, we were not "in sync" in how we expressed it to each other. This was something that we had just come to accept about ourselves and our relationship. However, through our Encounter weekend we have come to better understand each other's needs and have rediscovered the joy of sharing the words/deeds of affection as each of us needs to experience them. We are determined to build on this new beginning.

Finally, one of the most profound possibilities that was opened for us through the Marriage Encounter experience has been in our spiritual life. Our shared faith has been one of the strong and constant bonds of our relationship over the years. I think we have always had a strong sense that in living in a loving union we were living in harmony with God's plan for His creation. The possibility we had never entertained was that our "couple-power" could also play a role in God's plan for the world's redemption. What more tangible way to experience God's love than through the love and healing we share with each other through Christ? What better way to witness the "good news" than through the depth of our unconditional love for each other? Both of us like the idea that in working to strengthen our relationship, we not only create happiness for ourselves, but also are participating in God's plan to heal a broken world. This gives an increased urgency and meaning to the hard work involved and imparts new depth to the joy we experience in each other.

Though I didn't state it then (perhaps because I was afraid it couldn't last), the simple fact is that Julie and I had actually "fallen in love" all over again! We were like a couple of giddy newlyweds—delighting in each other and feeling a oneness that had seemed impossible just days before—but even better than newlyweds, since we now had so many wonderful shared memories!

What was this amazing new program that made such a difference in our relationship? Actually, Marriage Encounter has been around for quite some time. Originally conceived in the 1960s by a priest in the Catholic Church in Spain, it quickly spread to the United States

and was adopted by essentially all of the major Christian denominations. Today over 2 million couples in more than ninety countries
have experienced Marriage Encounter weekends, and the overwhelming majority, like us, state that they too fell in love all over
again! The program has been attended and enthusiastically endorsed
by a number of luminaries in the field of marriage and family enrichment. Dr. James C. Dobson, host of *Focus on the Family,* is one such
enthusiastic supporter, and columnist Michael McManus, developer
of the Marriage Savers program, simply states that Marriage Encounter is the *best* marriage saver of all.

Marriage Encounter weekends are, of course, only one of many
beneficial programs that a couple can participate in to strengthen
and/or rejuvenate their relationship. But the Marriage Encounter
formula is certainly one that has stood the test of time. The format
is actually quite simple. Weekends are held at hotels or retreat
centers with approximately twelve to thirty couples in attendance.
Protestant weekends are presented by four couples—an ordained
member of the clergy and spouse, and three lay couples, all of
whom must be members of the faith expression that is presenting
the weekend. On Catholic weekends, the presentations are led by
a priest and three lay couples.

Although weekends are presented by various faith expressions,
all couples are welcomed at all weekends regardless of faith. The
weekend unfolds as a series of presentations focused on specific
topics related to self- and mutual understanding. Sessions are
structured per a standard outline that is used by all Marriage Encounter weekends but periodically revised to keep it timely. However, each presenting couple illuminates the topic with personal
examples drawn from their own experience.

At the end of each presentation, there is a question related to
the topic. The couples separate, and husband and wife individually reflect on the question and the feelings it raises. Then each
couple is reunited in the privacy of their own room to share and
discuss their reflections. There is no counseling, no group sharing
and no point in the weekend when couples need expose their relationship to the scrutiny of others.

How does this simple format accomplish so much? There are undoubtedly many different answers to this question—but there are a couple of things that seem to be key:

1. All distractions are eliminated during the weekend so that participants can focus exclusively on their own relationships. This is no "getaway" weekend where couples lose themselves in pleasant distractions; rather, it is a time of focused sharing of a couple's most personal feelings.

2. The sharing of the presenters enables couples to relate and take hope in the experiences of others. Though the presenting couples are trained and their talks are carefully reviewed for relevancy, these are not "stock" presentations. Rather, presenting couples are encouraged to share deeply from their own marriage journeys—both the ups and the downs. These examples free attending couples to overcome their own inhibitions and share deeply with each other.

3. The material is structured to encourage sharing and acceptance, rather than confrontation and conflict. Couples are encouraged by word and example to seek the positive in their relationships.

4. The weekends are solidly anchored in Christian principles. Christ is invited into the marriages, and couples are encouraged to understand their relationships as extensions of God's encompassing covenant of love and grace.

A brief summary such as this can't begin to tell the story of what actually happens on a Marriage Encounter weekend. One reason is because what happens on a particular weekend is unique to each couple and their particular circumstances. Those couples whose relationship is already vital and loving are able to go to even deeper levels of intimacy in their communication and understanding. At the other extreme, many couples who have been struggling are able to discover a basis for healing and reconciliation. And for those couples who are "in the middle"—couples who are committed to each other but sense that something is "lacking" in their relationship (like Julie and me), the weekend is an opportunity to rediscover the pure joy that they have been missing. Regardless of where they begin the weekend, however, couples who are prepared to commit themselves to the effort will inevitably find their relationships enhanced.

I earlier stated that our own Marriage Encounter weekend was one in which we simply fell in love again. We left the weekend almost "walking on air." Of course, that giddy feeling of romantic love hasn't burned at the same level of intensity continuously since—"happily *ever* after" is a phrase that really does belong only in fairy tales! But the flame has continued to burn brightly. Though our relationship still has its ups and downs, the ups are better and the downs aren't nearly as low and lasting as they once were, since the weekend provided us with some tools that help us work through the rough spots. When we disagree, we do so as lovers, confident in the acceptance and caring of the other. The joy we find in each other has continued to grow. And we continue to discover new possibilities in our relationship!

How can you learn more about Marriage Encounter or register for a weekend? Here are two ways:

- Call 800.795.LOVE. The volunteer couple who takes your call will be able to answer your questions about weekends and, if you wish, connect you with your preferred faith expression active in your area.

- If you have Internet access, point your browser to www .wwme.org. This will connect you to the Worldwide Marriage Encounter (Catholic) Web site, which contains a wealth of information about weekends, when and where they are held, how to register, etc. For other faith expressions, click on "Learn More About M.E. Weekends," and then under "Other Information" click on "Other Denominations." From here you can access numerous other Marriage Encounter Web sites.

Part Four
Spiritual Foundations

A three-stranded rope isn't easily snapped.
(Ecclesiastes 4:12, The Message)

Cheri Fuller is a dynamic writer and speaker whose heartbeat is encouraging women to pursue a deeper experience with God. With transparency, energy and humor, she shares out of the richness of her life experiences and God's Word. Her desire to encourage people and her passion for prayer have inspired her messages and more than twenty-seven books that are full of hope, practical ideas and stories that impact hearts and change lives. Fuller's ministry, Families Pray USA, motivates and equips moms and dads, kids and teens to impact their world through prayer.

With a master's degree in English literature, Fuller uses her messages, magazine articles, books and tapes to provide encouragement to women throughout the United States and other countries. She speaks at women's conferences and events throughout the year and is a frequent guest on national radio and TV programs. She's a contributing editor for *Today's Christian Woman*, and hundreds of her articles have appeared in national magazines.

She and her husband Holmes have three grown children and live in Oklahoma.

Books

Christmas Treasures of the Heart
Fearless: Building a Faith That
  Overcomes Your Fear
The Fragrance of Kindness
The Mom You're Meant to Be
One Year of Praying Through the Bible
Opening Your Child's Spiritual
  Windows
When Children Pray
When Couples Pray
When Mothers Pray
When Teens Pray

Seminars/Retreat Packages
Amazing Grace

Couple Prayer: The Little Known
  Secret to Lifelong Happiness in
  Marriage
Getting Through the Winters of
  Marriage
Journey to a Fruitful Life
The Power of Encouragement
The Power of a Woman's Prayer
Prayer: The Great Adventure
Shining a Light—Loving Your
  Neighbor
Trading Your Worry for Wonder

Web
www.cherifuller.com

Praying Together 12

Cheri Fuller

When two people decide to become "one," they actually become a new entity. Their oneness is something that can deeply satisfy both husband and wife as well as serve God's purposes. Yet because they are imperfect people in a fallen world, this new entity faces incredible challenges from within and without. The couple must deal with each other's weaknesses and differences. Their sin natures war against their unity. Selfishness, childhood wounds or bitterness may oppose their best efforts to become one.

From without, a couple may be assailed by situations that can strain any marriage—serious, chronic illness, the loss of a child, business calamities, overloaded schedules and career pressures. They also are surrounded by a society that calls marriage irrelevant and says, "If it doesn't work out or make you happy, it's okay to call it quits." The cultural pressures to cheat, get divorced or go after material things instead of spiritual values can lead many couples to part ways in spite of their best intentions.

There are also spiritual attacks against this oneness. The enemy comes to kill, steal and destroy—and not just in our individual lives, but in our marriages and families as well. To counter his attack, we need the spiritual ammunition of prayer. "For though we walk (live) in the flesh, we are not carrying on our warfare . . . using mere human weapons. For the weapons of our warfare are not physical . . . but they are mighty before God for the overthrow and destruction of strongholds" (2 Corinthians 10:3-4, Amp.).

The reality is that half of all marriages today *do* end in divorce, both for Christians and non-Christians. Studies show that simply attending church does not guarantee a happy marriage or divorce-proof a relationship. However, couples who pray together regularly report enjoying the most satisfying marriages of all—and the divorce rate for praying couples is less than 1 percent!

All of us face obstacles and challenges in our marriages. But the good news is that *God is for you.* He wants your marriage to succeed, to be fulfilling and to reflect His glory to the world around you. And He offers incredible resources of grace, power and boundless amounts of forgiveness so that you can truly live in peace and harmony instead of anger and bitterness. He has an inexhaustible storehouse of love, wisdom and provision for every single day of your life—even new mercies every morning!

The key to accessing all these resources for your marriage and family is *prayer.* Prayer is the way you keep the unity candle lit, so to speak. It is the way you invite God into your everyday life and continue the dialogue with Him and your mate that began in that wonderful season of "first love" that brought you to the altar.

Whatever your age or stage of life, praying together as a couple is a powerful, little-known secret to lifelong happiness in marriage. It will help keep your marriage alive and well—even rekindle your love if the flame has died. Praying as a couple is a doorway to intimacy.

Of course, there are many other ways to build a strong marriage: spending time together, meeting your spouse's needs, writing love notes to each other, giving physical affection, keeping the romance alive. But prayer is the glue that binds everything together. It is the catalyst for God's power and blessing to be released in your life.

Perhaps you don't feel successful at praying as a couple. If so, let me assure you that you are normal and have lots of company. Maybe you are going in so many directions that you're not sure how to wedge in prayer. Again, join the crowd! Although most of us know that God wants us to pray as couples, the truth is that even people who have been Christians a long time struggle with it.

What if . . . your spouse is reluctant to pray—more interested in her latest craft project or his TV ball game than prayer time? Instead of approaching your spouse with an attitude that conveys, "You don't pray with me enough, you spiritual sluggard, so I'm going to take charge of this," remember that it's the gentle, loving, quiet spirit that wins a partner over. "I want to share" messages are usually more effective than scolding, nagging or giving orders. For example:

- "Here, dear. This story meant a lot to me [or was so inspiring to me] . . . I want to share it with you" could open the door to reading one of the devotionals together.

- "Honey, I need to pray with you about something that's worrying me." Or maybe a note left on the pillow saying, "By the way, I'd really like us to pray together for the kids once a week. Let's go out for breakfast Saturday morning and try it then." Most men or women, once they understand their husband or wife's need, will respond favorably.

If you are married to someone who, despite your best efforts, avoids praying with you or is disinterested in spiritual matters, let me encourage you to keep praying for your spouse. Know that when you're feeling alone in the prayer closet, heaven is watching and the God of the universe is listening. *You are not alone!* In fact, the spiritual reality is that when you pray—with or without your spouse—you are joining Jesus in intercession. He's seated at the right hand of the Father, making intercession for you (Hebrews 7:25), and He makes a terrific prayer partner!

Our divine Prayer Partner does not want us to give up praying for that reluctant spouse. He urges us to be like the persistent widow who, in her determination to receive justice from the unrighteous judge, kept on knocking, seeking and asking. And Christ assures us that the One who sees what we do in secret will reward us openly (Matthew 6:6) if we *P-U-S-H: Pray Until Something Happens!*

One of the most vital things prayer does is change our hearts and draw us to the Lord. And as each of us moves toward God in prayer, we grow closer to each other and the unity candle remains lit. God's blessing will touch your family for generations to come, and His eternal purposes will be fulfilled.

Someone once said, "It is the heart that prays; it is to the voice of the heart that God listens; and it is the heart that He answers." Maybe that is precisely why we sometimes avoid prayer with our spouse—it's just so heart-to-heart.

When you hear each other's "voice of the heart"—the feelings and longings underneath the surface—your hearts are knit together in new ways. Coldness and indifference can melt away in a few tender moments together. Who knows what might come from experiencing God's presence in prayer? You could find emotional healing, a new sense of unity, a physical relationship sparked anew when the embers were dying or a special blessing in the lives of your children.

Every time you pray together, you are letting God into your lives and into the particular situation you talk to Him about. In those moments of prayer as a couple, God wraps His arms around each of you and bridges any gaps between you. No matter how difficult the situation, there is no substitute for the flood of peace that results from a husband and wife praying together. There is no situation so dark or problem so hopeless that God can't shine His light and provide help. And most importantly, when you pray faithfully through a crisis or extremely painful situation, you'll find that the difficulty actually brings you closer together instead of tearing you apart.

So now let me encourage you to pray! As you do, the watching world will see in your marriage a living picture of the intimate relationship between Jesus and His bride, the Church.

*S*ince August of 2001, David Maitland has served as pastor of First Baptist Church in Butler, Pennsylvania. He is also the director of the Slippery Rock Baptist Camp, a position he has held since 1996.

The Butler-born pastor, orphaned at age eight, is a graduate of Milton Hershey High School in Hershey, Pennsylvania. He left his job at PNC Bank in Butler to become a youth pastor at Meadville, Pennsylvania's Calvary Baptist Church in 1977. During his ministry in Meadville, he doubled as athletic director and basketball coach at Calvary Baptist Christian Academy.

Maitland became youth pastor at Grove City's First Baptist Church in 1994 and received his ordination into the ministry on June 4, 1995. He resigned his Grove City youth pastorate in 1998 to become the full-time director of Slippery Rock Baptist Camp.

He and his wife Bonnie live in Grove City and are the parents of one daughter. During their youth ministries in Meadville and Grove City, they were involved in twenty mission trips.

Web
  www.butlerfbc.com

Puzzles *13*

David Maitland

My wife will sit for hours in the evenings putting together a jigsaw puzzle. Sometimes the process is enjoyable and relaxing, sometimes it is frustrating and challenging, but it is always time-consuming. It would be so much easier if the puzzles came put together rather than in hundreds of pieces! Marriage is like a puzzle. It can be enjoyable or frustrating, and it takes work, because there are many pieces to fit together.

First, men and women are different. I don't think I am surprising you with any new truth here! God made us different physically, emotionally and even in how we respond to various situations.

Second, opposites often attract—opposites in talents, personality traits and interests. We seem to forget this principle, and when we get married we become frustrated when our mates are weak in an area where we are strong. We cannot understand why they don't do things the way we do them.

Third, the only way to survive marriage is to stop and realize that your goal is to learn how you can fit together with your mate like pieces of a puzzle that unite to form a beautiful picture. So often we marry people who are opposite to us and try to shape them to become the same piece of the puzzle that we are. In the long run we design a puzzle that will never fit together.

I have learned many things in my thirty years of marriage to my wife Bonnie, but the story I am about to tell you gave me a whole new perspective on how I view my wife and respond to her.

Bonnie works as a merchandiser. That means that when you go into a store and look for a product but can't find it because someone has rearranged everything, she has been there. I guess stores do this to make everything look fresh, clean and new—and also to cause us to pick up unintended purchases while we search for the relocated item.

Sometimes on my day off, I go to work with Bonnie so I can spend a little extra time with her and take her to lunch. I have found that I have a hard time working with my wife! I put things on a shelf, and she takes them off. We approach the job from two different perspectives and constantly get in each other's way. Add to that a tight workspace, and it's a recipe for certain frustration. One day it got so bad that I said, "I can't work with you. We are driving each other crazy!"

Have you ever said that about your husband or wife? When I reached my breaking point, it hit me like a ton of bricks—I wanted Bonnie to look at what we were doing from my point of view. I was trying to make her a carbon copy of me. I was trying to shape her into the same piece of the puzzle that I was, and it wasn't working.

The Puzzle Principle

I realized that day that where I was weak, my wife seemed to shine, and where she seemed to be weak, I was strong. We were two different pieces of a puzzle. If we combined our strengths, we could eliminate our weaknesses and the puzzle would fit perfectly together.

We began carving out areas where we could use our strengths and help each other. We would try to stay out of the other's area or yield to the other's wisdom in his or her strong area. It took time and communication, but today there isn't anyone I would rather work with than my wife. We are working the puzzle principle, and we are tough to beat at things we endeavor to do together. We make a great team when we use our strengths to cover each other's weaknesses.

The puzzle principle has changed my perspective about the ministry my wife and I can have together. It all depends on our strengths and weaknesses and how we carry out our areas of responsibility, each doing his or her best to help the other and glorify God.

I wonder how many couples are fighting against each other, trying to prove each other wrong, frustrated that their mates do not do things like they do. Some of us may even be jealous of our spouses' strengths, feeling that their strengths only expose our own weaknesses. Then we criticize and belittle our mates with cutting remarks. We may be so conditioned to think our way is the only way that we show a lack of trust in our spouses. We worry that our mates' talents will become so strong that they won't need us anymore. As in my case, I could only see us tripping over one another, and my frustration neutralized my effectiveness and kept me from seeing the larger picture that a completed puzzle would create.

God made husbands and wives to be a team, to be helpmates, to become one. I want to encourage you to look at your wife or husband from a different perspective. Don't look down on your mate's weaknesses, but use your strengths to help him or her. Don't be jealous of your mate's accomplishments; let his or her strengths help *you* to become a better person. Our goal should be to use our talents and strengths to help complement our mates. Don't try to keep your mate under your thumb with cutting remarks; help him or her soar to great heights. If you do this, the pieces of the puzzle you are designing will come together. As you follow this principle, you will not lose your mate's love and need for you; instead, you will be astonished at how your puzzle pieces mesh.

The Missing Piece

When my wife puts puzzles together, she always hopes that the last piece will be there. If she gets to the end and a piece is missing, she searches all over for that piece. Sometimes she finds it and sometimes she doesn't. If we find a used puzzle in a thrift shop, we will stand right there and count the pieces before we buy it to make sure it is complete.

Life is like a big puzzle, and it will take your lifetime to put it together one piece at a time. But there is a secret to the puzzle of life: Everyone—regardless of skin color or background or location on earth—comes into this world with a piece missing. You may not know how to express it or put your finger on it, but there is an empty spot in your soul where that piece should go. And there is just one place to find it.

The missing piece is God. Romans tells us that everyone has knowledge of God, but unless we come to Him on His terms, that piece will always be missing. There is a longing in everyone's soul to fill the void. Our mates, our jobs, our children, fame, money— nothing can fit the hole in our puzzles. God is the only piece that will fit.

You see, where we are weak, He is strong! What we cannot do, He can do. Just like our mates complete us in an earthly way, God completes us in every way, for eternity. In this case, our weakness is sin, and our sin will not only keep us out of God's heaven but will keep us from God's plan for our lives and greatly affect our life puzzle.

God sent His only Son to die for our sin, and if we will confess our sin to God and ask His Son, Jesus Christ, into our hearts, we will have the missing piece of our life puzzle. Jesus Christ did what we could never do: He defeated sin on the cross. When we believe in Christ, He completes us and the missing piece falls into place.

This one act of deciding to follow Christ will affect your marriage and your home. This one piece will influence all the other pieces. God wants to help you complete your puzzle!

Many people, maybe even you, are ruining their lives. But you don't have to! There is hope, and it starts with realizing that you are a sinner, that you cannot live your life on your own, that you need help. Call out to God and ask His forgiveness right now by talking to Him in prayer and asking His Son, Jesus Christ, to come into your heart. If you have done this, the missing piece of life has been found. You have a new life, a new hope, a new goal and a promise of a full and complete puzzle.

My wife always keeps the top to the puzzle box close by because it has a picture of the whole puzzle on it. In the same way, God gave us a model for our lives. Although you won't see the completed picture until the end, you can see enough for each day to help you put the puzzle pieces in place. That model is the Holy Bible; you can depend on it and use it as you build your puzzle.

This is a book on marriage, and it is written to help marriages. There are too many divorces today, even among Christians. It's as if we are putting our own individual puzzles together and not working on the same one as husband-and-wife teams. It is not God's fault or the Bible's fault that we are having problems—it is our own fault! When we realize this and open our hearts to seek the help of God given to us in His Word, we can begin to put our lives and marriages back together one piece at a time. God wants to help you. No matter how bad your marriage is or how messed up your life is, God wants to help. He proved this by the ultimate sacrifice of His Son on the cross. Take the missing puzzle piece that God offers!

*D*avid Brown currently serves as senior pastor of North Main Street Church of God in Butler, Pennsylvania. Via his weekly pulpit ministry, he seeks to disciple and equip hundreds of people through the practical teaching and application of biblical truth to the daily issues of life. He and Jennifer, his wife of thirty-four years, have three adult children and have enjoyed more than thirty years of pastoral ministry together.

Brown has an abiding conviction that a church is only as strong as the families that make it up. That conviction has led him to devote much of his energy and ministry efforts to the strengthening of the family unit. Using foundational principles from God's Word, his experience as a pastor and counselor and his longtime role as husband and father, he teaches with a confident assurance that the Bible is, indeed, our handbook for life and the last word on the challenging issues and pressures facing the twenty-first-century family.

Building a Love That Lasts
a Lifetime

David Brown

Perhaps you've heard the story of the distraught husband who, try as he might, could not seem to convince his wife that he really did love her. He bought candy, he sent cards, he had flowers delivered, all to no avail. Nothing worked. Finally, desperate for a solution, he went to his pastor for help and counsel. His pastor said, "I'll tell you what to do. Take off work and go home early to surprise her. Walk into the house, take her into your arms and give her the biggest, most passionate kiss you've ever given her in your life. She will see how much you really love her."

Well, the man did exactly that. He went home in the middle of the day, found his wife in the kitchen and, without saying a word, pulled her into his arms and passionately kissed her. To his utter dismay, she pushed him away and ran crying hysterically into the bedroom. Following after her, he said, "Honey, what's wrong? What did I do?"

She looked at him, tears streaming down her cheeks, and said, "Well, you're just the icing on the cake today! First, our son got expelled from school for fighting in class, then the washing machine broke and flooded the house, and now you come home drunk!"

Has it really gotten that bad? Are we neglecting our marriages to the point that an honest, open display of love and affection would be so rare and unexpected as to cause our mates to wonder what we were up to? Sadly, in far too many marriages the answer is "yes," and it begs the question: How does what was a loving, caring, committed relationship on one's wedding day spiral downward into an angry, ugly divorce just a few years later? The national statistics on divorce are alarming and distressing to anyone who cares about couples and families. Most surveys reveal that fifty percent (some survey results are even higher) of all new marriages will end in divorce, most in less than five years. As disturbing as these numbers are, they do not begin to reveal the pain, hurt and emotional suffering caused by broken relationships. Broken relationships lead to broken lives. The pain is real, it is deep and it is often lifelong. Where can we go for help, and what can we do to turn the tide?

A good place to begin is at the beginning. Marriage is God's idea. Genesis 2:24 in the Amplified Bible says, "Therefore a man shall leave his father and his mother and shall become united and cleave to his wife, and they shall become one flesh." In this wonderful, mystical relationship we call marriage, God says that two become one. I submit to you that there would be a lot less "leaving" in marriage if there were more "cleaving."

When a marriage is built on the foundation of God's Word, with Christ at the center, it will be able to weather the storms and counter the crises that inevitably come. It will not just survive; it will thrive. Unity, oneness and intimacy in marriage are not elusive goals to be desperately sought after, but instead are results that naturally occur when God's pattern and plan for marriage are faithfully followed. Physical, emotional and spiritual intimacy are God's gifts to every married couple willing to build their marriage on the unchanging principles He has established in His Word. Let's discover how these principles can change *your* marriage for good and forever.

Physical Intimacy

A humorous story is told of an old fella who was walking down the road one day when he heard a voice. He looked down and, to his utter amazement, saw a talking frog. The frog looked up and said, "If you kiss me, I will become a beautiful princess." The old fella picked up that talking frog, put it in his pocket and continued on down the road. A little while later the frog repeated his promise from inside the pocket: "If you kiss me, I will become a beautiful princess." Undeterred, the old man kept on walking. More time passed, and then the determined frog said once again, "If you kiss me, I will become a beautiful princess." At that, the old man reached into his pocket, grabbed the frog and, looking him square in the eye, said, "Listen, you! You might as well shut up, because at my age I would rather have a talking frog!"

Sadly, I often encounter couples who find their physical relationships so unfulfilling, disappointing, boring, frustrating and unenjoyable that they will say or do almost anything to avoid the experience with their spouses. Were one available, they would much prefer a talking frog. They are completely in the dark as to the great things God has for them in this area of their marriages.

The sexual relationship, created and designed by God, is something to be enjoyed, not just endured. God has established clearly defined parameters in His Word for the sexual relationship which, when followed in faith and faithfulness, enhance love and intimacy in deeply profound ways. What are the parameters, the boundaries God has established to maximize fulfillment in this area? And, secondly, what are the benefits and blessings that result when we follow God's plan?

We live in a culture obsessed with sex. Sex sells. It sells movies; it sells TV sitcoms; it sells books and magazines, clothes and cars and anything else you can think of. From chocolate bars to deodorant bars, sex sells. But what is it, exactly, that the culture is selling?

For starters, what the culture is selling doesn't even remotely resemble the relationship defined and described in God's Word. That, by the way, is the number-one reason why Christians and the Church must begin to speak in an open and straightforward manner on this subject. The message of the culture on sex, a message that leads to bondage, must be effectively countered by the biblical message, which leads to liberty and wholeness. Let's compare these two messages in a couple of areas:

- Our culture says sex is all about me: "Meet my needs." . . . "Do what I want." . . . "Follow my schedule." . . . "Serve me."
    God says the purpose of the sexual relationship is to mu-

tually benefit both husband and wife. The Apostle Paul writes in First Corinthians 7:3, "The husband should fulfill his marital duty to his wife, and likewise the wife to her husband." It's not about getting—it's about giving. The wonderful, divine mystery I discover when I follow God's plan is that, in meeting my spouse's needs, I get my needs met. I find fulfillment. The exhilarating pleasure and enjoyment God always intended becomes mine through the selfless act of giving.

- Our culture says that sex is a purely physical act without implications or ramifications beyond the act itself. Therefore (as this hedonistic logic goes), it is perfectly acceptable to engage yourself sexually with any number of willing partners, be they one-night stands or short-term or long-term relationships. Since there are no emotional or spiritual consequences or accountability, you simply discard the current relationship and move on to the next relationship whenever you feel like it, because, remember, it's all about you and what you want.

  God, on the other hand, says that a profound bonding and unity occurs in the sexual relationship, a bonding and unity with emotional and spiritual implications that go far beyond the physical act itself. Implications, in fact, that last a lifetime.

What was in the mind of God when He established the husband/wife relationship?

When God speaks of a husband and wife becoming one flesh (see Genesis 2:24), He pictures for us, through physical intimacy, the intimacy that can occur between a husband and wife on the deeper emotional and spiritual levels. This is the depth of relationship that God desires for every married couple. It has always been His plan. It also pictures the kind of bonding and unity that God desires to have with every one of His children through the new birth, and the oneness Christ desires to have with His Body, the Church.

Do you understand that you never lose when you follow God's plan for your marriage? You always win! I challenge you to build your marriage on a foundation that will last. Build it on Christ and "do not conform any longer to the pattern of this world [the culture], but be transformed" (Romans 12:2).

Emotional Intimacy

God's design and desire for your marriage is intimacy and oneness on every level: physical, emotional and spiritual. A deep, intimate marital relationship on all these levels doesn't just happen automatically; it takes work, hard work, and lots of it. It also takes a willingness to learn and an openness to change. Yet this kind of intimacy is attainable, and it is God's will for your marriage.

Because of the frenetic pace at which couples so often live these days, emotional intimacy can be an especially elusive goal. Career pursuits, parenting responsibilities, recreational and social activities and, yes, even church or ministry commitments take their toll on our marriages. They not only require huge chunks of our time, but they also sap our energy and leave us physically and emotionally drained, often to the point of exhaustion. We have nothing left to give to our spouses. No time. No energy. No effort. We're just too tired. We can't give them any quantity of our time, and we certainly can't give them any quality time. If that describes you, you are overcommitted! And it is your marriage that is suffering for the lack of time and attention.

I am reminded of the story of the couple who went to see a counselor. The husband said, "My wife is so depressed. I'm really worried about her." The counselor said, "Would you mind if I talked to her privately?" "That's fine," the husband said. After talking with the woman, the counselor discovered that the woman was just starving for her husband's love and affection. He invited her husband back into the office, and to dramatically demonstrate this need, he walked over to the wife, pulled her into his arms and passionately kissed her right on the lips. He turned to her husband and said, "She needs that at least once every day of the week." The husband, with a puzzled and confused look on his face, said, "Well, OK, but I can only get her here on Mondays, Wednesdays and Fridays." Talk about a busy schedule! That little story illustrates how vitally important it is to make your marriage a priority, not just in your schedule, but in your personal commitment to building emotional intimacy.

Since good marriages don't just happen, what is the solution to this serious problem? What can you do to establish or reestablish emotional intimacy in your marriage? Frankly, you are going to have to make some choices, and, in all likelihood, many of them will be difficult and perhaps even painful to make. You will have to choose between good and best. You are going to have to give up some things. You can't be everything and do everything—there aren't enough "you's" to go around and there aren't enough hours in the day to do everything you want to do. It takes time to build emotional intimacy with your husband or wife. The one indispensable thing you must be willing to give to achieve emotional intimacy in your marriage is yourself.

And, yes, to do that requires the willingness to sacrifice. It's a sacrifice, however, that pays huge dividends, and it is well worth the cost. So what if you have to scale down your busy schedule and cut back on some of your commitments? We're talking about your marriage! Apart from your personal relationship with Jesus Christ, no commitment in your life is more important than the one you made on your wedding day. Make the decision now to put your marriage at the top of your priority list and you won't live to regret it—you'll live to enjoy it!

Spiritual Intimacy

Ecclesiastes 4:9 says, "Two are better than one. . . ." The writer continues in the next couple of verses to give various reasons why this is true. But then he concludes in verse 12 by stating, almost as an afterthought, "A cord of *three* strands is not easily broken." What was he thinking of? As he was describing the many positive benefits of two persons working in partnership together, it's as if he took pause and said, "Hey! Wait a minute! Two are better than one, but there's something even better than that! Add the presence and power of God to that relationship and you've really got something great!"

A husband and wife partnering together in a loving, caring and committed relationship is a wonderful thing. As great as that is, think how much greater it can be when the Creator of the marriage relationship Himself joins the partnership. The greatest thing you can do for your marriage is to make Jesus Christ the "managing partner" of the relationship. Turn all control over to Him. He will make you one, and when you and your spouse are one in Him, you will have a unity that is absolutely unattainable any other way. It is a unity that the world does not know and cannot give, because it comes from God and it is exclusively for those who trust in Him.

How do you develop spiritual intimacy? The key to spiritual intimacy in marriage is for both husband and wife to first be in right relationship with God themselves. When I am committed to Christ and my spouse is committed to Christ, He will join our hearts and lives together in a spiritual oneness that far surpasses anything we could ever attain on our own. He is the glue that bonds us together in an inseparable union.

It is then, and only then, that the mystery of "two becoming one" can be fully understood and appreciated. The relationship deepens and grows on every level. When we are committed to Christ, our commitment to one another and to our marriage is greater. When we are committed to Christ, our sexual relationship can become all that God intended it to be. When we are committed to Christ, we are able to share the sorrows and disappointments as well as the joys of life together, because we are one. When we are committed to Christ, we are able to treat one another the way He would treat us in the same circumstance—with love, grace, compassion and understanding.

Jesus makes us one. Nothing will draw you closer together as a husband and wife than having Him at the center of your lives and at the center of your marriage. Nothing will give you greater intimacy (physically, emotionally, spiritually) than joining your lives together and sharing life together in Him. The greater my relationship is with Christ, the greater my relationship will be with my spouse. In Him, we two "become one."

It is not a question of whether we need God's presence and power in our marriages. We do! The question is: Are we willing to accept the challenge of doing whatever it takes to build our lives and our marriages on the only foundation that will last, Jesus Christ? Spiritual intimacy will lead to physical intimacy, which leads to emotional intimacy. The divine mystery of "oneness" becomes a reality in marriage when Christ comes in. Accept the challenge today. Nothing will bring you greater fulfillment, and nothing will bring you greater joy.

Part Five
Sexual Intimacy

Honor marriage, and guard the sacredness of sexual intimacy between wife and husband. God draws a firm line against casual and illicit sex.
(Hebrews 13:4, The Message)

*D*r. Kevin Leman is an internationally known psychologist, author, radio and television personality and speaker. He has ministered to and entertained audiences worldwide with his wit and common-sense psychology and has written twenty-two books, several of which made the best-seller list. The "Relationship Doctor" has made house calls for numerous radio and television programs, including *Focus on the Family*, Moody Network's *Midday Connection* and *Open Line*, *The Oprah Winfrey Show*, *Live with Regis and Kelly*, *CBS This Morning* and the *Today* show. He is a consulting family psychologist for *Good Morning America*.

A master communicator, Leman is also a husband and a dad to five children. He attended North Park College and received his bachelor's degree in psychology from the University of Arizona, where he later earned his master's and doctorate degrees.

Books

Adolescence Isn't Terminal
Becoming a Couple of Promise
Becoming the Parent God Wants You to Be
The Birth Order Connection
Bringing Up Kids Without Tearing Them Down
Joy Breaks for Couples
Keeping Your Family Together When the World Is Falling Apart
Living in a Step-Family Without Getting Stepped On
Making Children Mind Without Losing Yours
Making Sense of the Men in Your Life

The New Birth Order Book
The Real You
Say Good-bye to Stress
The Six Stress Points in a Woman's Life
Sex Begins in the Kitchen
Sheet Music
Unlocking the Secrets of Your Childhood Memories
What a Difference a Daddy Makes
Women Who Try Too Hard

Web
www.realfamilies.com

Why Sex Begins (and Sometimes Ends) in the Kitchen

Kevin Leman

*I*t's one of those Friday nights when every member of the family has something to do. The two teenagers and their nine-year-old brother are going to the high school football game. It's Dad's night to bowl, and Mom has to go to church to work on decorations for a mother-daughter banquet coming up the following evening. At six-thirty, as soon as dinner is finished, everybody flies out of the house, headed toward their separate destinations.

It's about three hours later when Mom is turning her car into the driveway of her home. She's completely exhausted. It's been a long day, and the only thing she wants to do now is collapse into bed—but first maybe she'll relax in a tub full of bubbles for a while. And then, as she turns off the ignition and switches off the lights, it hits her: the dishes! She didn't have time to get to the dishes after dinner. In fact, the whole kitchen was a mess.

She thinks for a moment about the possibility of leaving it until morning, but quickly decides that's not possible. Well, so much for her plans for a hot bath and a warm, comfortable bed.

She walks up to the porch, unlocks the front door, tosses her purse on the table in the front hall, and heads straight for the kitchen. Might as well get this out of the way right now.

She stops dead in her tracks as she sees a beautiful, sparkling-clean kitchen. Her first reaction is to think that she got into the neighbor's house by mistake. But she goes back outside, checks the number, and finds that . . . yes, this is her house. She walks back into the house just in time to see her husband hanging up the wet dish towels in the laundry room.

And let me tell you: the guy may have a bald spot on the back of his head, his stomach may hang over his belt—just a little—and he may give the appearance that he's trying hard to grow a second chin. But the old fellow has never looked more desirable to his wife than he does right now.

And that's what I mean when I tell you that sex begins in the kitchen.

Too many people—especially those of us who are fortunate enough to be males—seem to believe that sex begins and ends in the bedroom, period. Some men grunt their way through the evening without showing their wives the least bit of attention. When a man's wife asks him if he thought the dinner she fixed was good, he grunts in response. She tells him about something important that happened to her during the day, and she gets another grunt out of him. She tries to talk to him about something cute that one of the kids did or said and hears the third grunt of the evening. After that, she just gives up trying to talk.

But then when bedtime comes, he's grabbing for her and wondering why she's so "cold" to him. That's just not how "good sex" happens. Sexual intimacy between a man and woman should be the culmination and expression of the intimacy they share in all areas of their life together. For sex to be what it is capable of being, it must be an act of loving and sharing, of giving to each other.

It is most definitely not a game of "I'm Tarzan, you Jane—gimme."

Now before I get myself into trouble, let me explain what I meant a moment ago, about those of us who were "fortunate" enough to be born males. That may have sounded like a sexist statement, but that's definitely not the way I meant it. What I did mean was that as far as I'm concerned, there couldn't be anything better than to be a man who has a deep and abiding relationship with a good woman.

Let me assure you that there have been many times, over the course of the years, when I have thanked the Lord above that he made me a man. And all of those times have had to do with my relationship with my wonderful wife, Sande.

When a man has the deepest sort of communion with a woman who is warm and wonderful and wise—well, he's really got something. My purpose in writing this book is to help men discover that sort of relationship with the women in their lives, and to help women find that sort of relationship with their men.

Let's go back for a moment to the story I told you at the beginning of this chapter.

If you're a woman, chances are that when I got to the part about the dishes having been washed and the kitchen cleaned up, you said something like, "Oh. I thought this was a *true* story."

Or if you're a man, you might have said, "You mean the guy did the dishes? What a wuss!"

Well, guys, if you really want to be macho, if you want to be the virile, manly sort of man every woman wants . . . then you'd be wise to tie on an apron once in a while and take a couple of steps in the direction of dishpan hands.

Your mate ought to be the number-one priority in your life. . . . A good marital relationship is based upon pleasing each other, being sensitive and tuned-in to each other's emotional—as well as sexual—needs. [We have a] need to be intimate with each other as husband and wife; to share our most intimate thoughts and feelings; to understand the different languages in which we express our love; to come together as one in marriage, both emotionally and physically.

Unfortunately, in most marriages, couples seem to live in a "married-singles" lifestyle. In too many of these homes nothing at all happens behind bedroom doors. And if a sexual relationship does exist, it occurs only as a ritual or a duty, a few minutes squeezed in after the late news and before Letterman.

It is hardly the culmination of an entire day full of affection, consideration, love and oneness.

Now this isn't to say that on Friday night when Dad did the dishes before Mom got home he was going to be rewarded with a sexual encounter with his wife. However, Mom's feelings when she walked into the house and saw what her husband had done had to be, "Hey! What a neat experience to walk in and find that he beat me home by a half hour and was thoughtful enough to clean the kitchen!" He was showing his wife that he loved her and not doing it because he was thinking, "Hey . . . maybe she'll make love to me if she sees that I did the dishes."

Motivation is important here as in every other area of life. False motives will be spotted a mile or more away, but acts done out of the motivation of love will produce dividends in all areas of your life together as husband and wife. What the husband in my illustration had done is an act of love toward his wife as surely as anything else he's ever done for her—and it lets her know that she is important enough to him that he will do what he can to make life more pleasurable for her. This kind of consideration in your own marriage can do nothing but bring you closer together as man and wife.

I have watched thousands of couples come to grips with the fact that they have to open up and take a good look at themselves in order to have a satisfying marriage. Most of us don't really understand ourselves. But if you are going to share with your mate and become one in marriage, you must be able to recognize your own feelings—why you do what you do, what preconditioning you have received, and so on. You have to see how these influences have affected your way of thinking and be able to "reprogram" yourself in the places where you need it.

You also need to know what it means to be committed to making whatever changes are needed in your own behavior.

And that's important. If you want to change somebody else's behavior, the best thing you can do is to change your own behavior first. Handing your husband a book and saying, "Here, George, I think you ought to read this," won't do you any good.

Telling your wife, "You know, I've been reading about the importance of good communication in marriage, and you really could do a better job," isn't going to win her over to your way of thinking. But if you demonstrate by your own actions that you want to make things better between you—if you'll begin doing those little things to show your mate how much you care—then I can almost guarantee that you're going to see a steady improvement in your marriage.

I want to tell you a couple of things about sex and marriage that I strongly believe in:

Sex belongs in marriage.

Sex belongs *only* in marriage.

Let me explain.

First of all, when I say that sex belongs in marriage, I mean that the sexual union is a vital part of the love that brought a man and woman together as husband and wife in the first place. A while ago I was flipping channels and came across a talk show where several married couples were talking about how happy they were to be taking part in the "new celibacy." Some of them hadn't made love in several years, and they seemed to be happy as clams about it. (Although I couldn't help but wonder if perhaps a couple of clams wouldn't have had a more exciting life.)

If a healthy man and woman who are husband and wife look me in the eye and tell me they are perfectly happy without any sort of sexual contact between them, my reaction is not, "That's great." My reaction is, "There's something wrong here." The sexual aspect of life is one of the great gifts from our Creator, and long-term celibacy between married couples is simply not normal or healthy, no matter how much it may be considered the "in" thing.

I do not believe that for a marriage to be healthy a husband and wife have to engage in sex five or six times a week—or even once a week. Frequency is entirely up to the couple and should be based on mutual respect and a desire to please the other partner. The couple should come together in this way often enough that they are both fulfilled sexually. Furthermore, the wife needs to know that her husband sees her as sexually desirable, and the husband needs to know that his wife enjoys being with him in this intimate way. In fact, one of the greatest needs of most married men is sexual fulfillment. Notice I didn't say sex. Men need to feel wanted sexually.

And as I mentioned earlier, in order for the sexual relationship to be healthy, all other aspects of the couple's relationship must also be healthy.

Now, the second point I made is that sex belongs *only* in marriage.

For many Christians this is a no-brainer. But many others would look at me as if I *am* a no-brainer. For centuries Christians and other religious folks have preached the value of fidelity, chastity, and monogamy. But the sexual revolution of our age has made premarital and extra-marital dalliances commonplace. For the last couple of decades, whenever I stood up in a public forum and promoted sex only within marriage, I was branded as some sort of religious kook.

But things are changing. More and more, as mental and physical health professionals grapple with the problems brought about by sexual promiscuity—which range from chronic depression all the way to AIDS—even the most libertine people are beginning to see that a lifetime monogamous relationship between one man and one woman is the ideal.

Sometimes I think the world has turned topsy-turvy when I see married couples on television talking about the joys of celibacy, and then I turn the channel and see a drama glorifying sex between two unmarried individuals.

Why do I believe that marriage is the only context in which a sexual relationship should take place?

- First, because I personally believe that's the way we were created. You might say that I believe the "divine plan" is for one man and one woman to pledge their lives to each other, to encourage one another, to support one another, to be totally loyal to each other in all areas of life, including sexuality. The Bible consistently restricts sex to the marriage relationship, and I believe God's laws are perfect. He knew what he was doing when he set up this marriage thing.

- Second, sex is a powerful experience that triggers extremely strong emotions. Some people insist they are immune to those emotions, but the truth is that they aren't. So even from a purely psychological, nonreligious perspective, sex was never meant to be an impersonal act. Like it or not, you become emotionally bonded to your sex partner.

- Third, my feeling is that sex is to be shared only with someone you love deeply, and if you love that person deeply enough to have sex with him or her, then you should also love that person deeply enough to commit your life to him or her through marriage.

- The final reason is simply that promiscuous sex is danger-ous—physically, mentally, and emotionally. I love a little verse tucked away in the next to the last book of the Bible: "Stay always within the boundaries where God's love can reach and bless you" (Jude 21, TLB). Sexual fidelity is not a matter of keeping our hands out of some delightful cookie jar. It's about enjoying a full and honest relationship in which God can bless us.

I honestly believe that if you and your spouse (or future spouse) will commit yourselves to each other, chances are very good that you are going to be richly blessed by a beautiful marriage.

Taken from Sex Begins in the Kitchen *by Kevin Leman, Copyright © 1999 by Kevin Leman. Published by Fleming H. Revell, a division of Baker Book House. Used by permission.*

Who is Jay Carty? An "unusual communicator" is a mild statement. Maybe "a little nuts" would be more accurate. He's not a preacher, not a teacher . . . more a storyteller with a very important message. He is fun, funny and provocative. Traditional, he is not; challenging, he is. Where some "deep" preachers are too "snoozy" for the rank and rile, and where some humorists don't have much to say, Jay's "stuff" is generally regarded as an unusual blending of humor and content.

Carty played basketball at Oregon State and coached there for two years. He was on John Wooden's staff for three years at UCLA and coached Kareem Abdul Jabbar. He then played for the Los Angeles Lakers. Following basketball and a time in the business world, Carty directed a Christian conference center, was a church consultant with Churches Alive and in 1982 began Yes! Ministries, an organization dedicated to helping people say "yes!" to God. He crosses denominations and relates to a changing contemporary society as well as a broad range of age groups. He speaks in churches, colleges, schools and retreat centers across the country.

Carty and his wife Mary make their home in Santa Barbara, California. They have two grown children.

Books

Coach Wooden One-On-One
Counter Attack (also audio, video and workshop)
Darrell Waltrip One-On-One
Discovering Your Natural Talents (also video)
O. Whillikers in the Hall of Champions
Playing with Fire (also audio)
Something's Fishy (also audio)

Web

www.jaycarty.com

God's Solution to Sexual Temptation

Jay Carty

I was in the San Francisco Bay area and had just come back from speaking. I parked my car in the motel parking lot and saw a woman struggling with her luggage. It would have been unkind not to have helped her. She invited me into her room.

I didn't have a decision to make. I had already decided to set the bags down outside her door and go straight back to my room. I made that decision in the parking lot. But even at that, a little mental discipline was required. I still remember her room number—203. Flattery is an enticing commodity.

Since most people have messed up in sexual areas, let's look at the biblical solution to staying pure. There's only one: You better RUUUUUUNNNNNNNN! Your passport to purity is a simple formula: Purity = beat feet.

The solution to the temptation of sexual sin is a twofold mandate: First Corinthians 6:18 says, "Flee immorality." Get out of there and don't sin in the first place.

Flee! Stay out of situations where trouble might find you. There is no other instruction. Just as God made only one way to Himself (through Jesus), and Christ reemphasized the point by saying spiritual birth must occur ("you must be born again"), it is also true of God's instruction on how to handle sexual temptation. Run! Set your rules, etch them in stone, make sure you follow them, and then when temptation comes—scram.

You may be thinking that I missed a great opportunity to share Jesus with a woman who probably didn't know him. Not so. I had to run to be safe. Let God raise up a woman to share with her. He can send someone to get her into a church. At times like that His highest commandment for me is to bug out.

We Can't Be Trusted

People need to learn to run from sexual sin, *including all situations that can lead to temptation*. It's the only solution God gives. He tells us to run because we can't be trusted.

I'm into Superman. I was raised on Superman. I think he's great. But in *Superman II,* Superman went to bed with Lois Lane. I was devastated. I couldn't believe he'd do a thing like that. Superman, my hero . . . the man of steel rusted in front of my very eyes.

Folks, if you can't trust Superman, who can you trust? Do you know what I mean? And that's the point. When it comes to sexual temptation nobody can be trusted. That's why there's only one instruction given as to how to handle sexual sin. Leave! Scram! Split! Jet! Get out of there! Never try to stand firm and be the mighty man or woman of steel. Ultimately you will rust for sure.

Ladies, remember when you were in high school and you had one of those talks with your folks when you wanted to stay out later than usual? They said no, but you were determined to go the limit to get your way. As the conversation progressed, tears began falling down your cheeks, tears led to sobbing, and your sobs progressed to mild convulsing sounds followed by deep whimperings. Remember? Finally, when you had run out of options, you resorted to the last weapon in your arsenal as you blurted out, "You . . . (sob), you . . . (sob, sob) . . . YOU JUST DON'T TRUST ME!" (boo hoo hoo hoo). Have you ever used that line on your folks? Just about every girl who has grown into womanhood has tried that one on her parents at one time or another.

The guys do it differently. They stand, looking Dad in the eye in a macho head-cocked-to-the-side stance and say, "Hey, Dad, why don't you trust me? Huh? Huh?" They then tilt their chin upward in a snapping, defiant kind of motion three or four times for emphasis.

Let me tell you something that's very important. When it comes to sex, I want my kids to know something absolutely, for certain, for sure: I DON'T TRUST 'EM! *I don't trust them because they can't be trusted.* And neither can you.

I was talking to an eighty-five-year-old man the other day. I asked him, "When did you stop noticing the ladies?"

He said, "I haven't yet. Perhaps you need to talk to someone who's a little older."

We can't be trusted. That means there should always be a few precautions taken to protect relationships from sexual compromise.

Police Yourself

The best precaution I know of is to police yourself. There are several policing tactics that I'd like to suggest. Granted, some of these may be in variable areas and may be just fine for you, but look out. About the time you think you're safe is the time you're closest to falling.

Counseling. I tell pastors not to talk to another man's wife more than once in a counseling session unless another woman is present or unless her husband is there. Why? Because neither the counselor nor the counseled can be trusted! Probably the biggest contributor to pastoral infidelity is the result of intimate, repeated, private counseling with women. Don't allow your pastor to do it. Make sure he's policing himself. Don't you do it either.

Praying. Never pray with a member of the opposite sex repeatedly unless you want the relationship to deepen. When I worked with large college departments in our previous churches, I found that when prayer partners were opposite sexes, their relationships usually went from friends to dating. *Married people should never pray repeatedly with a member of the opposite sex other than their spouses.* It's just too intimate—therefore, too dangerous. Police yourselves.

Hugging. I preach in quite a few churches where the people hug a lot. Some churches do some serious hugging. It's like greeting someone with a modern-day version of the biblical "holy kiss" Paul talked about, only they greet each other with a holy hug. It's the cultural thing to do and in the environment you can't avoid participating without being rude.

When I preach I represent God to the people and the people to God. Sometimes a woman sitting out there in the audience thinks, *Oh, what a godly man.* She doesn't know me. (The godliest person you know lives at least 150 miles away. Godly people are the ones we don't know very well, because after we get to know them we usually find they aren't so godly.)

Sometimes a lady who thinks that way, who is a part of a huggin' church, will get out of her seat and come straight at me after I finish speaking. She's thinking, *Oh, what a godly man.* I'm thinking, *Oh, what a woman.* Sometimes women forget that God wired men differently—and sometimes they know very well what they're doing.

At any rate, here she comes. It's going to be a full-on body press for sure. My practice is to rotate forty-five degrees to the side, put my left hand in my pocket and say, "Give me half a hug."

My actions say, "I care about you and I want to honor you, but let's make sure there is some godly distance between us. I want you to know I can't be trusted. I also want you to know that I don't trust you either." It's an effective policing action.

Call me old-fashioned but I never want my wife fully in somebody else's arms. I don't trust myself enough to allow somebody else's wife in mine. Many a spouse has a sinking heart when their mate fully embraces somebody else.

Back rubs. In married circles back rubs may become more than therapy, and it is a practice that ought to be scrutinized carefully. I for one don't want another man's hands on my wife's body. I'll keep my hands off theirs. It's a policing tactic.

What practices are you engaged in that fuel your fantasies and stimulate your senses? They may be legitimate activities and socially acceptable practices, but are they okay for you? Think through what policing action you need to take. You'll be staying on the offensive if you do.

Are You Playing with Fire?

If you are single, the following questions probably don't apply to you. Your yes is most likely a healthy response. But for a married person an affirmative answer could mean big trouble.

Is there a person at church you want to see on Sunday because you fantasized about them during the week?

Is there a person you look forward to hugging ahead of time? Is there a person you would like to be around because he or she stirs your emotions?

Do you find yourself hanging around to watch somebody walk by?

Do you find yourself looking forward to a committee meeting because that person will be there?

Is there something about that counseling appointment that makes you especially look forward to it?

Are you a chronic back-rubber or rubbee? Why?

Are you involved in any contact activity that might not be good for you?

If you answer yes to any of these questions, figure out how to run. You're playing with fire if you don't. A decision to keep messin' around is a decision that will probably lead to your downfall. And you're probably allowing Satan to gain a foothold in your life.

Pulling It Together

1. God offers only one solution to the problem of sexual temptation—don't allow yourself to be tempted. Run, avoid, stay away, leave, flee, turn it off, don't buy it, and get out of there. Beat feet when sexual temptation comes. Running is God's only solution to dealing with sexual temptation.

2. Nobody can be trusted with sexual temptation. Pastors, counselors, neighbors, friends and relatives shouldn't be trusted. Too much time in the wrong setting will cause anyone to fall to sexual sin.

3. Since you know you can't be trusted, police yourself. Think through an evaluation of your high-risk areas and determine what you are going to do about them.

Excerpted from Counter Attack *by Jay Carty, Copyright © 1988 by Yes! Ministries. Used by permission.*

*R*andy and Deb Kalmbach are living proof that God's amazing grace can carry you through even the most difficult times. In her book, *Because I Said Forever: Embracing Hope in a Not-So-Perfect Marriage*, Kalmbach tells about her own marriage, the struggle of living with her husband's alcoholism and how God mercifully brought them to a place of forgiveness, healing and restoration in their marriage.

Kalmbach offers encouragement, comfort and help for women in difficult marriages, especially where addictive behaviors are involved. She has been a guest speaker at treatment centers for alcoholism and drug addiction, conferences, retreats, Alcoholics Anonymous and Al-Anon. She cohosted a radio talk show, *Straight Talk,* in Seattle, Washington, and has worked as a DJ for a local radio station with her own daily program. Her faith in Jesus Christ and the changes in her own life since she became a Christian in 1976 motivate her to tell her story.

The Kalmbachs recently celebrated more than thirty years of "not-so-perfect" marriage. They make their home in Washington's beautiful Methow Valley with their dog, Kramer, and cat, Nip. Two grown sons, Chris and Jeremy, live in the Seattle area. Randy and Deb love the Methow Valley's quiet and peaceful surroundings (no traffic!) and recreation for all seasons.

Book with Heather Harpham Kopp
Because I Said Forever

*H*eather Harpham Kopp is an editor and author. For four years she wrote a popular column, "Out of the Ordinary," for *Virtue* magazine. She and her husband David make their home in Sisters, Oregon. They have five children between the ages of sixteen and twenty-two who often join them on hikes and camping trips in beautiful Central Oregon.

Books
Baby Stories God Told
The Dieter's Prayer Book
The Dream Giver
God's Little Book of Guarantees
God's Little Book of Guarantees for Marriage
God's Little Book of Guarantees for Moms
Lost Boys and the Moms Who Love Them (also journal)
Powerful Prayers for Your Baby
Powerful Prayers for Your Children

Powerful Prayers for Your Marriage
Praying the Bible for Your Baby
Praying the Bible for Your Children
Praying the Bible for Your Life
Praying the Bible for Your Marriage
Praying the Bible with Your Family
Treasured Friends

Book with Deb Kalmbach
Because I Said Forever

Sex Matters 17

Deb Kalmbach and Heather Kopp

> I have already gotten settled in bed, wearing my flannel night-
> gown and reading my book. Now that you're in the mood, I'm
> not sure I want to go to all the trouble. . . .
>
> A paraphrase of Song of Songs 5:3, 6

Sometimes the well-worn excuse, "I've got a headache, honey,"
is actually true. Just the thought of having sex makes your
head hurt, and maybe your heart as well. It's hard to feel amorous
when you're angry or disappointed, and it's equally difficult to desire your husband sexually if you're not attracted to him.

Many women in difficult marriages lack a desire for sexual intimacy with their mates—and you don't have to look far to understand why, at least in part. We're all aware that women are wired
differently than men when it comes to sex. While men are aroused
by physical and visual stimuli, women usually need to feel affection and trust in order to be responsive to a man's sexual advances.
When a wife receives her husband during intercourse, she is, in a
sense, allowing herself to be invaded by him—not just physically,
but on emotional and spiritual levels, as well. Wives who feel loved
and secure welcome this invasion as an opportunity to experience
intense intimacy and pleasure with their husbands. But wives who
lack sexual desire or who feel animosity toward their husbands often experience sex as a violation rather than as loving communion.

Many women in difficult marriages find sex undesirable. So, if you
have problems in this area, know that you're in good company—and
that you can take steps to have a more satisfying and healthy sexual
relationship with your husband.

You may be surprised to learn that Scripture can shed some insight into why you may be feeling resistant or resentful when it

comes to lovemaking. In a well-known but often misrepresented passage about marriage, Paul writes, "The husband should fulfill his marital duty to his wife, and likewise the wife to her husband. The wife's body does not belong to her alone but also to her husband. In the same way, the husband's body does not belong to him alone but also to his wife" (1 Corinthians 7:3-4).

These verses have been used to browbeat wives into feeling guilty for not wanting to have sex or for avoiding it. But notice that Paul doesn't say a wife's body belongs *only* to her spouse. It says it belongs *also* to her spouse. As "one flesh," a wife shares her body with her husband. Bible commentaries also point out that when Paul says we "belong" to one another, he's not just emphasizing our ownership rights over one another, but he's also clarifying that our exclusive conjugal rights belong to each other—no outsiders allowed.

This passage does not teach that a wife (or husband, for that matter) should submit to sex whenever, wherever, and however our partner demands it, no matter how we feel. Rather, it teaches that since my husband's body belongs to me, I should care about it enough to give it pleasure whenever I possibly can, and he likewise with my body. In the same way, since my husband's body belongs to me, I should also be understanding and generous when it's not "in the mood," and he likewise with my body. The emphasis is on mutuality, not selfishness.

At first reading, this passage may also seem to teach that sex is a duty, a required act. But duty is better translated as *sacred responsibility*. Paul is advising couples to continue to have sex on a regular basis because sex is at the heart of our sacred oneness and helps to protect our fidelity. The intent of this duty isn't that a wife complies with a husband's selfish appetite for sex on demand or vice versa, but to fulfill her sacred obligation to meet her husband's sexual needs, keep the marriage bed pure, and keep each other free of sexual temptation.

Let's look at another passage. In Ephesians, husbands are told to love their wives "as their own bodies" (Ephesians 5:28). "After all, no one ever hated his own body," Paul writes, "but he feeds and cares for it, just as Christ does the church" (v. 29). God describes a husband who loves his wife so much that he puts her needs as high on the chart as his own bodily needs! In regard to sex then, if a husband loves his wife this way, there's no danger that he'll mistreat her or take sexual advantage of her, because that would be like hating his own body.

In God's ideal picture of marriage, if a wife wasn't feeling up to sex, for whatever reason, the husband would honor and respect her feelings as if it were himself who wasn't in the mood. If a husband *doesn't* love his wife this way, he—not she—is sinning when he expects his wife to be available for intercourse on demand and without regard to her feelings.

Okay, so now we see that God didn't intend for a wife to be a slave to her husband's sexual needs. However, on the other extreme— saying that a wife has no responsibility or can shirk her obligation to nurture a healthy, ongoing sexual relationship—is equally wrong and unbiblical. A wife who regularly refuses to have sex or is only willing to be intimate with her husband on her terms is also acting selfishly. If you consistently rebuff your husband's sexual advances and resent intercourse, you need to take active, positive steps toward restoring consistent and mutually satisfying lovemaking to your marriage.

Here are some suggestions to start you on the path to discovery and change. For starters:

Tell your husband that you want to improve your lovemaking and you are actively pursuing positive changes. Assure him that you understand that you have a part in the sexual problems in your marriage. Be sure he knows that your goal is for both of you to be sexually satisfied.

Take a "time out" from sex. Paul said not to deny each other except for a time of prayer (1 Corinthians 7:5). The reason for a sexual hiatus isn't to avoid sex—it's to pray and to take active steps to bring about change. It's not to stop resentment from building, it's to bring healing so that resentment is no longer an issue. Talk about this with your husband. Tell him what you're doing and why. If he knows the goal isn't less sex, but more and better sex, he'll likely feel less threatened by a time out and be more willing to see a counselor together, read books together, or otherwise explore the problem. If he gets angry or refuses to respect your wishes, talk with a counselor in order to gain wisdom and support for what you can do.

Educate yourself. There's not enough room here to address the myriad of emotional and physical aspects of sexual dysfunction, and there are plenty of good books available. One or both of you may have grown up with ideas or teachings about sex that are inhibiting you now. Some good Christian books include:

- *Restoring the Pleasure* by Clifford L. Penner and Joyce J. Penner
- *Intimate Issues* by Linda Dillow and Lorraine Pintus
- *Intended for Pleasure* by Ed Wheat.

Check your history. Could it be that past sexual relationships are interfering in your present one? Were you involved in sexual activities earlier in life that left you feeling resentful and used? If you have a history of any kind of abuse, chances are great that you need healing from these hurtful experiences before you will begin to have a healthy attitude about lovemaking. Since this is a complex issue, you should seek help from a professional as soon as possible.

Rule out physical problems. Sometimes physical problems, such as hormone imbalances, inhibit a woman's desire for sex. If your troubles have more to do with a lack of physical responsiveness than with emotional resistance, see a physician who specializes in sexual dysfunction and explore possible causes and solutions. You should also visit your doctor if you don't experience orgasms, if you lack lubrication, if you find intercourse painful, or if you are on medications that might be interfering with your sexual drive.

Experiment with being the initiator. In most cases where a wife is reluctant to have sex, the husband is the designated initiator, which can lead to an unhelpful pattern in which the problem only gets worse. Authors Clifford and Joyce Penner point out:

> Because the wife does not show her interest in being together sexually, the husband begins to believe she has no interest in him sexually. His insecurity is triggered by her

apparent lack of interest, so he anxiously beings to initiate
sex more often than he would want it if he were feeling sure
of himself in relation to her. She feels pressured by his initia-
tion, so she begins to avoid him or pull away sexually. The
more he approaches, the more consistent is her avoidance.
The more frequent her avoidance, the more anxious is his
approach. It becomes a negative spiral.[1]

Talk with your husband about waiting for sex until you approach him. Many men, once assured that sex will take place,
aren't put off at all by waiting for the wives to signal their readi-
ness. If you are the initiator it may remove some of the feelings of
pressure and duty you experience. Instead, it becomes something
you are giving, versus something he is always approaching you to
take.

Spell it out for him! "If she [a wife] feels uncared for, she may believe the only interest her husband has in her is sex," write the
Penners. "He comes home from work, turns on the television, sits
quietly at dinner, and watches television after dinner. Then at bedtime he becomes friendly—and her anger sizzles."[2]

Sound familiar? Tell your husband exactly what it takes to please
you in bed and to make you feel happy to be invited there. You'd be
amazed how many men just don't realize that a wife needs to be
courted during the day, instead of only five minutes before lovemaking. And chances are, it probably doesn't take that much: a midday
phone call, kisses on the way out the door, a long hug when he gets
home. Be specific about what you'd enjoy and list for him several
small things he could do to help you be in the mood more often.

Consider sexual therapy. For some couples, the road to a healthy
sex life may require outside help. Often sexual therapy involves literally starting all over again with a clean slate. Couples typically
follow a program that begin with nonsexual touching; over the
course of weeks, homework assignments build back up to intercourse (*Restoring the Pleasure* contains a step-by-step program). If
your husband is unwilling to see a counselor with you, consider
seeking help alone. You'd be surprised how much progress you can
make this way. A therapist may not only be able to help you deal

with your own issues pertaining to sex, but may also help you find nonthreatening ways to talk about them with your husband.

Be honest about turnoffs. It's important to find a way to let your husband know what dampens your mood. For years, Catherine's husband Jason had no idea that his wife was repelled by the smell of a prescription lotion. When she finally mentioned it one night, he was hurt that she'd never been honest before. Now he never applies his bedtime dose of lotion until he's sure that they won't be making love.

If it's something he can change, let your husband know that while you accept and love him as he is, you'd think he were sexier if he could deal with this particular problem. If it's not something he can change, the problem then becomes yours. In truth, your sexual responsiveness to your husband, if all else is well, shouldn't be dampened by baldness, graying, or wrinkled skin. If they trouble you, you need to deal with your own thought patterns and values and try not to let them detract from lovemaking.

Making changes in your sex life won't necessarily come easily. Some changes might not come at all. However, never give up or relegate sex to the old days. A healthy sex life is foundational to every marriage. The Penners put it this way: "How important is sex in marriage? A simple answer is that when sex is compared to an automobile, sex is to the marriage what the oil is to the combustion engine. At least a little oil is necessary to keep the engine running—without sex, one's marriage will eventually break down."[3]

> *Dear Lord,*
> Thank You for the gift of sex! I want to become more and more grateful for this miracle of oneness You created. Help me, I pray, to do everything in my power to make my love life with the husband You gave me all that You would have it be. Restore our passion, revive our affections, and fill us with mercy and grace for one another. Amen.

Kendra's Story

Like most couples, Kendra and her husband Artie enjoyed lovemaking immensely during their early years of marriage. But after Kendra gave

birth to two boys two years apart, the frequency of their sexual relations
dramatically declined. Kendra didn't think Artie minded much. But could
it be that their flagging sex life was at the root of a host of other marital
troubles they were having?

When Artie and I were first married, we had a great sex life.
Then came two kids two years apart. After I had kids, it felt like
someone came along and just sucked any sexuality I had right out
of my body. To be honest, my "Not tonight, honey" turned into
"Not this week, honey." When things began to fall apart in other
areas of our marriage, I began to worry that if something didn't
change soon, I'd be saying to Artie, "Not in this lifetime, bucko!"

I had no idea marriage would be so hard and motherhood so
draining. The last thing I wanted at the end of the day was a man
making demands on my body. Whenever Artie approached me
with that look in his eye, I tried to act like I didn't notice. I made
sure our kisses were just smooches or pecks. I began to avoid wearing attractive nightgowns, thinking that this would help him not
think about having sex (I was still naive enough to imagine an hour
went by when a man didn't think of sex).

Our lack of lovemaking wasn't something we argued or even
talked about. Artie just backed off. When our marriage continued
to spiral, the last thing I would have traced our problems to was
our infrequent lovemaking. It seemed like our main problems had
to do with Artie and his immaturity. First he quit going to church,
and then he was beginning to hang out with his old crowd from
high school. He checked out as a dad, and it seemed like he wanted
to stay twenty forever.

Meanwhile, I began to feel more and more like a single mom.
My whole world revolved around doctor's appointments, pre-
school, grocery shopping, and housecleaning. And I completely
lost sight of why Artie and I were in all this together in the first
place: Oh yeah, we were supposedly so deeply in love that we
wanted to spend the rest of our lives together. What a joke!

Finally the fighting and arguing about his lack of help around
the house and his frequent nights out got so bad we decided to go

to counseling. It was either that or just give up. We'd even begun using the *D* word.

After several weeks of telling a Christian therapist everything we hated about each other and why we were so miserable, the counselor asked us about our sex life. Artie blushed and I played with my purse strap. "Uh . . . yeah . . . sex?" mumbled Artie. "Yeah, we have sex. Not enough, but once in a while."

That admission turned out to be the opening the therapist was looking for. He insisted that we got onto a regular program—a schedule!—of lovemaking. I was pretty certain I'd fallen victim to the whims of yet another dumb male. Couldn't this man see that we didn't need better sex, but a better marriage? But since this was the first thing the counselor suggested that Artie seemed to respond to (I should say, seized upon), I begrudgingly agreed to try it.

It was hard, uncomfortable. Just like I knew it would be. I think even Artie found it awkward that first week. Not knowing how to go about initiating something, he'd make a joke of it and say, "Hey, babe, tonight's the night. Doctor's orders."

At the next session I challenged our therapist. "Why should I make love when I'm not in the mood? Won't that just make me resent Artie more?"

He said, "As long as you see it as something you give to him to reward good behavior, yes, it will. Do you tell Artie what feels good and what doesn't? Do you both take it slow and try to pleasure each other? Lovemaking does not have to mean intercourse, by the way.

"And Artie," he continued, now directing his attention to my husband, "do you treat Kendra all day long in a way that leads naturally to lovemaking?"

Artie agreed he could try harder to show me affection during the day. I admitted I'd never really told him what I like in that department and promised to try.

So we kept at it. I prayed about it a lot, even if Artie didn't. Over the next few months, we began to make slow progress. Gradually, sex began to shift from something I saw as my duty to something I welcomed. I learned to resist the little lie that said, You're too tired tonight. You have a headache, remember? Instead, I reminded myself that once we got going, once I was aroused, it would be good. And afterward I'd sleep even better than if we hadn't made love.

One night Artie told me, "You seem like my lover again, not just a mom." And I realized it was true. Things had changed some. He'd been spending a lot more time with me and the kids and going out less.

With the rebirth of our sex life came a subtle rebirth in our marriage. All our problems didn't go away. But somehow, with that vital connection in place, we were reminded of the basics—that we are, first of all, lovers. And yes, we were in love. I've decided I'm in this marriage for the long haul. And I think Artie has too. Now I joke with him that if he does ever leave me, it had better not be for lack of sex!

Notes

1. Clifford L. Penner and Joyce J. Penner, *Restoring the Pleasure* (Nashville, TN: Word Publishing, 1993), 210.
2. Ibid., 216.
3. Ibid., 125.

Part Six
Keeping the Promise

*So guard yourself in your spirit,
and do not break faith with the
wife of your youth. (Malachi 2:15)*

*R*on Hostetler has spent most of his life dedicated to his mission of giving this generation, and the next, a hope and a future. As an author, educator and public speaker, he has inspired thousands of people to create a more powerful and purposeful future for themselves and their families by helping them recognize and use their God-given, innate abilities in their business, civic and personal lives. His message has universal appeal to all audiences because he speaks about things of the heart as well as the home.

Hostetler earned his bachelor's and master's degrees from Penn State Univeristy. He teaches at the Milton Hershey School, a private residential school for disadvantaged children in Hershey, Pennsylvania, and has coached at all interscholastic levels. He is a former congressional candidate for the US House of Representatives of Pennsylvania's 17th District, school board president, Penn State football team co-captain and preseason All-American linebacker. After the Los Angeles Rams drafted him for the NFL, he cut short his professional career due to a debilitating knee injury. He is the brother of former NFL quarterback and Super Bowl champion Jeff Hostetler and author of *What It Takes: More Than a Champion* (Multnomah Publishing, 1997) and *There IS No Joy In Gruntsville, But There's Plenty To Learn* (Executive Books, 1996). He has been a guest on local and national radio and television talk shows and has spoken throughout the United States and abroad to conventions, associations, nonprofit groups, businesses, churches and schools. He and his wife Holly have four children and live in Hershey, Pennsylvania.

Books

There Is No Joy in Gruntsville, But
    There's Plenty to Learn
What It Takes

Seminars

Message topics available upon request by calling 717.533.8349 or by e-mailing hossusa@msn.com

A No-Cut Contract

Ron Hostetler

Groping along in the dark, hand in hand, was exciting for me, puzzling for my girlfriend, Holly.

I had asked her to come with me on this excursion into the darkened unknown and was thrilled when she said yes. But sneaking into her own church late at night made her more than a little nervous.

But I had plans. Boy, did I have plans.

We entered through an unlocked side door and followed along the wall until we got to the front of the church. Once there, I took out some matches and lit a large church candle that was sitting on the communion table.

The Bible on the portable lectern, sitting adjacent to the candle, was opened to Proverbs 31 and I began reading it while Holly quietly but curiously listened. The passage described the characteristics of an excellent woman.

When I finished, I removed the lectern to reveal the purpose of my mission and the secret I had hidden underneath it. It was a bouquet of roses and a diamond ring. Both symbols of the love I had for her and the commitment I was about to make.

Kneeling down, I took her one hand in mine as I asked for the other in marriage. Her affirmation sealed our ceremony of betrothal, and a year later, before God and a host of witnesses, we made a marriage covenant—a solemn and binding promise to love and cherish each other until the day we died.

Giving her my heart was easy that night. Giving her my word as a guarantee was difficult. It is for all of us. Particularly because of the dark unknowns and uncertainties that lie ahead.

Sort of reminds me of Joe Paterno's proposal, the time he asked me to sign a letter of intent to play football for him at Penn State.

Saying yes and sealing my promise with a written contract was easy. Honoring it when I was a third-string linebacker groping along on the dark side of the maroon platoon practice squad was hard, particularly when I felt Paterno wasn't living up to his end of the agreement.

But I did. Things worked out. And the Lord honored me for it. Which brings us to the significance and benefits of honoring our covenant commitments.

You see, keeping one's word keeps faith fresh, hope hydrated, love lavish and trust taut. Breaking it causes faith to fracture, hope to hide, love to leave and trust to tatter. Just ask anyone who's been bitten by the teeth of broken promises and you'll see what I mean. It produces a hopeless, faithless, loveless and distrustful person. God knows this, and it's why He not only keeps His Word but He watches over it to perform it. We need to do the same. We need to watch our word(s) and keep our commitments. We need to say what we mean, mean what we say and deliver on it.

Professional basketball players have a slogan for this; it's called "delivering the mail." It's backing up words with action. It's coming through in the clutch when the chips are down and the game is on the line. And like a great follow-through on a jump shot, keeping your word scores points, wins games and benefits everyone involved.

This is why the Word of God became flesh. It was God's way of binding Himself to us and us to Him. His way of delivering the mail—pledging His Word, watching over His Word and following through on the covenant commitment He had made with us. And the great thing about His covenant is this—He's never broken it, never will.

Now, I don't intend to break my covenant commitment to Holly. Neither does she. We plan on fulfilling our word regardless of the future unknowns and groping along we might have to face. But over the years I have found that she needs to be reminded of my commitment to her. She needs to hear me say, "Holly, I will never leave you, nor send you away."

Speaking these words assures her heart.

Watching over these words affirms my declaration of troth.

Performing them backs up my commitment to her.

And when I look into her eyes when I speak, I can't hide anything. She knows if I mean what I say.

Our kids too. They know whether or not I'm living up to my promises. Especially my promise to love their mother. Can't fool them. Sometimes I think kids are God's secret messengers sent to hold me accountable by reminding me of my words. They always seem to be saying, "But Dad, you said. . . . You promised!" Guess it is also why someone once said, "The best gift a father can give his children is to love their mother."

"He remembers his covenant forever, the word he commanded, for a thousand generations, the covenant he made with Abraham, the oath he swore to Isaac" (1 Chronicles 16:15-16).

Highlights

A No-Cut Contract highlights three essentials to building strong, healthy relationships:
1. Giving your word
2. Watching over your word
3. Keeping your word

Extra Innings

Read First Chronicles 16:15-16 as it relates to *A No-Cut Contract*, making personal application.

The validity of the Christian faith rests solely on the infallible, inerrant, unchangeable Word of God. Why is this so?

How is marriage validated?

How is honor in a family relationship validated?

Go back in time for a moment and recall your wedding vows. Perhaps it's a good time to pull them out of the old family album and say them again while you look into your partner's eyes. Go ahead, we dare you! Then do the same with your kids; tell them you will never leave them or forsake them while you look into their eyes. Record your thoughts and feelings afterwards in your daily journal. And if you haven't been keeping a daily journal, start one today.

*L*aBreeska Rogers Hemphill has spent her life ministering to others through gospel music. In the early 1950s, she traveled as a member of The Happy Goodman Family and later for twenty-five years with her immediate family, The Hemphills. The Hemphill Family—LaBreeska, Joel and their three children, Joel, Jr., Trent and Candy—has received a total of seven Dove awards from the Gospel Music Association. They live in Nashville.

Books
The Hemphills: Partners in Emotion

Songbooks
Candy Christmas "Favorites"
Songs of Restoration and Revival

Video
Restoration

Recordings
20 Favorites by the Hemphills
Accepted
A Family Tradition
Good Days, Bad Days, and
  Restoration (audio cassette)
Walking in the Light

Web
www.thehemphills.com

Committed Through the Hard Times

LaBreeska Hemphill

Editor's Note: When we marry, we vow before God to have and to hold . . . in sickness and in health. But if a debilitating illness were to grip our partner, would our promise truly stand? LaBreeska Hemphill faced that trial of commitment without hesitation—though the struggle was immensely painful.

Refreshed and ready to assume my responsibility, I gathered Joel's belongings and took him home from the hospital. The first thing I did was draw him a hot bath and see that he styled his hair, shaved and put on the new clothes that I had bought for him. Then we went to a restaurant for a hot meal. It was good to have him back, but what I didn't know that day was that when he walked out of the hospital, full-scale clinical depression came with him.

Heavy medication was the only answer. Antidepressants and potent sleep medicine kept Joel sedated enough to live through it. His waking hours were spent engulfed in fear. He told me later that suicide rode his every thought. His emotions constantly ached like a bad toothache that never let up, and his only relief came when he was asleep. Every so often he would say to me, "Honey, if the Lord doesn't intervene, this is not going to have a happy ending."

> My soul chooseth strangling, and death rather than my life. I loathe it. (Job 7:15-16, KJV)

I didn't know what he was talking about. When I saw Joel, I didn't just see what he had become—I saw all that he ever was, and suicide had never been a remote possibility with him. When he was well he was very outspoken on that subject and couldn't fathom someone doing such a foolish thing. He had stated that before he would consider suicide as a way out, he'd just change his identity and get lost in California or some other remote area and start a new life.

He had never known that emotional pain could be so severe that there is no escape, no matter where you go, and that dying could seem easier than living. But with emotional problems, you can't die, and your living is joyless, so you just exist and suffer it out.

Here is where many, seeking relief, take matters into their own hands and tragically end their lives. Joel knew, even in his pain and confusion, that death was not the answer; but the only thing that kept him from it was his strong Christian foundation and his knowledge of the Word of God. The Enemy, whom the Bible describes as "the thief [who] comes only to steal and kill and destroy" (John 10:10) would then have done what he had set out to do.

When I say that Joel was in depression, I am saying that he faced every day with a feeling of foreboding and dread from the very moment he awoke. He was too paralyzed emotionally to do anything constructive. All he did from the time he shaved, showered and dressed, which took the greatest of effort on his part, was to come downstairs and collapse on the couch in the den.

I stood by helplessly and watched my strong, optimistic, hardworking husband regress and become fearful and withdrawn. He was like a little boy cowering with his arms up to shield himself from the next blow. He turned to me for comfort. I couldn't be out of his sight. Many days I'd sit and hold his head in my lap and talk soothingly to him as tears ran down his cheeks and remind him how much he was loved by all of us and especially the Lord.

None of it would sink in. Every positive word spoken to Joel at this time was like a candle in the wind: It didn't stand a chance. Even Joel's knowledge of the Bible became distorted and turned to accuse and condemn him. The Bible has been our guideline for living since we were both children. Both of us believe it to be the infallible Word of God. We have used it to measure ourselves by and to direct our actions and our goals. We believe the Bible holds the key to successful living. So naturally Joel began weighing his present situation by his knowledge of the Scriptures, and none of it made sense. He felt as if he must have done something terribly wrong to bring on all this suffering, but he couldn't figure out what it was.

Joel has been an avid reader and has always had a thirst for information. I have laughingly teased him through the years by accusing him of eating newspapers—several a day along with newsmagazines—yet that was never enough. The evening news on television or radio was always a must for him. Then suddenly all of that stopped.

He became overwhelmed by current events and could no longer handle the news, which seemed to be filled with plane crashes, tragedy and human suffering. Not only was he suffering, but the whole world was hurting, and all he had was questions. What had he done? Where had he gone wrong? The conclusion that had lodged in the depths of his soul was that he had miserably failed the Lord and blown his ministerial calling. This was something he could not live with. It had become a fixation in his mind that overshadowed everything else around him. He thought he was eternally lost, without hope, and all he could do was to lie on the couch in the den, stare at the ceiling, cry and break out in a cold sweat.

Where are You, Lord? was the silent cry of my heart. *Can anything good come from all this insanity?*

While reading the little books of Bible promises, Joel found what he thought to be the ticket out of the living hell that he was mired in. He clung to this verse tenaciously: "He that cometh to God must believe that he is, and that he is a rewarder of them that diligently seek him" (Hebrews 11:6, KJV).

Joel had found the solution, and it was simple.

Did he believe in God? Of course he did. Then he must also believe that God would reward our diligent effort to find Him in the midst of all our pain and confusion. This spark of hope found lodging in the depths of Joel's spirit and began to flame up into faith.

The hardest part for me was not knowing how much longer it would last and how much further I could carry on. At what point would I snap under the stress? I had no doubt that Joel was going to come out of this storm a stronger man. The spiritual encounter we had experienced in 1986 left me knowing that the Lord had a plan for his life. Until now I'd felt that I was included in that plan, but I was ready to confess that I was at the end of my endurance and facing the possibility that I might not make it. There was nothing left inside me to draw from.

Little did I know that this was the place where the Lord wanted me—depending not on my power nor might, but on His Spirit. "Fear thou not; for I am with thee: be not dismayed; for I am thy God: I will strengthen thee; yea, I will help thee; yea, I will uphold thee with the right hand of my righteousness" (Isaiah 41:10, KJV).

"But *when*, Lord?"

The ground beneath my feet continued to feel like shifting sand, but with prayer and praise I held on to the Lord, and He was my solid rock. "I will love thee, O LORD, my strength. The LORD is my rock, and my fortress, and my deliverer; my God, my strength, in whom I will trust" (Psalm 18:1-2, KJV).

I was learning that His grace is sufficient, and that He was all I needed.

> Hast thou not known? hast thou not heard, that the everlasting God, the LORD, the Creator of the ends of the earth, fainteth not, neither is weary? there is no searching of his understanding. He giveth power to the faint; and to them that have no might he increaseth strength. (Isaiah 40:28-29, KJV)

Then came November 8, 1992. When we walked into church that Sunday morning, the congregation was singing, and as always it soothed my aching soul. The warm feeling of being surrounded by our church family as they sang and worshiped was a comfort to both of us.

The tears flowed in abundance. I couldn't help it. I cried all the way through praise and worship. It had become the norm for me, along with the feeling that I would never smile again. I also knew that before the service was over Joel would embarrass me, as he had so many times, by going down front to petition Pastor Nolan and the elders of the church to pray for him.

We were like spiritual sponges trying to soak up every prayer we could get. This was not an easy place for me to be, as we had always been the ones doing the ministering, and now we were on the receiving end. This particular Sunday seemed no different than the rest, but what I didn't know was that our Heavenly Father had said, "Enough."

Joel did walk down front for prayer, but it was at the request of Pastor Nolan. As the worship service was coming to a close, Brother Nolan stepped to the podium and halted the music. Then he looked directly at us and motioned Joel forward. He said, "Brother Hemphill, would you please come and let us pray for you? The Lord just spoke to me that He's going to heal you today."

With that invitation, Joel left his seat and walked down the aisle for prayer. Brother Nolan and the elders gathered around and prayed for Joel, and he was *instantly healed.* That was the last day of depression he ever had! The fear, the dread, the gnawing ache inside him were all lifted away during prayer that morning, never to return again.

When Joel told me the next morning that it was gone, I wanted to believe him, but my faith had been exhausted, and I couldn't grasp what had happened. It was practically impossible for me, after all the muck and mire that we had been bogged in for so long, to clap my hands in joy and say, "Yes, I believe you are healed!" At one time I had been that kind of person, so trusting, so believing, so innocently naive. But now I had come to view life with skepticism. This had caused me to accept Joel's healing experience with much more caution. I wasn't going to let myself in for more disappointment. Time would tell if he was really healed—and it did.

The healing was instant, but the restoration was gradual. I made a short entry in my diary just a week later, stating, "Joel is laughing, telling funny stories and doing great."

When we went back to see his doctor for his regular two-week appointment, he was amazed. Dr. Fishbein asked, "What happened to you?"

Joel replied, "I was prayed for at church and the Lord healed me."

The doctor wrote in his journal: "Prayers lifted his depression." He moved Joel's next visit to six weeks, and on that occasion, January 20, 1993, the physician discontinued Joel's medications. At the next appointment Dr. Fishbein was again amazed at the changes in Joel. "Man, you're doing great! You look athletic and tanned!" When we started to leave he added, "No need to come back. Just call me if you ever need me."

Joel has not been back since. He walked out of the doctor's office a new man. From that day forward I was convinced of Joel's complete healing and never again feared his depression would return.

From The Hemphills: Partners in Emotion, *Copyright © 2001 by LaBreeska Hemphill. Used by permission of Horizon Books.*

*M*arJean Miller is from Fond du Lac, Wisconsin, where she lived until she finished school at City College in Appleton, Wisconsin. She worked at a radio station as a commercial writer and as an on-air personality. Her diverse career path also led her to a secretarial position at a nuclear power generation facility and the position of assistant manager at a hotel. It was during this time in her life that she married and had two boys.

In 1975 Miller and her family moved to the Pittsburgh, Pennsylvania, home of her husband Gary, where she furthered her interest in advertising by attending broadcasting classes. In 1978 she and Gary surrendered their hearts and lives to the Lord and quickly became immersed in ministry. She and Gary began singing together as well as with an ensemble group called The Faith Singers, and they traveled around the Pittsburgh area spreading the good news of Jesus Christ through song and testimony.

In 1993 the Millers started a gospel trio called Promise. Then, in 2001 they went back to being a duet. They are presently working on their ninth recording project. Promise is part of the Marriage Enthusiasm Renewal Team.

Over the past decade, Miller has used her love for teaching and her knowledge of music to teach voice lessons to a variety of students. She has a studio in her home where she sees her students during the week. She also writes a monthly column for the *Southern Gospel Music Forum*, an on-line magazine. On weekends she is out singing with Promise. It is her prayer that whatever she does brings honor to the Lord and Savior whom she loves so very much.

Recordings
It's Called Love
Keeping Promises
Led by His Hand
Right Place and Right Time (also video)
Safe in His Arms
Shine Through Me
Sold Out for Christ
Something Special
Yesterday and Today

Web
www.southerngospelpa.com/promise/

God's Amazing Answer

MarJean Miller

When I was a little girl growing up in a Christian family, my parents taught me to pray. We had family devotions, prayer at mealtime and bedtime prayers. My mother always told me to ask God for something special, so that when the answer came, I'd know that God had answered my prayer. So, as an obedient child, I said all my prayers. Usually my prayers ended with something like, "Take care of my dog," or "Help me to be a good girl." But one night during my "now-I-lay-me-down-to-sleep" prayer, I asked God for something very special.

As I grew up and became a teenager and young adult, I rebelled against God, religion and my parents' lifestyle. I certainly didn't care about praying or answers to prayer. My life got all messed up, and I made some huge mistakes. To me, God was only a 911 call.

It wasn't until I was thirty years old that I finally recognized my sinfulness and rebellion. I realized that I needed to have a personal relationship with Jesus, and I finally gave my heart to Christ. Through a long series of events, my husband Gary also gave his heart and life to Jesus. Together, as young Christians, we took our first step in serving our Lord—we joined the choir in the church we began attending.

On the day we sang our first song, I suddenly remembered the prayer that I had prayed as a child so many years earlier. It was as though I had *just* prayed it. After the "now I lay me down to sleep," I had added a special request. I had prayed, "Please let me marry a nice boy, and let me sing with him in church"!

Can you believe it? God heard my prayer and answered it some twenty-six years later. He knew that I wasn't ready to receive the answer when I prayed to Him, so He held it in His hand until I was. And then, in His amazing grace, He opened His hand and gave me the desire of my heart. He truly gave me a "nice boy," but I didn't yet understand what else God had in mind. All I knew was that I had a desire to do more for Christ.

Gary also felt an incredible desire to do more than just be a church member and a choir member, but we had to mature as Christians first. We had a lot to learn, and we praise God for all the lessons learned—and the lessons we are still learning. We began singing more often, in smaller church groups and as a duet wherever we could.

Out of this desire that was planted in our hearts so many years earlier, the ministry of Promise was born. Through our experiences, we can testify of the love and faithfulness of the Lord in our lives. Our ministry is that of encouragement and hope.

Marriage and ministry are both commitments. In today's society, *commitment* seems to be an old-fashioned word. We commit only if it's convenient, only if it fits into our schedules or until we are bored with it. I believe that Satan began attacking commitment as far back as the Garden of Eden and he hasn't stopped yet. We are sending a wrong message to our young people. They watch Christian couples getting divorced at an alarming rate, preachers quitting, ministries falling apart—all because we are enticed by Satan's deceptions: "Check it out! The grass might be greener someplace else." But God honors faithfulness and He blesses commitment.

Our marriage got off to a very rocky start. We had six strikes against us before we ever got together. You see, this was a second marriage for both of us, and between us we had six small children who just couldn't understand why their world was falling apart. Besides that, neither Gary nor I knew the Lord in a personal way. There are two specific things that I can credit for the "success" of our marriage. Without these two components, our marriage would have gone the way of most second marriages. The first was *God*— He had a plan for us, and from the very beginning His hand was on us, but we only know that now, through hindsight. And the second was *Gary*. It was because of the kind of person he is, along with his love and wisdom, that we have made it this far. He has taught me so much about myself and makes me feel safe and loved.

Looking back on our relationship, I can see that God was working from the onset and against all odds. We became best friends first, because for the first year after we met, we were living over 600 miles apart and never saw each other. We have boxes of letters and cards that we wrote to each other in that year. I could write a book about the way we met and the years before we got married.

I have learned that communication is a key to any successful union. Even learning how to disagree is essential to a marriage. Two people will never agree on everything. When there are two opposing opinions, it is essential to know how to talk it through. Making accusations, bringing up past mistakes, yelling and name-calling will never produce positive results. I like to be right all the time, and Gary believes in "peace at any price." So that's why we get along so well. I'm always right . . . and he's peaceful with that. Just kidding!

Which brings up another very important point. A sense of humor is essential to a lasting relationship. The ability to laugh at yourself and the ability to laugh your way through trying circumstances are invaluable to a healthy marriage. Just don't laugh *at* each other.

A bad memory is also a plus. I don't accumulate problems in my head, simply because I can't remember them. I choose to forget the times when I think Gary has not done what he "should" have done or said what I thought was the right thing. In other words, don't bring up the past during an argument. (Of course, Christians never argue—they just have intense fellowship!)

And finally, we're back to where we started—commitment. Gary and I entered this marriage with the attitude that we both made one mistake already and we didn't want to have a repeat. Our mindset from the beginning was that this was going to work—period! And it has. Our marriage of twenty-four years is stronger now than ever. We have a common goal—to be committed and faithful to each other and to God, and to spread the message of His love wherever we go. Only eternity will tell just how the Lord is using our lives and the ministry that He has entrusted to us. We are certainly not perfect, nor do we have all the answers. We pray constantly.

If you have ever doubted God's ability to answer prayer, just remember that His timetable is not ours. He will answer your prayer—in His time. Just be faithful to Him, continue to pray and He will direct your path—even if it takes twenty-six years! God is faithful and He desires to have a relationship with you. It gives Him pleasure when you honor Him through your marriage.

*D*rs. Les and Leslie Parrott are founders and codirectors of the Center for Relationship Development on the campus of Seattle Pacific University. They have recently served as "marriage ambassadors" for the governor of Oklahoma's statewide marriage initiative. The Parrotts are award-winning authors of more than a dozen best-selling books. Their work with couples has been featured in such periodicals as *Family Circle, Redbook, Focus on the Family, USA Today* and the *New York Times*. They have appeared on a variety of television programs including CNN, *CBS This Morning,* Barbara Walters' *The View, NBC Nightly News with Tom Brokaw* and *The Oprah Winfrey Show.*

Books

7 Secrets of a Healthy Dating Relationship (also leader's guide and video kit)
Becoming Soul Mates (also video and seminar)
The Control Freak (also audio)
Escaping the Guilt Trap
Getting Ready for the Wedding
High-Maintenance Relationships
Joy Breaks for Couples
Love Is
The Love List
The Marriage Devotional Bible
Once Upon a Family
Proverbs for Couples
Questions Couples Ask
Relationships (also groupware, guide and workbook)

Relationships 101
Saving Your Marriage Before It Starts (also curriculum, workbook and audio)
Saving Your Second Marriage Before It Starts (also workbook and audio)
The Smart Start Church Resource Marriage Kit
When Bad Things Happen to Good Marriages (also workbook and audio)

Video

Mentoring Engaged and Newlywed Couples

Web

www.RealRelationships.com

Developing the Habit of Happiness

21

Les and Leslie Parrott

Happy couples *decide* to be happy. It is *your* attitude that will determine whether you and your partner "live happily ever after." How do we cultivate positive attitudes when our spouses do something we dislike? The answer lies in *taking responsibility for our own feelings*. Everyone is responsible for his or her own attitude.

Learning how to rise above difficult circumstances may be the greatest gift you can give your spouse. Too many marriages have unknowingly missed out on happiness because of self-pity. A great deal of unhappiness in marriage can be traced to a mate's habitual tendency to blame his or her spouse. Resentment is like a cancer to relationships, at first small and imperceptible, but over time growing larger and spreading its poison through the entire relationship.

At some point every husband and wife realizes that theirs is not a perfect match. Marriages can never be perfect because people are not perfect. Living happily ever after only works when you *make* it work. When you take the raw materials of marriage—the good and the bad that you've brought together as persons—to design, create, and build a lasting bond, the result is an enduring and meaningful sense of genuine fulfillment. If, on the other hand, you are counting on the magic of marriage to make you happy, the relationship will leave you crushed, lonely, feeling like a failure, and resigned to your despair.

The habit of happiness is an inside job. If you find the right attitude in spite of atmospheric conditions, if you program your mind with positive impulses, and if you adjust to things beyond your control, you will discover that living happily ever after need not be a myth.

For Reflection

- In recent years, more and more people have come to view happiness as the major purpose of marriage. What do you think?

- Part of your vows say something like: "to love and cherish your partner in sickness and in health." How can a person cultivate the habit of happiness even when things are not going well?

- Can you think of some examples from your own life where you rose above your difficult circumstances and *chose* to be happy? What keeps you from doing this sometimes?

- In one survey after another, researchers have found that people who rate their marriage as "very happy" also rate life as a whole as "very happy." In your mind, what does this have to say about cultivating the habit of happiness?

- While the culture into which we are born and our family background significantly influence our attitudes, each of us is ultimately responsible for how we choose to cope with life. On a scale of one to ten, how strongly do you agree with that statement?

Part Seven
Character Counts

Keep a firm grasp on both your
character and your teaching.
Don't be diverted. Just keep at it.
(1 Timothy 4:16, The Message)

*W*hile Dr. Chuck Borsellino has accomplished much throughout his professional career, his most prized accomplishment to date is that of becoming husband and father. Traveling extensively throughout the United States and Canada, he has spoken to more than 1 million people in seminars and workshops and is currently host and executive producer of the nationally syndicated daily television program *At Home Live with Chuck and Jenni*, which is aired to more than 35 million households on the FamilyNet Network. It was honored in 2001 as a finalist for the "Program of the Year" at the National Religious Broadcasters Convention, which oversees 1,750 Christian programs. In 2002 the program received a Telly Award for Outstanding Program.

Borsellino earned a Ph.D. from the University of North Texas and a Psy.D. from Forest Institute of Professional Psychology. In addition to being a licensed psychologist, he is an ordained minister with the Assemblies of God and serves as founder and president of OpenHouse Family Ministries. His wife Jenni earned a master's degree in communication from Southwest Missouri State University and cohosts the live daily program with Chuck.

Previously, Dr. Borsellino served as vice president of ministry with Crossroads Christian Communications, Inc., and while there he was also clinical director of the Family Center, a Christian mental health clinic staged by physicians, psychologists and marriage and family therapists.

Though born and raised in Hamilton, Ontario, he spent the majority of his adult life in the United States. He returned to Canada in 1993 to work at Crossroads and relocated to the Dallas/Fort Worth area in 2000, where he currently resides with Jenni and their three children, Brittany (sixteen), Cody (twelve) and Courtney (eleven). Chuck and Jenni have been married for twenty-five years.

Books
How to Raise Totally Awesome Kids

Web
www.athomelive.com

Media
At Home Live (11 a.m. ET on FamilyNet)

When Little White Lies . . . Begin to Color Your Character

Chuck and Jenni Borsellino

Let's Talk with Jenni

Well, it's time you knew the truth about me: I was a perfect child. I made my bed, I put away my clothes, and I even turned out the lights when I left a room.

I followed the rules.

I obeyed my parents.

I went to Sunday school.

I did the right thing.

In fact, I felt it was my responsibility to promote Truth, Justice and the American Way. I was the hall monitor, the teacher's pet, the class tattletale and a card-carrying member of the Polite Police. (And I had no idea why I always ate lunch by myself in the cafeteria!) While everyone else was at recess, I was doing extra-credit work, cleaning the chalkboard or conducting a survey.

In college, my roommates attended parties; I attended prayer meetings. The other kids challenged the dean of students, the campus police and the college president; I was a Republican. My classmates followed the theories of Plato, Freud, Marx and Darwin; I followed the theology of Jesus. I was a certifiable Jesus Freak and had a leather-bound, red-letter edition of the King James Bible to prove it! Sure of my convictions, steadfast in my faith and unwavering in my values, I could have been a poster child for the Moral Majority. Back then I had only two shoes in my closet—and both were named "Goody."

Well, guess what? This perfect little child grew up to become a perfect little adult. Isn't that amazing? I know that Chuck is amazed every time I remind him of it!

So when it came time for me to progress from marriage to motherhood, I was enthusiastic about passing on my "perfection" to my children. It was the least I could do. That way they could carry on this heritage of perfection from generation to generation—as long as Chuck's genes didn't get in the way! I thought to myself, *How fortunate these children are to have* me, *the model of perfection, as their mother!*

Then reality set in.

It's true when they say, "Out of the mouths of babes. . . ." In my case, it couldn't have been more accurate. In fact, it took the voice of my child (actually, I think it was Chuck's child) to set me straight and show me how high (or how low) my standards of integrity really were:

"Mommy, why did you tell that person on the phone that you were busy when you were just watching TV?"

Well, honey . . .

"Mommy, why didn't you tell Daddy about your new red shoes when he asked if you bought anything at the mall today?"

Sometimes it's okay if . . .

"Mommy, why do we have so many pens and pencils here from your office?"

You don't always . . .

"Mommy, why do we only buckle our seat belts when you see a police car?"

Oh, never mind . . . it's time for you to go outside and play!

Then I have to ask myself why it's not unusual to hear about people who . . .

- return clothing for a refund after it's been worn.
- switch a size-eight suit top to go with a size-ten suit bottom in the dressing room.
- tell the beggar on the street that they have no money when their wallet is full.
- fail to return the five-dollar bill when the cashier gives them too much change.
- "forget" to report that extra income each year on April 15.

White Lies Become Willful Compromise

Somewhere along the way, we let our guard down. A door that was once shut, locked and bolted is now cracked open ever so slightly. The deceiver has his toe in the door of our integrity, and he's whispering to us:

- Everybody's doing it . . .
- It's no big deal . . .
- Just this once . . .
- They'll never notice . . .
- What's the harm . . .
- God understands . . .

Excuses. Compromises. Explanations.

Soon we become Plan B people living Plan B parenting before our children. It goes like this: "Don't have sex before marriage! *But if you do,* use a condom." "Don't drink alcohol. *But if you do,* make sure you don't drink and drive." You get the idea.

Can we really promote integrity in the lives of our kids when we encourage them to have Plan B in their back pockets? Mixed messages lead our kids to one conclusion: If our parents aren't committed to Plan A, why should we be?

You know, I've learned a lot since my hall monitor days:

- I've learned that being the right kind of person makes it easier to do the right kinds of things. That's why God always builds people from the inside out.
- I've learned that there's always a good reason to cut corners, but there are a lot of better reasons not to.
- And I've learned that *small compromises* produce *large consequences.*
- I've also learned that if the devil can't make you bad, he'll make you busy. Because when you're busy, doing what's "easy" always comes before doing what's right.

Oh yeah, as I've grown older, I've also grown wiser. I've discovered that creative minds are rarely tidy. That fact alone gives me a lot of free time!

Let's Talk with Chuck

Integrity is doing the right thing, regardless of the circumstances, in spite of the costs, whatever the consequences.

Most of us view integrity as an all-or-nothing quality. Clergy have it; criminals don't. Actually, both are capable of telling little white lies. Most of us see integrity as a quality that is developed in ten-pound increments. Actually, integrity is developed one ounce at a time: at the grocery sore, in the dressing room, on the phone—when nobody's looking. Most of us believe that unprincipled people lose their integrity by the mile rather than by the foot—over big-ticket items and million-dollar deals. Actually, integrity is lost at the same rate it is gained—one ounce at a time. But Jenni's right. When you add yesterday's compromises to today's, collectively they can sink a ship . . . in no time.

Shipwrecked

Claims were made.
Deadlines were established.
Guarantees were given.

But they failed to account for one small problem—the ice.

Nothing but frozen water, but it brought her to her knees . . . and left her to lie at the bottom of the frigid North Atlantic, 12,468 feet below sea level. It also sent countless passengers into a nautical nightmare and over 1,500 souls to a premature maritime grave.

Go beyond the movie, the diamond pendant and the love story between Jack and Rose. Go to the real lesson to be learned aboard this luxury liner. If we miss this point, we're likely to sink our parental prospects as well.

Look carefully, 41 degrees north and 50 degrees west. Make your way beyond the two and a half miles of frigid blue saltwater. Buried beneath the mud, hidden by coral and guarded by marine life, lies the most immense ship that had ever been built. The year was 1912. It took 15,000 yard workers 7 million man-hours to construct this opulent symbol of power and prestige.

She was unsinkable. She was majestic. She was the RMS Titanic.

For years, the most widely held theory about the *Titanic's* sinking was that she hit an iceberg so immense that it cut a massive gash deep below the waterline on the port side of this proud, 882-foot ocean liner. However, an international team of divers and scientists came to a different conclusion. The truth was exposed by sound waves used to probe the wreckage and was later visually confirmed through the eyes of a submarine named *Alvin* and her remote camera. Rather than a huge gash, the gateway for destruction was actually more like a calculated incision made by a seasoned cardiologist.

Their discovery? The damage was small, but the outcome was severe. Instead of the large gash they had expected, the divers found six narrow slits that cut across several watertight compartments. Together, these slits accounted for only twelve square feet of disfigured iron.

Relatively speaking, the damage was nominal when compared to the number of square miles of steel that made up the ship. But collectively, those small blemishes sank the largest moveable object on the seas at that time.

As a result,

- a widow grieved the loss of her husband.
- a child grieved the loss of his father.
- a family grieved the loss of their lineage.

How could damage so minute create consequences so far-reaching?

Just ask David.

Following his incredible defeat of Goliath, David appeared to be unsinkable. In his day, he was the symbol of power and prestige. But there was a problem below the waterline. Although David was skillful enough to slaughter a giant on a hillside, he was powerless to resist a woman by the poolside (see 2 Samuel 11).

It began with an innocent stroll late one night when David couldn't sleep. His troops were on the battlefield, and his eyes were on a potential minefield. During his walk, David discovered a woman named Bathsheba on a rooftop, taking a bath. His discovery led to a decision. His glance became a goal. He made choices.

Invisible to most, these choices clouded his conscience and scarred his character. Soon lust became adultery, adultery became murder . . . and his relationship with God went from sacred to scarred.

So many times before, David had taken the high road. But not this time. He quickly progressed from looking to lusting, from fantasy to fulfillment. Satan had his foot in the door. One small slit was found in the armor of David's character, and like the *Titanic*, he began to take on water.

You know what I'm talking about. Maybe you've been there yourself.

Rules of Engagement

A coworker catches your eye. He tells you that you look good in blue. He notices your perfume. He listens when you speak. He remembers your birthday. You find a reason to talk together and then work together. You bring him home with you—first in your mind and then in your heart. No one seems to notice, but the *Titanic* is in trouble. You send out an SOS to your husband. But he's twenty miles away . . . on a golf course.

There's no response.

According to some researchers, as many as twenty-five percent of women and thirty-three percent of men will be unfaithful during the course of their marriage—and will admit to it.[1] First we rationalize; then we justify. Instead of raising our integrity, we find it more convenient to lower our standards. Our guard falls and so does our faith. Satan is in the process of sinking another marriage. Unfortunately, when a marriage sinks, the kids go down with the ship.

But it's never too late to do the right thing. It's never too late to turn things around.

While his ship was on its way down, David looked up. He concluded that no one is too wrong to do right. No one is too bad to do good. No one is too lost to find grace. David confronted his behavior. He confessed his sin and experienced God's grace. He found an oasis in the desert.

With God . . .
  every thoughtless mistake
  every loveless marriage
  every rebellious child
  every hurting heart
  and every sinking ship
  has a lifeboat.

Integrity begins with truth in our hearts and ends with action in our homes. It will keep a train on its tracks. It provides a moral compass to help parents and kids navigate the "relative" world we live in. Integrity will cost us a lot to live by, but will cost us even more to live without. It's hard to define, but easy to spot. It is applicable at home, at school and at the office. Integrity—or the lack thereof—can define you or destroy you. It's an issue of will, not wisdom. It's developed, not demanded. A lack of integrity can turn the unacceptable into the tolerable, the prohibited into the permissible.

Integrity is the backbone of character, and that's why we need to teach our kids.

It's Never Right to Do Wrong.

Throw Me a Lifesaver

Some people mistake reputation for integrity. But they're cousins, not twins. Reputation is external and is based on what people think of us. Integrity, on the other hand, is internal and is based on who we are when nobody's looking.

Reputation can vary by person, place, time and situation. For example, your spouse sees you as a loving provider, while at the same time your manager sees you as a ruthless salesman. Both may be true; both may be rewarded. But integrity is internal. It's a moral compass that cuts across circumstances, costs and consequences. It describes what we do, not what we claim to be.

But some people say they have a defense, grounds for dismissal. Some of those defenses are better than others.

During twenty years of private practice as a psychologist, I've heard it all. From the mouth of an inmate I heard, "It was the drugs. You should be locking up the drug dealers who sold them to me!" From an incorrigible adolescent I heard, "If my father had been home more often I wouldn't have stolen all of his stuff." From the lips of a promiscuous woman I heard, "If someone would have loved me when I was growing up, I wouldn't have looked for it in the arms of a paying client."

We intellectualize, rationalize and spiritualize. And when that doesn't work, we simply justify. I've sat with many a wayward husband and heard many a weary defense explaining an affair and the beliefs behind the behavior. It typically begins with "I didn't really love her when we got married." It doesn't take long until those words are followed by:

- "This will be better for the kids, you know."
- "This will give us both a chance to be happy."
- "I've prayed about it and God understands."

The slippery slope . . . at its worst.

I heard these very words from a successful pastor whose future was earmarked by the denomination as having "headquarters" potential. I've had a lot of difficult days while in clinical practice, but none more painful than the afternoon when this pastor told his wife and three children about his decision to leave them and the church . . . for another lover. His wife was crushed; his children were crippled. They sat motionless, tears filling their eyes and fears filling their hearts. Their father's faith—the faith he preached about every Sunday morning, the faith they cut their spiritual teeth on—was now about as appetizing as a bowl of artificial fruit.

Integrity.

> *A pastor assigned to teach it*
> *was a person unable to live it.*

While parents do their best to hold the moral banner high, others—from the pastorate to the presidency—have let their children down. Time and time again.

Modern-Day Mishaps

As far as presidents go, most have concluded that William Jefferson Clinton was one of the most gifted of all time. Many credit him with being a consummate communicator. Indeed, he was a master at connecting with the American public. But though he did much for our country's economy, he did little for our country's integrity. In fact, he lowered the bar to a new low in 1999.

Ability is a blessing; character is a choice.

In Clinton's case, "truth" was determined by definition. Lawyers dueled, journalists investigated and spin doctors spun their "strategic misinformation." Leno and Letterman had him for lunch, and the country grew weary. As the truth unfolded, Republicans called his behavior "perjury" while Democrats labeled it "trivial." And as the debate raged on, few noticed a wife and daughter sitting on the emotional sidelines, with hearts in hand and home hanging in the balance. With two years left in office, this ship took on water and barely made it back to port. At the same time, our kids watched and took notes. And many of them concluded that right and wrong are no longer absolutes.

But Clinton wasn't the first. . . .

More than twenty-five hundred years ago, this falsehood was designed to save a man's life—not just politically but literally. Once again, it all came down to "the definition": six inches of truth and a half-foot of lie, not once but twice. Fearful for his life, he told the pharaoh that his wife was his sister. Her name is Sarai; his is Abraham. While his faith became famous (see Hebrews 11:8-19), his character became flawed (see Genesis 12 and 20).

In our world today, headlines give gruesome details and tragic stories of broken promises, broken dreams and broken hearts. Families are constantly bombarded with reports ranging from corporate capitalists who trade inside information to misguided ministers who fumble their affections.

First we ask ourselves, "Who's next?" Then we say, "If they couldn't keep their behavior on the moral plumb line, then how can I?" Finally we conclude, "If everybody's doing it, why can't I?"

This lack of integrity has shipwrecked many sailors. And now, as our kids drift on the sea, we faintly hear their cries: "Would somebody please throw me a lifesaver?"

Jenni's Tips from the Trenches . . . to Turn Things Around

1. Examine your beliefs. They determine your behavior.

Behavior follows beliefs. Period. The majority of the time parents focus on a child's misguided behavior, but we need to back up the boat and examine the underlying *beliefs* that form the birthplace for that behavior. They sound like this:

- "I can't help it. It's just the way I was brought up."
- "Nobody reports all their income."
- "The company won't miss a few tools from the shop."
- "If I don't lie for the boss, he'll fire me."
- "If the customer doesn't ask, it's not my job to tell him."
- "What's the problem? Everybody pads their expense report."
- "If the cashier gives me too much change, I see it as a gift from God."

We place compromise above conviction when we believe that the end justifies the means. Character takes a backseat to convenience and integrity suffers another slash below the waterline, where most people believe it will go unnoticed.

To a wayward church in Rome, the Apostle Paul said, "Do not conform any longer to the pattern of this world, but be transformed by the renewing of your mind" (Romans 12:2). The bottom line? A renewed faith within the heart of a parent produces renewed beliefs within the mind of a parent. The Apostle Paul implies that renewed beliefs will result in righteous behavior. He also reminds us of a fundamental principle of human conduct: Beliefs determine behavior.

An Example from Chuck

I was selling our car. I advertised it as a "Cream Puff: one owner, driven to church on Sundays." Well, it was true . . . as long as you didn't count the trips taken Monday through Saturday. I figured, *Hey, they'll never notice. They'll kick the tires. They'll pop the hood. They'll take it for a spin around the block. Sold.*

Jenni asks me if I told them that the transmission slips.

I say they didn't ask.

Jenni asks me if I told them the wipers don't work.
  I say they didn't notice.
Jenni asks me if I told them that the spare tire in the trunk is flat.
  I say they didn't look.
Jenni asks me about the condition of my integrity.
  I must admit that I needed a moral makeover.

2. Teach by example. "Well done" is better than "well said."

In a letter to Titus, his "partner and fellow worker" (2 Corinthians 8:23), the Apostle Paul once again addressed the issue of teaching integrity. The method he recommended in the first century is what we call "modeling" in the twenty-first century:

> In everything set them an example by doing what is good. In your teaching show integrity, seriousness and soundness of speech. (Titus 2:7-8)

Teach by example. Model what you desire. For our children to develop character of integrity, they must first see the integrity of our character. In a world that endorses situational ethics and moral flexibility, the Apostle Paul reminds us to "set them an example by doing." Like Paul, I believe that the most meaningful classroom your children will ever attend is located in your home.

An Example from Chuck

Jenni asks me, "Why is there a radar detector on the dashboard of our car?"
  I say, "Everybody's got one . . . we live in Texas."
Jenni asks me, "Do you plan on breaking the law by speeding today?"
  I feel like a deer caught in the headlights of an eighteen-wheeler.
  Enough said.
Your kids are watching.

3. It's never right to do wrong.

Integrity is never easy to initiate. It's even harder to maintain. Tests of our integrity will occur when we least expect them:

- at the cash register
- in the dressing room

- on an expense account
- on a tax return
- when no one's looking.

Everyone knows that when it comes to parenting, consistency is our best ally (unless of course we're consistently inconsistent). The consistency of our integrity is equally critical. In all probability, sometime today your character will be challenged.

What will you do?

Abraham Lincoln said, "Pay the price, and reap the rewards."

Throughout his administration, Abraham Lincoln was under fire, especially during the scarring years of the Civil War. Although he knew he would make errors in office, he resolved never to compromise his integrity. His resolve was so strong that he once declared, "I desire so to conduct the affairs of this administration that if at the end, when I come to lay down the reins of power, if I have lost every other friend on earth, I shall at least have one friend left, and that friend shall be down inside of me."[2]

He determined that it's never right to do wrong.

Not even a little wrong. It costs too much.

The Apostle Paul challenged the church in Corinth. They wanted their spirituality to be graded on a curve. But he reminded them that "a little leaven leavens the whole lump" (1 Corinthians 5:6, NKJV).

Never compromise yourself.

Not today. Not tomorrow.

Never.

You're the most influential role model your kids will ever have. They need you to model integrity, teach integrity and reward integrity when they demonstrate it.

An Example from Chuck

Jenni asks me, "Why didn't you come to a complete stop at the stop sign?"

I say, "I didn't see anybody else at the intersection, so why stop?"

Jenni asks me, "Did you notice the police officer behind the tree over there?"

Jenni is really starting to bother me!

Notes

1. Dr. Samuel S. Janus and Cynthia Janus, *The Janus Report on Sexual Behavior* (New York: John Wiley and Sons, 1993), 169.
2. *Today in the World* (August 1989), 21.

*I*n November of 1949, sixteen-year-old Gerald Williams' music career was launched when his mentor, Herschel Foshee of the Stamps Baxter Quartet, died suddenly and young Williams was hired as his replacement. The group then became Smilin' Joe Roper and The Melody Boys Quartet.

Between then and now, Williams has been a constant in the music industry, singing for such groups as Rosie Roselle & the Searchers and the Plainsmen, and working with such luminaries as Roy Clark, Loretta Lynn, Grandpa Jones and many other Grand Ole Opry stars. And though his career took many interesting turns throughout the years, his heart never strayed far from his Southern Gospel roots and his beloved Melody Boys Quartet, where he still anchors the bass spot today.

"I accepted the Lord as a young teenager," Williams says, "and will never forget the peace I felt in my heart as I lay down to sleep that night, knowing that my heart was free from the sin that bound me. It holds good to this day, over fifty years later. God has always been faithful and my confidence is still in Him."

Books
 Mighty Lot of Singin'

Recordings
 Basically Bass (cassette only)
 Classics Collection
 Faith in My Savior
 Get Happy

 The Melody Boys Quartet Live
  (50th Anniversary) (also video)
 Mercy Called Me by Name
 Sing Me a Song
 Talkin' 'Bout Jesus

Web
 www.themelodyboysquartet.com

Character Built Through 23 Struggle

Gerald Williams

Nineteen-sixty was a banner year for me both professionally and on the home front. That was the year Martha gave birth to our son, Stephen Gerald Williams.

I had always vowed I would never raise a child by him or herself. Although there was a loving bond between Mother, Dad and me, I always missed not having any brothers or sisters. With ten sisters and one brother, Martha also believed in the value of children growing up together. With our two precious girls, we had already accomplished that much of our family goal. But Martha and I decided we didn't want to leave our family at just two children because of the sibling competition for parental attention that can occur.

For instance, when the girls were small, they drew an invisible line down the middle of everything we owned! Specifically, Judy always rode in the back car seat behind me and Loretta always rode in the seat behind Martha. If either one of them crossed even a big toe over the imaginary line down the middle of the floorboard, we'd hear, "She's on my side!" Though Martha and I wanted to break up this tug-of-war, we didn't want to live up to the Bevill tradition of twelve. So we decided three children was just the right number.

I have always been a sucker for my girls. Either one of them can still wrap me around her little finger. But like most men, I wanted to have a son to carry on our family name. Since our third try would likely be my last chance at having a son, I jokingly bribed Martha with a five-pound box of her favorite Millionaires candies if she had a boy. When Steve was born on December 22, 1960, I bought her the biggest box of Millionaires I could find!

When Steve was only a couple of weeks old, he gave us a real scare. He was hospitalized with a serious case of pneumonia. A couple of times we were afraid we were losing him. I will never forget the anguish of having to leave with the quartet while Martha stayed with our new son at the hospital. It still grieves me to think of all the times Martha had to handle family emergencies on her own. Those of us in this business have to rely heavily on our wives to keep the home fires burning while we're burning up the road. In spite of her own fluctuating health, Martha somehow managed to keep everything going. Thank God for her.

The nurses knew my situation, so they were good to let me sneak into Steve's private room for a little while when I came in off the road. At that time, the standard treatment for Steve's condition was to keep him bundled up under a cold vaporizing tent designed to help keep his lungs open. It would break my heart to look down through the transparent tent and see frost on his little eyebrows from the cold mist.

Thanks to God, our son was spared, and now Steve has three terrific sons of his own. The panic I felt at the prospect of losing my child reminds me of how great a sacrifice God made when He did not spare His own Son, but sent Him to die for me.

Nineteen-sixty was also the year Martha and I began to realize our own "American Dream." We decided to build a new home! Mind you, we were still just making ends meet at the time. But for a couple who had survived living on a creek bank eating nothing but pork and beans and hanging our baby's diapers in the tree limbs to dry, building a home of our own was a dream come true! And when I tell you we bought that house and lot for only $8,500 and had it completely ready to move in before spending a dime, you might accuse me of "dreaming up" our dream house. But that's what we did, by the grace of God and a lot of teamwork!

Jerry Venable's family owned the Venable Lumber Company, one of the quartet's first TV sponsors. Jerry worked there during the day as a draftsman, learning the lumber business inside and out. So, when he found out Martha and I wanted to build a house, he agreed to draw our plans. Venable Lumber Company then let us have all the lumber, electrical, plumbing and other building supplies without any money up front. We agreed on a price of $1,875 for our lot with Mr. Suggs, the owner, who also agreed to wait on his money until we got our loan. Dad, Mr. Suggs and I framed out the house and did all the finish work.

Martha, big and pregnant with Steve, worked side by side with us helping to string wiring, float sheetrock, hang light fixtures and anything else she could find to do while the girls were in school. After Steve's birth and recovery from the scary pneumonia episode, Martha would bring him to the construction site with her and let him sleep in his bassinet while she painted walls and varnished hardwood floors. On the weekends, the entire family could be found at our "new house." We made quite a construction crew!

By the time I presented the appraisal of our completed new home to the bank, it was finished and ready for occupancy. The loan officer looked up from our paperwork and said, "Well, Mr. Williams, everything looks to be in good order. All we need now is the deed to your lot."

This was a wrinkle I hadn't anticipated.

"Well," I restrained a gulp. "We don't exactly have the deed yet."

When that loan officer realized Mr. Suggs had allowed us to build an entire house on his lot without having yet received a dime for it, his eyes kind of glazed over for a second. Then, with a kind of "water-under-the-bridge" resolve, he cut me a check for the $1,875 lot cost so I could have the Abstract Company prepare a deed. We then closed the rest of the loan, paid everyone off and moved in!

Building our first house was like an old-fashioned barn-raising where all the family and neighbors pitched in. There's no better glue for cementing family and friends together than the sweat of mutual labor. I believe the world would be far more "neighborly" if we had more "barn-raisin's" today!

By 1963, Martha and I had spent twelve years of marriage without ever taking a vacation. I had done a lot of traveling during those years with the quartets, but Martha had spent nearly all of her time at home with the kids. I had often felt guilty about never having much fun-time with the family. We finally decided that if we ever intended to have a family vacation, we would have to make it a priority. So somehow, I managed to save a grand total of $100 in cash, and we decided to take the kids on a trip to Florida.

We had just bought a new Fiat four-door sedan. The Fiat was only slightly larger than a Volkswagen Beetle and typically got great gas mileage. So with gasoline at 28 cents a gallon, the transportation cost was within reach. Then, we bought the biggest ice chest we could find and packed it with all kinds of cheese, lunch meats and drinks and wedged it in behind the backseat. We then wedged ourselves into the tiny car and took off for the white beaches of Pensacola.

Reminiscent of my $15-a-week Melody Boys days, we stretched that $100 as thin as cheap whitewash on a picket fence and had an absolute blast on our week-long trip. We ate cinnamon rolls for breakfast, sandwiches from the ice chest for lunch, and splurged on a restaurant every night for dinner. We spent the night in a motel on the way down, and rented a little cabin on the beach in Pensacola for two nights at $18 per night. It was the first time Martha and the kids had ever seen the "ocean." And even though it was really just the Gulf, it was the ocean to us!

The kids were ecstatic over the beautiful white sands of Pensacola Beach. "Look!" they exclaimed. "It looks just like snow!" Jumping over the swelling waves of the gulf and sailing back to the beach on a crest was more fun than any amusement park ride. Martha was more uninhibited playing in the water with the kids than I was. I've never been big on getting water in my ears! But it was great fun for me to sit on the beach and watch them all running back and forth, squealing with excitement over every fun new discovery.

On the way home, the muffler broke loose from the exhaust pipe on the little Fiat, which cost $4 to repair. But in spite of that unexpected expense, I still had $4 of our original $100 in my pocket when we arrived back home!

People who never have to figure out how to do what they want to do in spite of limited means miss out on a lot of fun. For all the times

I've had to come up with inventive ways to make something work or just to keep going in general, you could call me "Thomas Edison Williams." Even though I admit there were times I would have gladly traded the "fun" of being inventive for the relief of financial security, I thank God for what I've learned from the struggle!

Struggling and learning: I believe that is the process through which we all grow, both as human and spiritual beings. Like they say, "No pain, no gain." But so often the struggling seems to go on for a long time before the learning takes place.

Excerpted from Mighty Lot of Singin' *by Gerald Williams, Copyright © 1999 by TMBQ Publishing.*

*R*aleigh B. Washington, president and CEO of Road to Jerusalem, is the former executive vice president of global ministries for Promise Keepers. Prior to holding that position, he served as vice president for Reconciliation and was a member of the Promise Keepers board of directors.

Washington is the founder and pastor emeritus of Rock of Our Salvation Evangelical Free Church in Chicago, Illinois, an urban church reaching across racial barriers within the inner city of Chicago. In 1993 he was voted Pastor of the Year by the Greater Chicago Sunday School Association. He is a member of the board of trustees of Azusa Pacific University and the board director for Reconciliation and Peace Ministries, Inc. He co-authored a book with Glen Kehrein entitled *Breaking Down Walls: A Model of Reconciliation in an Age of Racial Strife*, which received the 1994 Gold Medallion Award from the Christian Booksellers Association.

A Florida native with a bachelor's degree from Florida A&M University, he attained the rank of lieutenant colonel in the US Army, earning the Bronze Star for meritorious service in Vietnam.

He has been a featured speaker for Promise Keepers; Moody Bible Institute's Founder's Week and Pastors' Conference; the National Religious Broadcasters' Conference; the Evangelical Free Church of America Conference; college and seminary commencements; as well as missions, urban outreach and racial reconciliation conferences across the United States and globally.

He lives in Denver with his wife Paulette and attends Church in the City, a thriving multicultural, inner-city church. The Washingtons have eight children and eleven grandchildren.

Books
Breaking Down Walls
Break Down the Walls (workbook)

Relationship: How Your Character Is Key to Your Family Life

Raleigh Washington

The family represents an earthly model of God's perspective on relationship. The foundational relationship in the family is that between husband and wife. When children arrive, the partners acquire the added roles of mother and father. Today, however, the family is under siege. The gay community seeks to redefine marriage and family; divorce among Christians, reportedly as high as 54 percent, is destroying the foundational relationship in the family; and deadbeat dads, who father children out of wedlock, are creating the fatherless family.

Family, the way God intended it to be, can be defined and sustained by one word: *relationship!* The answer to quality, fulfilling and successful family life can be summed up in that one word. Considering that this appears to be a very simplistic definition, we can easily miss the real value of the dynamic of relationship. I shall unfold six irrefutable, biblical principles of relationship that, if they are understood, complied with and built into your character, will guarantee a successful and gratifying marriage and family experience.

Principle #1: Call

Marriage begins with a biblical call. When a Christian man and woman confirm that Christ is calling them into holy matrimony, they begin a life together.

The call to marriage is permanent. The Bible reveals in the book of Malachi that God hates divorce (see 2:16). The only honorable way for a marriage to end is when one of the partners dies. Any other method that ends the marriage is not honorable in God's eyes.

A biblical call to marriage is best validated through thorough and intense counseling. I never marry a couple without conducting ten premarital counseling sessions with them. I administer a temperament test that helps them evaluate the way they will likely respond in conflict and identify the areas in their interpersonal relationship that could lead to serious conflict. I also require the couple to sign a chastity vow based on First Thessalonians 4:1-8. This vow is a signed covenant between each party and God that they will abstain from all intimate contact until they are married.

When I begin my premarital counseling, the prospective bride and groom enter into a covenant with me. We all agree that we are in the marriage process because of their belief that they have been called by God into marriage. The covenant agreement states that any one of the three of us, at any time before the counseling sessions are completed, can bring the counseling process and the marriage plans to a halt if he or she feels that there is any reason to do so. The agreement states that whatever reason brought things to a halt must be resolved to the satisfaction of all before the counseling resumes. I have delayed several marriages as much as six months, and a couple of times I have refused to go forward with a marriage.

While this might seem harsh to some, I believe that it is the godliest way to approach preparation for marriage. The marriage is the foundation of the family. If it is sound, then the family will be sound. I wonder how many divorced Christian couples never should have married in the first place. Marriage is permanent; appropriate, thorough preparations for it are indispensable.

Principle #2: Commitment to Relationship

The success of marriage and family depends on a relentless commitment by all parties involved (see Ruth 1:16-17).

Commitment to relationship is really contained in a commitment to resolve any and every conflict that enters a marriage. Into every marriage and family conflict will come over and over again. Joy in the family depends directly upon the ability of the persons involved to resolve the conflicts successfully.

The danger to conflict resolution is conflict avoidance, which is practiced by the majority of families. Loving confrontation of differences will never start out joyfully, but it will always end joyfully. I am not suggesting that conflict resolution is a given when you earnestly seek it. Conflict is always a formidable challenge. Personality, temperament, emotions, quality of faith, humility, control, perception and competitive spirits all find their places during conflict. However, the ability to resolve conflict consistently and successfully will set the tone for joy in a marriage and create an effective pattern for addressing and resolving conflicts between parents and children. This successful pattern will facilitate conflict resolution between siblings as well.

The keys to successful conflict resolution are commitment and dialogue. In the Bible Ruth makes a commitment to Naomi, her people, her God and her place of residence—for life (see Ruth 1:16-17). For many couples covenant and commitment do not have lasting value. And commitment alone is not enough—you must apply dialogue. Ruel Howe describes dialogue as being "as critical to love as blood is to the body." When the flow of blood stops, the body dies. When dialogue stops, love dies and resentment is born. Dialogue is the vehicle for achieving success in relationships. According to Howe, dialogue can start, resurrect or sustain a relationship. Both or all parties involved must be committed to pursuing dialogue relentlessly.

Men frequently seek to bypass dialogue to quickly arrive at a solution. In many instances, dialogue is more important than the solution. When men bypass dialogue with their wives, or when parents do so with their children, the frequent result is keeping true feelings hidden. This bypass of dialogue often leads to extramarital affairs—with someone else who *is* willing to dialogue. Failure to discuss conflicts can also lead to alcohol and drug addiction and running away from home.

Principle #3: Intentionality

Intentionality is the purposeful, positive and planned behavior that facilitates marriage and family (see Ephesians 2:14-15).

Dating, engagement and marriage are all purposeful, positive and planned. Appropriate preparations for marriage must be intentional. Intentionality drives romance during the courtship before marriage. When husbands and wives cease to be intentional about dating, giving gifts for no special reason, and spending quality time with each other, romance departs from the union.

My wife Paulette reminds me often that she needs to be romanced. I desperately need those reminders, because I am geared for convenience, and the intentionality required to plan for and carry out elements of romance does not come naturally to me. I am blessed because Paulette reminds me. How many wives do not remind their husbands, feeling that to do so takes away the joy of feeling that their husbands really wanted to do romantic things? The truth is that romance is not a felt need for me until I get in touch with the reminder that it is a felt need for Paulette. And every so often I think of romantic things on my own—always reaping the reward of a thousand marital bonus points! Such activity can become habit-forming.

Parents should always date their kids individually. Get them to talk—you'll be shocked! (See the tips on dialoguing with your kids under Principle #5.)

Principle #4: Sincerity

The willingness to be vulnerable, disclosing your feelings, attitude, perceptions and differences with a goal to resolve and build a foundation of trust, is sincerity (see John 15:15).

Transparency and vulnerability do not come easily, yet they are critical to trust. The absence of trust will bring certain corrosion to any relationship. Trust is essential to success in marriage and effectiveness in raising and guiding your children. The most important words between husbands and wives and parents and children are "I believe in you." These words communicate love, trust and confidence.

You cannot express love, trust and confidence apart from the principle of sincerity. When your partner knows you are being vulnerable and transparent, it removes the need to guess what your true thoughts are. Such interaction builds a foundation of trust, and a trusting environment generates peace and tranquility. Perhaps one of the most detrimental actions to marriage and family is failing to be sincere. When a person refuses to dialogue and does not make himself vulnerable and transparent, his true innermost feelings remain hidden. If you are, in dialogue, seeking to resolve conflict and yet do not share your true inner feelings, you are building relationship on a faulty premise. There will be no genuine trust, especially when the truth is made known. The principle of sincerity contributes immeasurably toward the critical need for trust in relationships.

Having served as a pastor for many years, I have counseled many troubled marriages. One significant reality consistently finds its way into these marriages: One or both partners find it easy to disclose their genuine feelings to another family member or close friend but have great difficulty in expressing those same genuine feelings to one another. A relationship without genuine, sincere, transparent and vulnerable dialogue is a relationship that is superficial and without depth. Such communications reflect an absence of trust. No one is willing to be vulnerable in a situation where trust is not evident. Building a foundation of trust is building security for a long and successful marriage.

A children's psychologist once stated that the closest confidant to a teenager is an older sibling, and the second closest confidant is a peer. This means that even the best parents generally can get no higher than third on the ladder of confidentiality with their children. This is a scary thought. However, there is a way to break this general pattern. Dialogue with your children. Insist on it; create the atmosphere for it; take each one on a date and encourage him or her to open up. Once you create an environment for transparent dialogue with your children, you can move to first place as a confidant with your children. I believe this is the critical missing element in interpersonal relations between parents and children.

Principle #5: Sensitivity

Sensitivity is gaining the knowledge needed to relate empathetically with your spouse or children (see Ephesians 4:15-16).

Intentional efforts to relate sensitively to your spouse and children will yield the fruit of joy and success in family relationship. Each person in the family is unique. This uniqueness requires a lifetime to fully understand all of its dimensions. The challenge is to enter intentionally into a lifelong process of seeking greater understanding of your spouse or your child. The key here is never taking one another for granted. There is a three-word request that facilitates in-depth understanding of one another in an interpersonal, family-connected relationship. It is "Help me understand." Whenever you are engaged in dialogue and you perceive that there is information being withheld, rather than go after it in a dogmatic fashion, simply pose the question: "Help me understand. What are you feeling now? What are you thinking now?" This sensitive approach to getting another person to open up can prove exceedingly effective.

My wife Paulette carried a deep emotional scar that came as a result of her mother and father's separation when she was five years old. Her sister, who was three years older, remained with her father while Paulette remained with her mother. During this ten-year separation, my wife endured multiple hurts from the rejection of her father, separation from her sister and the rejection that she felt from the men who entered her mother's life. This emotional scar was not only deep, but it caused Paulette to adjust her behavior and life to protect herself from hurt. This adjustment was subconscious but very real. For twenty-five years of our relationship, she was like a person wounded and half-dead emotionally, while my insensitivity caused me to walk by her on the other side of the street, never having a clue as to what she was going through. However, in the midst of a heated argument, after all those years, I sensed that her reaction was motivated by more than the discussion at hand. This prompted me to say to her those precious words, "Help me understand. Why you are reacting so strongly right now?"

She immediately broke into tears, and for the next couple of hours, I learned of her emotional scars, and God used my sensitivity to unlock the door and set her free from a vicious, inward, emotional prison that had plagued her for forty years. I believe emotional prisons such as this often lead to divorce. I also believe that many teenagers experience emotional scars that parents never recognize. The result of these unhealed emotional wounds can be devastating. Relationship demands that we dialogue to probe for understanding of the cause of any excessive behavior in the lives of our spouses or children. When we probe from a standpoint of love and compassion, our loved ones will make themselves vulnerable and share with us the information we need to help them walk through the valley of the shadow of death.

I would encourage you to begin immediately to practice using these three innocent, intimate and powerful words—"Help me understand." They are the key to gaining knowledge so that you can relate to the deep inner feelings of your loved ones. "Help me understand" can deepen and strengthen the relationship between husband and wife. "Help me understand" can help parents connect with their teenagers. In today's world, particularly in America, the gap between parents and children is wider than it has ever been in any former period. The age of television and the Internet has provided a maturity and dynamic in teenagers of today that catapults them into a lifestyle drastically different from that of their parents. The only possible way to bridge this gap with your child is through intentional, sincere and sensitive dialogue.

My youngest daughter would dialogue with her mother but never with me, mainly because I would not seek to dialogue with her. I would ask her, "How did your day go today?" She would consistently answer me with "Fine" or "OK," and I would never press any further. A few years ago, my wonderful, sensitive wife challenged me to talk more with our daughter. I responded by saying, "I try, but she never wants to talk." My wife replied, "You're not trying hard enough."

The next day, I took my wife's suggestion. When my daughter responded to me with a single word, I said, "That's not good enough. I really want to know what happened." She said two words: "Not much." I pressed her further until she became convinced that I really wanted to hear about her day. What happened next literally brought me to tears. She began to dialogue about her day and her life, and she didn't stop talking for nearly twenty minutes. I had never had a one-on-one conversation with her of this duration, and I was blown away by the depth of her interaction.

The key that unlocked the door to this dialogue was when I continued to press her with "Help me understand what really happened in your life today." Nothing is more helpful to sustaining a high-quality relationship than gaining knowledge so that you can relate empathetically with one another. From the point of that conversation with my daughter, I had loads of launch points for interpersonal interactions with her in the future.

Principle #6: Sacrifice

Sacrifice is the willingness to give up a position of comfort and accept a position that is uncomfortable for the express purpose of facilitating relationship (see 2 Corinthians 8:9).

A relationship will never deepen beyond the surface if both or all parties are not willing to sacrifice for the purpose of strengthening and deepening the relationship. The essence of the principle of sacrifice demands that you be willing to step out of your comfort zone for the express purpose of facilitating relationship. Most husbands enjoy sports and can spend the entire day on Saturday watching football, basketball or golf. Many wives would much rather go shopping on Saturday. Although they will rarely ask, nothing would give them greater joy than if we would leave the TV, go shopping with them and, after shopping, stop at a favorite deli for a snack. If this happens while Tiger Woods is on the hunt for another championship, she is liable to get her head chopped off if she makes such a request.

I remember one Sunday a few months ago when Tiger was going into the final day of the tournament and was leading by two strokes. The network promised to cover Tiger from the first hole through the eighteenth hole, never missing a shot. I was so pumped up for this match that I planned for us to go to early service at 8:30. This would give me lots of time to get back home, unwind, get into my "special" easy chair and take in the full eighteen holes with Tiger. About a block from the church, there was a farmer's market loaded with fresh fruits, vegetables and the like. This market was not there every week, and on this particular Sunday it was set up with seemingly ten times as many stations as it normally would have. My wife said aloud, "Wow! Let's go get some fresh fruits and vegetables." At that point I was straining with every muscle in my body to present a happy face and to muster up the words to say, "OK, dear." Somehow I managed to do it, but then she remembered that I had wanted to go to church early to get home for Tiger. True to her nature, she began to insist that we not stop because she did not want to cause me to miss out on any golf.

Her reaction brought deep conviction to me. She was willing to give up what she wanted to do to embrace what I wanted to do. This conviction motivated me to absolutely insist that we go to the farmer's market, and so we did. We loaded up with vegetables and fruit, and as we took off she said, "Let's stop by Dozens" (our favorite breakfast place). Once again, I needed to respond in a way that demonstrated that I really wanted to do this. Any indication to the contrary would once again ruin the whole event. Somehow I succeeded. We got home in time enough for me to watch the second nine holes (which was very enjoyable because Tiger did win), but my greatest joy came when my wife realized the sacrifice that I had made. I had bonus points in my marriage that were good for six solid months!

If you are willing to build your character in a way that will strengthen and give joy to your marriage, begin to practice these six principles of relationship—today!

*N*ancy Cobb has been the director of women's ministries at Christ Community Church, a church of 6,000, since 1997. She is also a retreat and conference speaker and a frequent radio guest. She came to a saving relationship with Christ in 1981 through the ministry of Anne Graham Lotz, daughter of Billy Graham, who was her teacher and mentor. Seven years later, Lotz, who taught a Bible-study fellowship class of 500 women in Raleigh, North Carolina, providentially chose Cobb to take her place as the teacher of the class. Lotz also selected Cobb to be a seminar leader when she began teaching women at the Billy Graham Training Center at the Cove in North Carolina. Cobb continued in these two ministries until she and her husband Ray moved to Omaha in 1992.

Cobb has coauthored three books with Connie Grigsby. The first was a finalist for the Gold Medallion Award and has just been rereleased as *The Politically Incorrect Wife*. Their second book, *How to Get Your Husband to Talk to You*, was a finalist for The Books for a Better Life Award. Their third book was released in September 2003.

The Cobbs have four children and one grandson.

Books with Nancy Cobb
The Best Thing I Ever Did for My
 Marriage
How to Get Your Husband to Talk to
 You
The Politically Incorrect Wife

Media
Lifewalk (KHBI, Omaha's
 Christian radio station)

*C*onnie Grigsby, a popular teacher and speaker, is coauthor of *The Politically Incorrect Wife* (formerly titled *Is There a Moose in Your Marriage?* and a finalist for the prestigious Gold Medallion Award) and *How to Get Your Husband to Talk to You* (a finalist for The Books for a Better Life Award) and has also written *How to Get Your Teen to Talk to You*. Another book, *The Best Thing I Ever Did for My Marriage*, was released by Multnomah Publishers in the fall of 2003.

With her trademark love for people and enthusiasm for life, Grigsby enjoys pointing others toward life's "bottom line." With warmth and humor, she exhorts others to refuse to be content with a "ho-hum" relationship with their Savior—which she herself was for over twenty-five years. Calling others to live beyond the casual is her passion.

Grigsby enjoys spending time with family and friends, playing tennis and eating other people's cooking. A graduate of the University of Oklahoma, she and her husband Wesley have been married for twenty-three years. They have three teenage daughters and make their home in Omaha, Nebraska.

Books
How to Get Your Teen to Talk to You

Books with Nancy Cobb
The Best Thing I Ever Did for My Marriage
How to Get Your Husband to Talk to You
The Politically Incorrect Wife

Media
Lifewalk (KHBI, Omaha's Christian radio station)

Who Says Beauty Is Only Skin Deep?

Nancy Cobb and Connie Grigsby

The world today puts tremendous emphasis on external appearances. People flock to gyms in droves, searching for better bodies. Imaginary stairs are climbed and bicycles going nowhere are pedaled madly. Women sweat to the oldies and the not-so-oldies. *Surely if we work a little harder*, we think, *we can be ten pounds thinner by summer*. Cosmetic sales are soaring, and age-defying products are flying off the shelves as never before. We have become a nation bent on maintaining youth and beauty at all costs. This is especially true for women.

An overabundance of material tells us that if we are outwardly attractive we are more valuable, more desirable and more respectable. A recent ad in a women's magazine touted make-up as a woman's most important accessory.

We agree completely. A woman's make-up is the most important thing about her, period. Her *inner make-up*, that is. We call this "holy beauty." It is not based on the world's standard of beauty; it is based on the Lord's standard. It is a beauty that God calls unfading, and we are told in His Word how we can have it. It doesn't have to be wiped on, rubbed in, ripped off or reapplied in the morning. It is a twenty-four-hour-a-day beauty package, and it can be yours if you're willing to obey God's Word.

Holy beauty . . . God's idea of beautiful!

She is forever beautiful, the one who resembles Christ.

She was barely five feet tall and had to stretch to see above the steering wheel when she drove. Her hair was a beautiful silver gray, her face caressed with wrinkles. Joy danced in her eyes, and she spoke with a lilt in her voice. She was so magnetic, yet her life seemed so ordinary. What made her the way she was? I (Connie) couldn't quite figure it out. I was a young girl, and she was my great-aunt.

When I was nine, she gave me a Bible with my name inscribed on the front in gold lettering. Up to this time, I had shared a Bible with my sisters. Now I had my very own. I was so proud! She told me it was the greatest book I would ever own. Just the way she held it in her hands told me she dearly loved it.

Like my family, she lived on a farm, which was only a few miles from us. She had made the country house charming. The single bathroom, with a claw-foot tub, was accessible only by first walking through two bedrooms. The kitchen was small, but oh, the generosity and love that could be felt when a special treat or meal was shared with a guest. Every time we visited, announced or unannounced, we received a grand welcome. "You've just made my day," she'd say cheerfully. "How kind of you to visit. Come in!"

My great-aunt had known hard times and heartache, but she bore no ill will or bitterness. These were foreign words to her. She loved to attend church, but her husband was not a churchgoing man. Never do I recall her complaining or wishing aloud to my mother (when we girls were listening from an adjoining room) that he would go with her. "He's in God's hands," she'd say. She loved him with a loyalty and fervor that was rare even then. She treated him as a prized jewel, although he wasn't one to display such emotion in return. She didn't gossip or judge, and she had a way about her that made you want to behave in the same manner.

I observed all of this for some time and even as a young girl knew she was special. Although she lived an everyday kind of life—her world humble, her days predictable—she radiated something that made me want what she had.

It would be years before I realized what it was that made her so special. She had committed her life to Jesus and lived it trying to be like Him. Because of that, she had been transformed from the inside out. *She was holy beautiful.* What I had observed for years was a reflection of what He had done in her life. Her beauty came straight from the Maker Himself. No wonder I was so attracted to her.

Holy beauty, unlike external beauty, never fades and, in fact, is enhanced with each passing year. It's the ultimate beauty product and is produced in us by God Himself. That's what we'll be discussing in this chapter, but first we'll look briefly at external beauty.

External Beauty

Say what you will, a woman's external appearance is important to her husband. A friend of ours says, "If you ask one hundred men if their wife's appearance matters to them, ninety-five of them will say yes, and the other five won't have understood the question!"

When I (Nancy) was a little girl, my mother would actually change her clothes and mine before Dad came home. Somehow that heightened the anticipation of his arrival. She wanted us to look nice when he came home from his workday, and he always seemed to appreciate that she did this.

In many households today, both the husband and wife work outside the home. We believe that all women are working women—whether in the home, out of the home, or both. Every woman's role is vital and touches dozens of lives around her. How much time you have to freshen up at the end of the day depends on your personal circumstances. Some women have ample opportunity to do this, while some don't. Regardless, it is a fortunate man who has a wife who makes an effort to look nice for him.

A Man's Perspective

It's a well-known fact that men are more visual than women. It is one of the ways we're different. If you show a man a picture of an attractive woman, frequently his eyes will linger. If you show a woman a picture of a nice-looking man, often his appearance won't even register in her mind.

I (Connie) remember many years ago visiting a newlywed couple. We decided to drive to the ice cream shop for dessert. The wife ordered two scoops of vanilla. Her husband suggested she get just one.

She assured him she wanted two. He assured her he thought one was more than enough. After energetically discussing the issue for a few moments, she left the store without buying anything.

We saw these friends recently and laughed at the memory. Our friend readily admitted that he was attempting to make certain that his wife's physical appearance stayed the same following the wedding. "I hope I no longer try to control her like that," he said, "but I can't say enough about how much I appreciate her staying in shape after all these years. I think if any man were honest, he'd say that his wife's physical appearance matters greatly to him."

It's frustrating to many women that men place such a high value on external appearances. To a woman, this seems superficial and relatively unimportant. It's difficult for her to understand why this often seems to carry as much or more weight with her husband as her inner beauty.

We talked to several men to glean insight into this matter. Their opinions, though varied, all came down to the same basic conclusion: Most men wish they *were* able to see beyond the external to the internal, but few are able to do so. As one man said, "I don't know why men are so visually stimulated. I'd like to say I'm not, but I am! I know this sounds awfully shallow, but that's the way it is. I'm in a large Bible study, and it's an issue for every man in the group. We've talked about it many times. It is an ongoing struggle and temptation is never far away, even for godly men. Not the temptation to fall into adultery, perhaps, but certainly the temptation to look too long or imagine too much. You can hardly go to your mailbox anymore without this issue hitting you in the face.

"It makes a world of difference to a man when his wife *makes an effort* to look nice for him. To a man, this shows love, care, and respect for him. Men see their wives as a reflection of themselves. We're around well-dressed women all day in the workplace. To come home to a woman who is disheveled and unkempt is not something any man I know looks forward to. I think if wives realized how important this is to their husbands, they might consider changing."

This can be a difficult issue for a man to broach with his wife. One man said, "I don't mention this issue anymore because my wife becomes extremely defensive and argumentative. She accuses me of not loving the 'real' her. In an effort to keep the peace, I no longer bring it up. However, my desire for her to look nice hasn't changed. The only thing that has changed is that it's no longer verbalized. It's still an issue to me, just an unspoken one."

Most men care how their wives look, whether they say it or not. A wise woman would consider giving some thought to this and asking God if she needs to work on this. Without making any announcements, you might begin to make improvements. Do it with a joyful, glad heart, and don't get discouraged if he doesn't say anything. Many times it is awkward for a husband to say much, especially if there's been conflict in the past. Not only will you enjoy doing this for your husband, but many women find this makes them feel better about themselves as well.

Exercise

Is exercise part of your schedule? Women are busier than ever before and think they don't have time for exercise, yet often exercise actually gives them a renewed sense of energy. Most experts recommend exercising for twenty to thirty minutes at least three times a week. Exercise is good for you both physically and emotionally.

Some women get up early to fit exercise into their schedules. Many have found that it helps to exercise with a partner or in a group. This provides companionship as well as accountability. One woman we know walks every morning and uses this time to pray and reflect on the Lord. Is exercise a must for the godly woman? No! Some women are physically unable to do so. But for those of you who are able, you might find it beneficial.

Other Ideas

The ways for a woman to care for her external appearance are innumerable. Magazines are replete with simple tips. Fix your hair in a flattering way. If you don't have much time, find a low-maintenance cut that works well for you. You can wear inexpensive jewelry to offset your clothes, or you might find a scarf that makes an outfit really shine. There is a huge assortment of women's clothes to choose from these days, which fit all sizes and budgets. We both frequent consignment shops and find things that work for us at a fraction of their retail prices. A minimal amount of makeup can go a long way in making you look your best and takes just moments to apply.

Have you noticed that when you wear an old shirt with paint stains and your husband's oversized sweat pants, you actually *feel* tired? Try taking the time to dress for your day, and don't sacrifice looking nice for comfort. It's easy to have both. Most women wear 20 percent of their clothing 80 percent of the time. Find clothes that work for you and that you can see yourself wearing immediately. If you catch yourself thinking, *I'll probably wear this sometime*, when you're considering purchasing an item, chances are you won't! Put it back on the rack and find something that you'll wear often. It doesn't take long to distinguish between what you'll wear often and what you'll hardly wear.

A Surprise Party

I'll (Nancy) never forget attending a "come as you are" birthday party. The women who planned the event had selected several drivers to pick up the invited women around 9:30 p.m.

I was quite surprised when our doorbell rang. We had just put our four young children to bed. When I answered the door, I had only enough time to grab my purse before being whisked away to the hostess's home.

About twenty women had been invited, and we knew one another well. What fun it was for us to suddenly find ourselves out for an impromptu evening. As we talked about our rapid getaways, we began to look at each other. Normally at such a gathering, we all looked our best. But not that night! Most of us were embarrassed. Traces of lipstick gave evidence of faces that had been fussed over much earlier. Almost everyone's hair had not seen a brush in hours. And where in the world did we get those old sweat pants, unmatched tops and ragged bathrobes? After perusing one another's outfits, our eyes rested on one friend in particular, and the questions began:

"You knew about this, didn't you?" we said in chorus.

"No!" she exclaimed. "Why would you think that?"

"Because you look so nice. Your hair is in place, you're wearing a matching outfit, and you have on fresh lipstick. You look better than we do when we're getting ready to leave the house!"

"Really, I didn't know!" We weren't convinced. Obviously, she took far more care with her dress at home than the rest of us did. Blessed is the husband whose wife pays attention to the way she looks for his sake, as well as her own.

The woman commended in Proverbs 31 wore good clothes—fine linen and purple (v. 22, NASB). However, this is not to be the focal point of who you are. More important than this by far is the hidden person of your heart.

Inner Beauty

> Let it be the inward adorning and beauty of the hidden person of the heart, with the incorruptible and unfading charm of a gentle and peaceful spirit, which [is not anxious or wrought up, but] is very precious in the sign of God. (1 Peter 3:4, Amp.)

What makes a woman beautiful? It is the imperishable quality of a gentle and quiet spirit. A time will come when your physical beauty will fade. A time will also come when your sexuality is not as enticing to your husband as it is now. What are you doing now to prepare for these future changes? Are you allowing God to develop your *inner beauty*?

How can you develop the qualities of a gentle and quiet spirit? By *cultivating* them.

A Gentle Spirit

What does it mean to be gentle? One of the definitions may surprise you: to belong to a family of high station, of noble birth.[1]

It is incredible to realize that a Christian is of noble birth, born into the family of God.

To be gentle is to be free of harshness, sternness, and violence. Do you scream at your children or husband? Do you have a quick temper? Try softening your voice—it's surprising to see a child respond to the whispers of his mother and a husband blossom because of a soft-spoken wife.

Choose to be a gentlewoman! Here's our definition of a gentlewoman: one who is born again and is submissive to and surrendered to the lordship of Christ.

Jesus was gentle and humble in heart (Matthew 11:28-30, NASB). Don't you want to become like Him? The more you learn about Jesus and surrender to Him, the more this will happen.

A Quiet Spirit

Peacefulness is becoming a valuable commodity in our culture. Have you noticed that it is for sale these days? Aromatherapy, candles, soaps, creams, and elixirs all claim to be the antidote for stress. Small, soft, lavender-scented pillows or bedside machines that mimic the sounds of waves, rain, birds, and wind are helping the sleeping habits of the restless.

But what can compare to a *spirit that is peaceful*, not anxious or overwrought? No price tag can be put on a soul that is tranquil, calm, and still—free from noise or uproar. That comes from having a right relationship with God and is freely offered by Him.

> Peace I leave with you; My peace I give to you; not as the world gives do I give to you. Do not let your heart be troubled, nor let it be fearful. (John 14:27, NASB)

Here are some simple, practical things a woman can do to maintain a quiet spirit.

- Start the day with prayer.
- Spend time with and abide in Christ.
- Ask for God's help in developing a quiet spirit.
- Grocery shop for a week with a complete list.
- Don't go to bed, if possible, with the kitchen and living areas unsightly. (This causes you to begin the next day behind schedule.)
- Watch your caffeine and sugar intake.
- Don't overcommit yourself.

- Don't sign up your children for too many after-school activities.
- Plan for a day at home—we call them "home days"—and put it on the calendar.
- Don't overspend.
- Try to fold the laundry as it comes out of the dryer. This can be a real time-saver.
- Take a bubble bath. You can purchase a small tub pillow to lean against; read an uplifting book as you soak.
- Put the children to bed earlier. Play praise music.
- Ask your husband to massage your shoulders and neck; offer to do this for him if he enjoys it.
- Forgive quickly; don't bear grudges.

A Hopeful Spirit

> For in this way in former times the holy women also, who hoped in God, used to adorn themselves, being submissive to their own husbands. (1 Peter 3:5, NASB)

Your hope in God is a necessary part of developing inner beauty. To be holy beautiful, you must believe in God and also hope in Him. Hope is to "cherish a desire with anticipation and to expect with confidence and trust that God is working on your behalf."[2]

Sarah placed her hope in God. How wise she was, and what a leap of faith her life demonstrates to us. For ninety years she was childless, and she had come to deeply regret her own plan that Abraham should have a child with her maid, Hagar (Genesis 16:1-16). Then one day the Lord appeared to Abraham and told him that the next year Sarah would have a son. Sarah laughed when she heard this, saying, "After I have become old, shall I have pleasure, my lord being old also?" After the Lord Himself confronted her, revealing to her that He knew her thoughts, Sarah's faith was born (Genesis 18:1-15, NASB). She placed her hope and faith in God and considered Him faithful to what he had promised. And what God had promised came to be just as He said it would. Sarah gave birth to Isaac.

Sarah is an example of a woman who obeyed her husband and responded to him as the leader of her household. And God considered this so noteworthy that He put her in His "Hall of Fame" as one who triumphed in her faith (Hebrews 11).

Where do you place your hope? Sarah placed hers in God, expectantly and with confidence. She knew God would do as He said even though she had never conceived a child as a young woman. It would seem she anticipated that God would work on her behalf even in the most difficult circumstances.

The Key

Peter, who gives us Sarah as an example, tells us:

> You are now her true daughters if you do right and let nothing terrify you [not giving way to hysterical fears or letting anxieties unnerve you.] (1 Peter 3:6, Amp.)

Fearlessness seems to be intertwined with a woman's choice to acknowledge her husband's leadership. If you are a fearful person, ask yourself, "Have I taken the leadership of the home away from my husband and neglected verbal and heartfelt acknowledgment that my husband is responsible *before God* to be the leader?"

To take over the leadership in the home, it seems to us, results in emotional unrest and fearfulness in the heart of a wife.

Are You a Controlling Woman?

In a recent discussion, a woman confessed to being a "control freak." As she described herself and her controlling ways, she acknowledged that she had indeed become a very anxious woman. Examine yourself if you are fearful. Could it be that you need to give back the leadership role in your family to your husband?

This involves a conscious decision on your part. Once you do this, don't be quick with "constructive" criticism or second-guess your husband. If you've led the family for any length of time, give him a while to hit his stride. Encourage him! Both of you will be blessed by God as you fulfill your roles. Remember, your hope is in God, not in your husband and his abilities.

A Considerate Spirit

> In the same way you married men should live considerately
> with [your wives], with an intelligent recognition [of the mar-
> riage relation], honoring the woman as [physically] the weaker,
> but [realizing that you] are joint heirs of the grace (God's un-
> merited favor) of life, in order that your prayers may not be
> hindered and cut off. [Otherwise you cannot pray effectively.]
> (1 Peter 3:7, Amp.)

It seems to us that a woman can help her husband in this regard.
How can she do this?

She can choose behavior that her husband can respect. She can
be cooperative and pleasant. A friend recently said to us, "I don't
know if my wife knows how much I love her, but I know for certain
how much she loves me because of the way she treats me." This
same man, at a Valentine's banquet, was asked to list ten things he
valued in his wife. His number one reason: "I love the way she
loves me." What a fortunate man! And what a godly woman!
Surely that's the way God intended it to be. Even if a wife fails to
do this, it is still the husband's responsibility to love his wife.
There will come a day when he will answer to God regarding this
issue.

Can you imagine what your home life would become if both of
you respected, loved, and supported each other—even if one of
you is having a bad day?

The Road That Matters

Regardless of where you marriage is at this point, you are in the
place of blessing when you choose to do what is right. One aspect
of doing so is striving to have a harmonious home. Peter sums up
what he has been saying:

> Finally, all of you, live in harmony with one another; be sympa-
> thetic, love as brothers, be compassionate and humble. (1 Peter
> 3:8)

These virtues are Jesus' own character. He lives in you and can
exhibit these traits through you.

Loving the Unlovable

It is easy to live in harmony when your husband is treating you well. But what if he's not? How do you treat your husband when he is unloving and moody? Listen to what Jesus says regarding difficult relationships:

> Love your enemies. Let them bring out the best in you, not the worst. When someone gives you a hard time, respond with the energies of prayers for that person. . . . If someone takes unfair advantage of you, use the occasion to practice the servant life. No more tit-for-tat stuff. Live generously.
>
> Here is a simple rule of thumb for behavior: Ask yourself what you want people to do for you; then grab the initiative and do it for them! If you only love the lovable, do you expect a pat on the back? . . . I tell you, love your enemies. Help and give without expecting a return. You'll never—I promise—regret it. Live out this God-created identity the way our Father lives toward us, generously and graciously, even when we're at our worst. Our Father is kind; you be kind.
>
> Don't pick on people, jump on their failures, criticize their faults—unless, of course, you want the same treatment. Don't condemn those who are down; that hardness can boomerang. Be easy on people; you'll find life a lot easier. Give away your life; you'll find life given back, but not merely given back—given back with bonus and blessing. Giving, not getting, is the way. Generosity begets generosity. (Luke 6:27-38, *The Message*)

One way you can tell that you are walking in the Spirit in your marriage is to ask: Is my husband's response my goal, or am I doing this to please the Lord?

God will enable you to be compassionate to someone who doesn't deserve it, just as He was and is to you.

Ask yourself, "Why is my husband moody and sharp with me?" Often the answer is that you are simply catching the overflow of what happened to him at work, with his parents, or with some other problem. *Is this fair?* No, but life isn't always fair. Consider other reasons as well: Is he stressed about something in particular? Is he fatigued due to extra hours he's putting in at work? Is he going through a difficult time with someone? Ask God to give you understanding and patience during these times and continue to treat your husband lovingly, regardless of how he may be treating you.

Don't be so sensitive that you let your feelings and emotions be set by another's treatment of you. Jesus didn't do that. He continued to live His life with honor, dignity, love, and mercy through the most difficult times. Don't be judgmental or unfriendly. Don't allow yourself to be too easily wounded, crushed, or hurt. Guard against bitterness by being quick to forgive. Ask Jesus to help develop these attitudes in you when you face challenging times.

Be a Blessing

Your job is to bless (1 Peter 3:9, The Message). Put another way, it reads like this:

> Never return evil for evil or insult for insult (scolding, tongue-lashing, berating), but on the contrary blessing [praying for their welfare, happiness, and protection, and truly pitying and loving them]. For *know that* to this you have been called, that you may yourselves inherit a blessing [from God—that you may obtain a blessing as heirs, bringing welfare and happiness and protection]. (1 Peter 3:9, Amp.)

Holy, beautiful women never return harsh words, but instead give a blessing back! One way to do this is through prayer. Do you see that the blessed outcome of our unselfish prayer for our husbands' welfare, happiness, and protection is that we may inherit these things as well?

Have you and your husband ever been in the following cycle? He raises his voice; you raise yours. He becomes louder; you retaliate.

This is an endless cycle, but the dynamics of it can be broken quickly if you no longer react. You can choose to act instead in a manner the Bible says is right. Your consistent, sweet, silent response to poor behavior may be the very thing God uses to change your husband. Don't give in to the urge to let your silence be cold and stony.

When Jesus was oppressed and afflicted, He did not open His mouth (Isaiah 53:7; Matthew 26:63, 27:12-14). Mark says that Pilate was amazed at how Jesus stayed silent in the midst of the accusations that were swirling around Him. Only when He was placed under oath and asked whether He was the King of the Jews did He humbly reply, "Yes, it is as you say" (Mark 15:2).

If your husband is short-tempered and impatient, try remaining silent, in love. Stop participating in the vicious cycle of "he gets angry; I get angry." Choose not to react during heated times. Wait until your husband has cooled down or is more rested before discussing things.

Suppose you had two dogs. Let's say one was red and the other blue. What would happen if you fed only the red dog and not the blue one? The red dog would become bigger and stronger, while the blue one became weaker. Over time, Red would thrive, while Blue shriveled away.

Every time you act in a loving way toward your husband, it's as if you're feeding the red dog and refusing to feed the blue one. The basic principle is simple: *Feed Red, and starve Blue!* Each time you do this, it becomes more and more a part of your natural response. What you're doing is training your mind to think in a new way, and each successive time becomes easier.

Begin now to pray that you will have the strength to do this, and begin praying scripturally and fervently for your husband.

How to Pray Scripturally

An example is given in Colossians of a powerful way to pray. You might consider praying for your husband in such a way. Pray that he will:

- be filled with the knowledge of God's will,
- have spiritual wisdom and understanding,
- walk in a manner worthy of the Lord, living a life full of integrity,
- please the Lord in all respects and do those things that bring glory to God,
- bear fruit in every good work,
- increase in the knowledge of God,
- be strengthened with all power according to the Lord's glorious might,

- attain steadfastness and patience,

- joyously give thanks to the Father, who has qualified us to share in the inheritance of the saints in the kingdom of light. (Colossians 1:9-12, NASB)

Pursuing Peaceful Relationships

For let [her] who wants to enjoy life and see good days [good— whether apparent or not] keep [her] tongue free from evil and [her] lips from guile (treachery, deceit). . . . Let [her] search for peace (harmony; undisturbedness from fears, agitating passions, and moral conflicts) and seek it eagerly. [Do not merely desire peaceful relations with God, with your fellowmen, and with yourself, *but pursue, go after them*!] (1 Peter 3:10-11, Amp.)

We are to actively pursue peaceful relations, not just desire them or wait on them to come our way. Many times our hurt or pride paralyzes us and prevents us from seeking peace with our husbands.

Not long after I (Nancy) had begun to study and apply God's Word to my marriage, I was given an opportunity to live what I was learning. Our daughter Anne had been looking for a vintage 1966 Mustang automobile. She and her dad eventually found the perfect car: yellow with a black leather interior. Ray generously bought it for her and instructed her to watch the oil gauge since it was an older car and used oil more quickly. One day he got a call from Anne, who had just arrived at work.

"Dad, the car is acting strangely. I don't think it has any oil."

Ray was not pleased! We went to Anne's rescue, taking along our other daughter, Christine. As we drove, he verbalized his annoyance with Anne. Since I was completely innocent, I was quite unhappy to listen to what he really should have been telling her.

We arrived at her workplace, and Ray replenished the oil. As we were driving home, he continued to express his disbelief that this could have happened after all the warnings he gave her. I hadn't wanted to hear about it on the way over, and certainly I didn't want to hear about it again on the drive back! Yet what I had learned about pursuing peaceful relations with my husband was fresh in my mind. With great effort, I chose to remain quiet.

This was new to me! My old reaction would have been to utter a few choice words. Instead, I thought about what had just happened. My husband is a wonderful man. He had bought our daughter a beautiful car, and she had been careless with it. And instead of leaving her in the middle of a parking lot trying to figure out what to do, he came to her rescue willingly.

As we drove home, in the midst of his reprise of disbelief, I commented to him, "What a loving dad you are to help Anne when she didn't really deserve it." This comment mysteriously and completely defused him. He immediately returned to his pleasant self.

When we got home, our daughter Christine whispered to me, "Mom, how did you do that?"

"It was God's grace," I told her. She knew it was true because she knew how I usually reacted.

There is no limit to what can happen in a marriage when you begin to apply what you've learned. The blessings are showered down not only on yourself, but also on those around you. One of the sweetest is knowing that God is attentive to your prayers.

> The eyes of the Lord are upon the righteous . . . and His ears are attentive to their prayer. But the face of the Lord is against those who practice evil. (1 Peter 3:12, Amp.)

It is almighty God Himself who will oppose, frustrate, and defeat the one who chooses ungodly ways.

Life is full of opportunities to live out what you profess to believe, and not only your children are watching you. God is observing you as well. As He focuses on you and your life, is He pleased? Are you honoring the Lord by the way you embrace your role as a wife?

Classic Beauty

It is wonderful to realize that when we live God's way and through His power, something happens to us *inwardly* and *outwardly*:

> . . . our faces shining with the brightness of his face. And so we are transfigured much like the Messiah, our lives gradually becoming brighter and more beautiful as God enters our lives and we become like him. (2 Corinthians 3:18, *The Message*)

This is classic beauty in the timeless sense. No blushes, powders, creams, or lotions can give what is being talked about here. *It comes from God alone.* As we allow Him entry into our hearts, the royal paintbrush of His glory is stroked across our lives, and we find ourselves becoming more and more like Him. This is the only beauty that really matters.

Holy beauty.

Simply put, her makeup doesn't make a woman beautiful—her *Maker* does!

Notes

1. *New Webster's Dictionary and Thesaurus of the English Language* (Danbury, CN: Lexico Publications, 1993), 511.
2. Ibid.

Part Eight
Open to Change

*I tell you the truth, unless you change
and become like little children, you
will never enter the kingdom of heaven.
(Matthew 18:3)*

*B*ob and Yvonne Turnbull are a husband-and-wife team who for the past twenty-four years have traveled thousands of miles and spoken before thousands of people, as well as authored nine books, to give their message of hope and help in building relationships that last.

For two and a half years in the 1980s, Yvonne was the on-air nutritionist for *The 700 Club* TV show (CBN). She has a degree in counseling psychology and graduate work in business administration and nutrition.

For thirteen years Bob was a high school and college football and track coach. In the 1970s he served as "The Chaplain of Waikiki Beach," a title given to him by Hawaii Governor John Burns. Bob also served nine years with the Honolulu Police Department. He was also once a professional actor with a credit of nine motion pictures and forty-one TV shows, with the more recent ones being *Highway to Heaven, L.A. Law, Cagney and Lacey* and *Family Ties*. Bob has a master's degree in journalism and a Ph.D. in social psychology.

In the late '80s Bob and Yvonne worked together with another couple ministering to the professional athletes and the wives of the Dodgers, Angels, Rams and Raiders.

The Turnbulls live in the Washington, DC, area after having lived in Orange County, California, for fifteen years. They have a married son, Bob Turnbull V, and he and his family live in the Atlanta area.

Books
I Take Thee
Marriage Mentors
Team Mates

Audio (Series)
Four Secrets for a Successful Family
Out-Smarting Stress

Personality Puzzle
The Power of Goal-Setting and Time
  Management
The Six Habits of a Great
  Communicator

Web
www.turnbullministries.org

The Power Source for Change

Bob and Yvonne Turnbull

"*I* can't believe you said such a stupid thing! That was really dumb!" Yvonne informed Bob while they were sitting in Chicago's O'Hare Airport between flights.

Whoa! thought Bob. *Where did* that *come from?* He was jolted by her sudden outburst, since in the past several years both had veered away from taking cheap, mouthy shots at each other.

Bob didn't say anything. He just gave Yvonne a neutral glance for a second and then went back to the newspaper he was reading. At that particular moment it was the best thing he could have done, because if he had fired back with one of his old-style smart remarks, they would have wasted a lot of energy on an argument. If that had occurred, the Holy Spirit wouldn't have been allowed the opportunity to bring about a needed change in Yvonne.

When Bob didn't respond, Yvonne picked up a magazine and tried to read it, all the while justifying in her mind the way she had spoken to Bob. *Well, he needed to hear what I think is the truth. If he doesn't like it, that's his problem, not mine.* (It's amusing what we say to ourselves when we are wrong in our actions or words.)

Have you ever found yourself reading something that doesn't stick in your brain, so you reread it over and over and over, *hoping* it'll stick? That was happening to Yvonne. She was reading the same paragraph repeatedly, trying to focus on it, while at the same time replaying that last scene with Bob in her mind to justify that she was right.

While she was "reading," Bob, who was sitting right next to her with a newspaper in his face, was quietly praying, *Lord, take her down!* And He was. The Holy Spirit was starting the process of convicting Yvonne of her sin. This was why she couldn't get past the first paragraph of her reading.

It is through conviction of sin that positive change can occur in a person, which, of course, can impact a marriage relationship. This process of change is promised to anyone who has turned control of his or her life over to Jesus Christ. When that happens, God's Spirit—the Holy Spirit—takes residence in our lives and gives us the power to live the lives God desires us to live (see Ephesians 1:19-20). The way that transformation takes place is through conviction of sin—seeing that we are wrong.

But admitting she was wrong was not easy for Yvonne. She felt like "the Fonz" from the '70s TV sitcom *Happy Days,* who would stammer and sputter trying to say the *W* word. Yvonne adds, "We recently saw a similar situation with our five-year-old grandson, Jackson, who needed to apologize for something he'd done to his three-year-old sister, Hannah. He stood stone-jawed with arms tightly crossed over his chest, and he wasn't about to budge from his nonapologetic stance, even though he was told he needed to admit he was wrong. At times I realize I handle life the same way as my grandson. What got Jackson to admit he was wrong was when Hannah reached out and gave him a hug. That melted him."

What melted Yvonne's heart was the Holy Spirit working on her by bringing a Scripture verse to her mind. It was a verse she had recently memorized, Ephesians 4:29: "Do not let any unwholesome talk come out of your mouths, but only what is helpful for building others up according to their needs, that it may benefit those who listen."

It was as though the Holy Spirit was saying, "Excuse me, Yvonne. A few moments ago, weren't you just putting your husband down by telling him he was dumb? That is what is meant by 'unwholesome words.' What would benefit your marriage more is to speak words that would build Bob up, not belittle him."

Yvonne continues, "When these thoughts happen I have a choice: I can respond by admitting I was wrong and asking God's forgiveness, or I can just shrug it off, saying, 'It wasn't really that bad.' What I found in my life is that when I shrugged it off on a regular basis I eventually became insensitive to the conviction of the Holy Spirit. Once that happened I stopped growing and changing. This had a major impact on my marriage, because I started to rationalize that it was Bob who needed to change, not me. Thus everything got out of order. It was only when I decided to stop fooling myself and admit I was wrong that our marriage would grow and stop being hindered by hurt feelings and resentment."

So, there in the airport, Yvonne took a deep breath, put down the magazine (she really wasn't reading it anyway), turned to Bob and said, quite humbly, "Honey, I was wrong in speaking to you the way I did. Please forgive me." Bob gave her a hug, smiled and said, "Hon, thank you. I forgive you."

Bob went back to reading the newspaper and Yvonne went back to her magazine, but this time what she was reading made sense!

Our desire for you as we share this story about an incident in our lives is this: If you haven't been seeing changes in your marriage, you can begin right now by making a commitment daily to surrender your will to God's will. You may want to say the prayer that we use every day:

> Lord, You are in charge of my life today. Direct my thoughts, control my words and guide my actions, that they may bring glory to You. Please do whatever You need to do to change me today. I pray this in the name of Jesus. Amen.

If you pray a prayer like this, watch how God will mightily work in your life and marriage.

Since the late 1980s, Patrick Morley has been one of America's most respected authorities on the unique challenges and opportunities that men face. In 1973 he founded Morley Properties, which for several years was hailed as one of Florida's 100 largest privately held companies. During this time he was the president or managing partner of fifty-nine companies and partnerships. In 1989 he wrote *The Man in the Mirror*, a landmark book that poured from his own search for meaning, purpose and a deeper relationship with God. This best-selling book captured the imaginations of hundreds of thousands of men worldwide. As a result, in 1991 Morley sold his business and founded Man in the Mirror, a ministry to men. Through his speaking and writing, he has become a tireless advocate for men, encouraging and inspiring them to change their lives in Christ.

Every Friday morning Morley teaches a Bible study to 150 businessmen in Orlando, Florida, where he lives with his wife Patsy and their dog, Katie. They have two grown children.

Books

Coming Back to God
The Dad in the Mirror
Devotions for Couples
Devotions for the Man in the Mirror
Discipleship for the Man in the Mirror
Effective Men's Ministry
The Man in the Mirror (also audio)
The Rest of Your Life
Second Half for the Man in the Mirror
Seven Seasons of the Man in the Mirror
Ten Secrets for the Man in the Mirror
Understanding Your Man in the Mirror
The Young Man in the Mirror

Audio

Biblical Manhood
Book of James
Family and the Man in the Mirror
Finding a New Best Friend in Your
   Wife

Finding Respect and Honor at Home
God and the Man in the Mirror
Great Feats of Leadership
How to Make Major Decisions
Living in Two-Part Harmony
Money and the Man in the Mirror
Prayer and the Man in the Mirror
Principles of Success
Sex and the Man in the Mirror
Solomon's Twelve Secrets
Spiritual Disciplines for the Man in
   the Mirror
Success and the Man in the Mirror
Success That Matters
Twelve Tasks of an Effective Father
Work and the Man in the Mirror
and Bible study subscriptions

Web

www.maninthemirror.org

Steps Toward Change

Patrick Morley

Practical Daily Steps to Change

Each year the Minnesota Twins come to Orlando for spring training. Over the course of several weeks, what do you think these million-dollar thoroughbred athletes do? Do they come to Florida to learn about obscure but rarely used baseball strategies? No. They practice fielding, running, batting and conditioning—the basics. Every day they hit, run and field. In the same way the Christian should return to the basics daily.

Daily Preparation

A man's first spiritual discipline is to prepare daily for life among the "weeds." Whether done in early morning or in the evening hour, daily *Bible reading and study* coupled with *prayer* comprise the first essential building block for helping a man to change.

Underline passages that capture your interest. *Memorize* passages for strength, courage and faith. Establish a daily *routine* of seeking God *as He really is* as an act of discipline and an expression of faith.

Write down impressions, ideas and prayers. Keep a *journal* of what you pray about and record the answers in it. I use the acronym ACTS to help me pray. "A" is for adoration—praising God for His attributes. "C" is for confession—asking forgiveness for the sins I have committed. Learn to keep "short accounts" with God. "T" is for thanksgiving—expressing gratitude for His blessings and answers to my prayers. "S" is for supplication—asking for anything and everything that comes to mind for myself and for others. Be persistent in prayer (see Luke 11:5-13).

Daily Temptation

Everyone is tempted to sin every day. God promises He will provide an escape—a safety valve—if we will choose it. When tempted, reject the thought and thank the Lord for giving you the power to have victory over temptation.

> No temptation has seized you except what is common to man. And God is faithful; he will not let you be tempted beyond what you can bear. But when you are tempted, he will also provide a way out so that you can stand up under it. (1 Corinthians 10:13)

Whatever thought pops into our minds, we should take it captive to make it obedient to Christ.

Daily Sin

Everyone sins. Seneca said, "We have all sinned, some more, some less." Inevitably, we are overcome and give way to temptation. When you become aware of your sin, confess it to the Lord and thank Him for forgiving your sins—past, present and future—according to His promise in First John 1:9. Invite Christ to again take control of your life, and get on with the next part of your life. This is the essence of living in the power of the Holy Spirit.

> If we claim to be without sin, we deceive ourselves and the truth is not in us. If we confess our sins, he is faithful and just and will forgive us our sins and purify us from all unrighteousness. (1 John 1:8-9)

Daily Power

When Jesus controls our lives, the power of the Holy Spirit is at work in us (John 14:26; 16:13; Romans 8:9). The Holy Spirit is given to *all* believers (see 1 Corinthians 3:16).

Not all believers enjoy this power because they resist Him or otherwise sin. Even more, most Christians do not understand how to live in a moment-by-moment, daily fellowship with God. The fruit of God's Spirit—love, joy, peace, patience, kindness, goodness, faithfulness, gentleness and self-control—belong to the surrendered man who yields control of his life to the mind of Christ every moment.

If we crucify our own ambition, confess our sins and give Jesus Christ first place in our lives, then the power of the Holy Spirit is available to meet every need. Living by the power of the Holy Spirit is that intense moment-by-moment love relationship with the living Christ in which we soar on wings like eagles, or, having sinned, we tearfully confess and are restored.

Daily Witnessing

If Christ is truly preeminent in our lives, then we will want to tell others about Him. Every Christian has the *command* and the *power* to witness (Acts 1:8). The Great Commission does not say, "Therefore, *37 percent* of you go and make disciples of all nations"—it just says, "go." Do you have the *desire* to see others come to faith in Christ? If not, why? Do you have the *ability* to show someone how to trust Christ for the first time? If not, obtain training (1 Timothy 2:3-4; 1 Peter 3:15).

After all has been heard and considered, it is the human soul alone which passes from this world to the next. Can anything else matter, then, unless we address the need of the human soul first?

Daily Pilgrimage

Life is a struggle. Each day is part of a pilgrimage that prepares us for our eternal destiny. Each day we should set apart Christ in our hearts as Lord. Focus on the good you see and hear. Testify, just as a witness to the jury, about the *changes* occurring in your own life.

Encourage those around you, and meet together regularly for friendship, accountability, Bible study and prayer. To encourage someone is to inspire them to have courage. Attend church where the Bible is believed and Christ is honored. Join a weekly Bible study group. Form an accountable relationship. Pursue your job as a holy vocation. Remember the poor when you give your resources. Be a faithful steward. Stand against bigotry and racial prejudice. Increase your love for God and for people. Remember, no amount of success at the office can compensate for failure at home.

The Sin of Partial Surrender

Many of us go back and forth between the life with Christ and the life in the world—we compromise; we have only partially surrendered to the Lord Jesus Christ. The challenge is to be a certain kind of man—a man committed to the Christian life view, a biblical Christian.

Conclusion

It is time for you to stop just going through the motions and get serious about your eternal destiny and earthly purpose! The examined life *is* worth living! Determine to let Christ explore every inner room of your mind. Christ wants to empower us to break out of the mold of this world and lead an *authentic* Christian life. But it requires daily effort on our part.

My father once had an employee who said, "Mr. Morley, I need to make more money. If you will just pay me more money, I promise I'll work harder."

With a twinkle in his wise eyes my dad responded, "I can see you really have a need. I'll tell you what. I'd like to help. Why don't you go ahead and work harder, and then I'll pay you more money."

We often want God to increase our "pay" without putting forth any effort. To receive the higher wage, though, we need to take some daily steps to know Him as He is.

The pen is in your hands now, so go ahead—write the next chapter! And may God grant you every desire of your heart.

 *L*ori Salierno is the founder and CEO of Celebrate Life International, Inc., which takes character-based leadership training to public schools and other public arenas. A nationally recognized speaker, she has a passion to work for causes that shape culture and aid in the well-being of the youth of today. She travels throughout the United States speaking to audiences of thousands on topics such as personal development, abstinence and faith-based initiatives. Salierno is currently working on the dissertation for her doctorate in leadership development. She resides in Kennesaw, Georgia, with her husband Kurt.

Books
Designed for Excellence
Going the Distance with God
Mercy Beyond Measure
Ordering Your Private Life
When Roosters Crow (also audio)

Audio
Catch a Vision
Creative Communication for Any Audience
Developing a Power-Packed Prayer Life (also CD)
Get Under the Umbrella (also CD)

Going the Distance
Knowing God's Will
Sexual Purity

Video
Balance Is Beautiful (also audio and CD)
Celebrate Life (also audio and CD)
High-Impact Christianity (also audio)

Web
www.celebratelife.org

A Balancing Act 28

Lori Salierno

Editor's Note: There may come a time in our marriage when we realize that we (not only our spouses!) need to change our way of thinking and living. Author Lori Salierno offers some reminders of how we can focus in on the One who can change us like no other.

Most of us today run in the fast lane of life. There are many different reasons why we choose this lane. Yet it is here that we absolutely must pause and examine the bulky weight of constant busy-ness that comes with running in the fast lane. The fact is, we are going to have difficulty finishing our race if we continue at the speed at which we are running. If we are going to persevere, then we must learn to run a balanced race. This will require spiritual nourishment; physical, mental and emotional health; and balance in our various relationships, from families to church to work, and everywhere in between. Busy-ness must be countered with rest, comfort and refreshment.

Please understand right here, at the beginning, that I am speaking to you as one who is still learning. Like you, I continue to struggle to find the best balance in my own life. Yet I also speak to you out of the depth of my experience—what I have learned from others and what I have learned from the hard knocks I've suffered in family life and in serving the Lord in ministry. Let me share with you my two rock-bottom reminders and my three basic axioms for achieving balance in life.

First, the reminders:

Rock-Bottom Reminder #1: The One Good Thing Rule

This is a great thing to make a part of your daily life: Every day, in every area of your life, find the one good thing.

Now, I don't like negative thinking. Negative thinking drains us of our spiritual power. It drains us of creative well-being.

You say you can't find one good thing in your situation? I know it may not be easy to get started. Ask God to show you the redeeming factor right where you are.

Once you find that one good thing, say it out loud. Yes, even if you are all alone. We need to hear ourselves say, "You know what, Lord? I found the one good thing here. It is . . ."

Rock-Bottom Reminder #2: Each Day, Determine Something for Which to Be Thankful

The companion to reminder #1 is to identify one thing each day that is worthy of your gratitude. Again, speak it out loud: "Dear Lord, today I want to thank You for . . ."

Each day, in any and every situation, make these two rules an automatic part of your life. Speak aloud those things that are true, honorable, right, pure, lovely, admirable, excellent or praiseworthy. After all, these are the things about which the Apostle Paul tells us to think (see Philippians 4:8). When you think about these things, you're going to have a balance to your mentality, a balance emotionally and a balance in your perspective. That, right there, is a redeeming factor.

Now, the axioms.

Axiom #1: Find the Positive in Each Situation

If you can find the positive in every situation you face, your most negative feelings will be replaced with a sense of joy and laughter that can bring a calmness to a heavy-laden heart, even one that is working through extremely difficult things. You say you doubt that it's possible to see anything positive in your current situation? Don't be so sure. Take a look at the cross of Jesus Christ. As Jesus' followers watched Him suffer that most pathetic, disgusting of deaths, they must have thought, *There can be nothing positive in this!* Yet God knew otherwise. Three days later, He showed them the positive in all its magnificent glory: Jesus Christ, risen from the grave! Jesus Christ, Redeemer of humanity! Jesus

Christ, Savior of the world. Talk about finding a p̶
tive situation!

If you are a child of God, you have every reason to think pos̶
tively. In fact, a positive perspective should be your regular out-
look on life.

Axiom #2: Discover One Thing to Laugh About Each Day

Did you know that you will be much more likely to solve a problem if you take time for something fun and delightful before you go
on to that problem? You were created for laughter! God Himself created it. He is a God of hope, love and joy—and, yes, of laughter too.

We need to let go and not take ourselves so seriously.

I know that some personalities have a more difficult time laughing than others. I realize some people just don't see things in a very
humorous light. Yet ask the Lord for little moments of humor, and
pause from your busy day to laugh. Just watch what lightness and
balance will come about!

Axiom #3: Look Forward to One Thing Each Week

Every week, find something to which you can look forward. It
might be nothing more than going to the library and reading a
good book, or watching a ball game on television. It might be calling up a friend and saying, "Let's go out for coffee." It might be
something as great as a big date with your spouse.

A Sense of God's Spirit

Can we ever hope to maintain a sense of God's Spirit in this cha-
otic, unpredictable world? Only if we make a definite, concen-
trated effort to do so. It won't just happen, that's for sure. If we
rely on external structures to provide continuity and security in
our day-to-day living, we're going to be in trouble, because the external structures of our lives often go through complete changes.
Therefore, we must have inner strength to handle whatever circumstances or external structures may alter our lives.

"But," some people insist, "I sense God's Spirit in me by the ways in which He uses me." This is great, but here is one very important thing we must understand: God works *in* us before He works *through* us.

Spiritual balance means yielding ourselves completely to God and resting in Him. To help you do this, consider Psalm 91. This psalm is a glowing testimony to the security of those who put their trust in the provision and safety of God. Verses 1 and 2 tell us:

> He who dwells in the shelter of the Most High
>   will rest in the shadow of the Almighty.
> I will say of the LORD, "He is my refuge and my fortress,
>   my God, in whom I trust."

Do you want a sense of God's Spirit? Then dwell in the shadow of the Most High. Rest in His presence. Claim Him as your refuge and your fortress. Ahhh, now that is real peace.

Yes, this is not easy to do in our culture. We are in such a mode of producing and doing that we have forgotten the importance of *being*. The fact is, however, our *being* must precede our *doing*. Only then will we have the maturity to lean back and receive God's best from His merciful hands.

How can we gain the inner strength we need to run the race well? The only way I know is to spend time with God each day.

Time with the Lord, sitting at His feet in worship, doesn't need to take a specific amount of time. It doesn't have to happen at a particular hour or place, and it need not have a distinct format.

I truly believe that it is in seeing the humor in life, and in rediscovering simple pleasures, that we discover why we were created. We can be in Christ, and be aware of His presence, even in the midst of all the different things going on in our lives, if we just train our senses to become aware of Him.

An Attitude of Servanthood

An attitude of servanthood enables us, by the power of the Holy Spirit, to submit to the Lord and serve Him by serving others with humility and joy. When we have the right kind of servant attitude, we will not be easily offended by cynical, critical people or upset when the ones we serve don't appreciate us. When it comes right down to it, the Lord is the only one we serve. So what difference do the praises and affirmation of people make? That's not to say we don't appreciate and enjoy the support and encouragement of others. Of course we do. Yet in true servanthood we can live and serve without it. The Lord's affirmation is enough.

Certainly one aspect of servanthood is developing a meaningful volunteer life, giving out with nothing tangible coming back in return. This might be done under the auspices of a Christian organization, but it doesn't have to be. To do something that takes time and effort on our part and expect nothing in return adds a sense of purpose and meaning to our lives.

Part Nine
Love Restored

And this provides a good picture of how each husband is to treat his wife, loving himself in loving her, and how each wife is to honor her husband. (Ephesians 5:33, The Message)

*R*andy and Deb Kalmbach are living proof that God's amazing grace can carry you through even the most difficult times. In her book, *Because I Said Forever: Embracing Hope in a Not-So-Perfect Marriage*, Kalmbach tells about her own marriage, the struggle of living with her husband's alcoholism and how God mercifully brought them to a place of forgiveness, healing and restoration in their marriage.

Kalmbach offers encouragement, comfort and help for women in difficult marriages, especially where addictive behaviors are involved. She has been a guest speaker at treatment centers for alcoholism and drug addiction, conferences, retreats, Alcoholics Anonymous and Al-Anon. She cohosted a radio talk show, *Straight Talk,* in Seattle, Washington, and has worked as a DJ for a local radio station with her own daily program. Her faith in Jesus Christ and the changes in her own life since she became a Christian in 1976 motivate her to tell her story.

The Kalmbachs recently celebrated more than thirty years of "not-so-perfect" marriage. They make their home in Washington's beautiful Methow Valley with their dog, Kramer, and cat, Nip. Two grown sons, Chris and Jeremy, live in the Seattle area. Randy and Deb love the Methow Valley's quiet and peaceful surroundings (no traffic!) and recreation for all seasons.

Book with Heather Harpham Kopp
Because I Said Forever

*H*eather Harpham Kopp is an editor and author. For four years she wrote a popular column, "Out of the Ordinary," for *Virtue* magazine. She and her husband David make their home in Sisters, Oregon. They have five children between the ages of sixteen and twenty-two who often join them on hikes and camping trips in beautiful Central Oregon.

Books

Baby Stories God Told
The Dieter's Prayer Book
The Dream Giver
God's Little Book of Guarantees
God's Little Book of Guarantees for
Marriage
God's Little Book of Guarantees for
Moms
Lost Boys and the Moms Who Love
Them (also journal)
Powerful Prayers for Your Baby
Powerful Prayers for Your Children

Powerful Prayers for Your
Marriage
Praying the Bible for Your Baby
Praying the Bible for Your Children
Praying the Bible for Your Life
Praying the Bible for Your Marriage
Praying the Bible with Your
Family
Treasured Friends

Book with Deb Kalmbach

Because I Said Forever

Can This Marriage Be Saved?

Deb Kalmbach and Heather Kopp

Restore us, O God Almighty; make Your face shine upon us, that we and our marriage may be saved. (A paraphrase of Psalm 80:7)

"Can This Marriage Be Saved?" is a regular feature in a popular women's magazine. Maybe you've seen it. First a therapist fills us in on the husband's perspective on his ailing marriage. Then we get the scoop from the wife. Often there's a glaring chasm between the two views. The article concludes with recommendations and a prognosis. Sometimes the marriage simply can't be saved and the couple parts.

Is there such a thing as a marriage that can't be saved, one that is too far gone?

Molly thinks so. "My marriage is already dead," she states. "There are no feelings of affection, much less romance. It's like we're already divorced; we just haven't signed the papers or moved out yet. It feels like I'm hauling around a dead body in the trunk of my car, and I need to just admit it's there and dump it."

Sometimes a marriage like the one Molly is describing is in deeper trouble than a marriage where two people are constantly fighting. Where there is fighting, there is passion, emotion and at least some connection between the people. But where there is only a sense of deadness and neither spouse even cares anymore . . . how can you resurrect such a relationship? Is it even possible?

It might take a miracle, but that's what God is in the business of doing.

Experts tell us that a marriage can be brought back from the brink if at least one partner is willing to try, willing to invest energy and effort. Feelings can be reborn and affection restored.

If you identify with Molly but truly want to save your marriage, you need to make some conscious and dramatic changes—beginning with the decision to change almost everything about the way you relate to your husband. Decide that with God's miraculous power and help, you are going to do everything you can to resurrect this marriage. Tell your husband, "I want to save this marriage. I really want to try. I know that we both feel it's dead, a goner. But I also know that God can do miracles."

Ask your husband if he's willing to help. If not, don't let his disinterest dissuade you. Simply proceed on your own to make as many of these changes as possible.

Be willing to reengage emotionally. As unresolved conflicts and feelings pile up over the course of years in a marriage, partners gradually begin to harden their hearts. Maybe you and your husband both disengaged emotionally because it was safer. You learned not to care in order to protect yourself from further hurt and disappointment. But what you may not have realized is that stifling your feelings not only harms your marriage, it harms your emotional health as well. When you stop letting yourself feel pain, you also block your ability to feel deep joy and other positive emotions, including love and affection for your spouse.

In order to reengage emotionally, you must be willing to care again, to be vulnerable and risk pain and rejection. In order to do this, be sure you have fully forgiven your husband for past offenses. You just begin with a clean slate, and then make a conscious decision to reopen your heart.

Renegotiate your relationship. Every relationship has invisible terms that have to do with our expectations. In marriage we have jointly, often wordlessly, agreed on the way things will be, the way they will work. Molly says, "Our terms looked like this: We will go our separate ways in the evening. We will not talk about the relationship unless it's to make negative comments. We don't let each other see our pain or tears. We have an unspoken agreement that we're staying together for the kids' sake. We are expected to be civil. I'm expected to clean house. John is expected to bring home the bacon."

If your husband is willing, ask for his input about what changes to negotiate. Set up a meeting and take notes. Ask each other: What do we want this marriage to be? How can we take one small step toward togetherness? What routines or patterns can we purposely change in order to create more intimacy or unity between us?

If your husband is unwilling to talk or negotiate, you can renegotiate your part by yourself. Decide what you want to change. Write it down. Pray over it. If you begin to implement changes, it will dramatically affect the relationship. When one partner changes his or her patterns, the other partner always reacts. For example, if you stop yelling at him when you argue, you'll be changing the usual dynamics and he won't be able to yell back if that's his usual response.

Try to have new conversations. Many couples fall into a conversation rut. Molly says, "I think one reason John and I didn't talk anymore is that we had a repertoire of exactly five conversations which we had over and over. We talked about the kids and their problems. We talked about John's latest peeves with a peer at his work. We talked about money. We often talked about how we both really should have been exercising more and needed to lose weight. Sometimes it struck me as funny, and I'd tell John we should just make tapes of our five conversations and play them back instead of saying the same things all over again."

It may sound hokey and feel artificial, but it is crucial for you to find new topics for discussion. The trick is to find things that you both are interested in. Try to ask questions that probe the other's personality. Go see an unusual movie together and talk about it. Ask your husband something ridiculous like, "What would you do if you won the lottery?" At first such conversation might seem forced, but often the discussion will gradually lead into a genuine exploration of a topic.

Find a way to have fun together. Or at least find a way to both be enjoying yourselves in the same vicinity. The path back to a marriage with feeling is the path of friendship. And friendships are formed when two people have fun together. If your husband is at all amenable, try to find a new activity you both might enjoy. Join a volleyball league. Take up fishing together. If he doesn't want to try something new, see if he might be willing to involve you in something he already enjoys. In fact, it might be as small as deciding to run two miles together every day after dinner instead of watching the local news. Making one small change like this can be the catalyst to a changed life and marriage.

Get nostalgic. One way to revive the feelings of love that you experienced early on in marriage is to revisit those times. Pull out old scrapbooks. Find that letter he wrote you. Spend time reminiscing about how you fell in love. What did you feel? How did you see your husband? What was it about him that really attracted you to him?

Invite your husband to join you by asking him a question like, "Can you remember our first three dates?" A long conversation about the early days can do wonders to rekindle the desire to feel love again.

Dream a new dream. One of the most painful things about a not-so-perfect marriage is the death of a dream. You may not even realize that you had one, but you did. You pictured how your marriage would be. And it wasn't this. Maybe you thought you were marrying a man with money and a future full of promise, but now he's unemployed and you're miles from the white picket fence.

Your husband had a dream too. And guess what? You're probably not it either. Remember, he's likely just as disappointed and disillusioned as you are.

Sometimes when a dream dies, we need to consciously acknowledge its death, have a cry and let it go. Only then can we begin to dream a new dream, much less embrace it.

The Bible tells us, "Where there is no vision, the people perish" (Proverbs 29:18, KJV). It could also be said that "where there is no dream, the people divorce." One of the best ways to improve your marriage is to begin to dream dreams with your husband.

And if he's content to be stuck where he is and isn't willing to dream with you, dream on your own and pray that God will resurrect the desire to dream in his heart. As much as possible, share with him your own thoughts and hopes for the future. When your husband sees that you're excited, he just might catch the dream bug himself.

Whether you dream together or alone, it's important to get outrageous. Throw out all the preconceived notions and limitations like "We can't move to another town" or "I make too much money at this job to quit." Sometimes making a big change—moving out of the city to a small town or going back to graduate school—can reenergize a marriage.

Do you believe God wants to do a new thing in your lives? Pray for a vision of a different future. Seek Him and His power with all your heart for your marriage. If you haven't ever fasted and prayed, try it. Now!

Remember, God loves your marriage even when you can't feel love for each other. God has plans for the two of you to become something wonderful together even when you can't see it. And God will never ever give up on your marriage even when you want to.

Dear God,
When I feel no hope for my marriage, when love feels like it's died, remind me of what's true: There is always hope because of Your resurrection power at work. Keep teaching the truth of the cliché: Love is not something I feel, but something I do. Please restore in both of us a desire for change and growth. Lead us to the path that will bring healing and fresh starts. I choose to believe that You can save this marriage. Only help me to do my part. Amen.

*D*r. Henry Cloud is a clinical psychologist with an extensive background in both inpatient and outpatient treatment programs and a private practice in Newport Beach, California. He is a specialist on such topics as adult psychotherapy, biblical models of personality functioning and character growth and spiritual issues of psychopathology. He also does extensive organizational consulting and speaking.

Born and raised in Vicksburg, Mississippi, he attended college at Southern Methodist University in Dallas, Texas, where he earned his bachelor's degree in psychology with honors. He attended Rosemead Graduate School of Psychology at Biola University, where he received his M.A. and Ph.D. in clinical psychology with additional graduate-level theological training. He also completed a clinical internship at Los Angeles County Department of Mental Health.

A best-selling author, he has been a guest on *Focus on the Family* with Dr. James Dobson, CBN's *The 700 Club*, Trinity Broadcasting Network and Fox News Network, as well as many other television and radio broadcasts.

Together with Dr. John Townsend, he is cofounder and codirector of Cloud-Townsend, Inc. He cofounded the Minirth-Meier Clinic West, where he served along with Dr. Townsend as its clinical codirector for nine years.

Cloud is an international speaker and the author of *Changes That Heal*. He is the coauthor of many books, including the best-seller *Boundaries*, which was awarded the Gold Medallion Book Award in 1993.

He lives in Southern California with his wife and two daughters.

For a list of resources shared by Drs. Cloud and Townsend, see following page.

Dr. John Townsend was raised in Wilson, North Carolina. He attended college in Raleigh at North Carolina State University, where he received his B.A. in psychology with honors. He then attended Dallas Theological Seminary, where he received his master of theology degree, also with honors. He did further studies at Rosemead Graduate School of Psychology, Biola University, and received his M.A. and Ph.D. in clinical psychology.

Townsend is a clinical psychologist and marriage, family and child therapist. He has an extensive background in both inpatient and outpatient treatment programs and has a private practice in Newport Beach, California. He is a specialist on such topics as biblical models of personality and character growth and spiritual issues of psychopathology.

A best-selling author, international speaker, cofounder and codirector of Cloud-Townsend, Inc. and cofounder of the Minirth-Meier Clinic West, he is the author of the best-selling *Hiding from Love* and coauthor of the Gold Medallion Award-winning *Boundaries* and the Boundaries series.

Townsend lives in Southern California with his wife Barbi and their two sons.

Books

12 "Christian" Beliefs That Can Drive
    You Crazy
Boundaries (also seminar)
Boundaries in Dating
Boundaries in Marriage
Changes That Heal
God Will Make a Way (also seminar)
Hiding from Love
How People Grow
Making Small Groups Work
Safe People

Dealing with Emotional Problems
Growing Your Relationships
Heart's Desire
Keys to Successful Relationships
Learning About Love
Maturity: Becoming the Person God
    Wants You to Be
Relationships, Romance and Reality
Secrets of Soul Mates
Six Steps to Spiritual Freedom
Spiritual Nature of Psychological
    Problems
Top 24 Monday Night Solutions
Why Emotional Problems Are
    Spiritual Issues

Audio (Series)

13 Keys to Spiritual Growth
Boundary Conversations
Boundaries for Life
Crazy Nature of Love

Web

www.cloudtownsend.com

Setting Healthy Boundaries

Henry Cloud and John Townsend

Many times one of the partners [in a failing marriage] will justify unfaithfulness by the other's lack of safety. "Well, if she hadn't been so critical, I wouldn't have had to turn to someone else for love." Or, a wife who has an affair will say, "Well, it wouldn't have happened if he had been meeting my needs."

Nothing is further from the truth. An act of unfaithfulness is something that one person does, not two. As the Bible says of God, "If we are faithless, he will remain faithful, for he cannot disown himself" (2 Timothy 2:13). God does not become unfaithful if we do not love Him correctly. He remains faithful no matter what we do. Marriage requires this as well. Do not let your spouse's failures of love be an excuse for your unfaithfulness.

In short, make a commitment to each other that you will not allow anything to come between you. You will be trustworthy. You will be dependable. You will be sexually and emotionally faithful.

If you struggle with wanting to take some part of yourself to someone or something other than your spouse, find out why. Your actions may be okay; your spouse can't identify with all parts of you. Different interests and different aspects of personal identity keep spouses from totally identifying with each other. One person cannot be all that you need in life. Friends can connect with some parts of you better than your spouse. This is okay. For example, you may like skiing, but your spouse hates it. Find some friends to ski with while your spouse pursues the loves that you don't share. A circle of friends can round out your life.

What is not okay is using some lust to keep you split and keep you from integrating your heart to your commitment. Duplicity is taking your heart away from your marriage and bringing it somewhere else. This is unfaithfulness, in love or in deed. As God says, "Remain faithful until the end."

Often people will get to a point in a boundary-less marriage when they just cannot take it anymore. And they are right. God never meant any relationship to be lived without boundaries, for boundaries enforce His righteous principles. But God never meant for divorce to be the boundary either, and he certainly did not mean for it to be the first real stand that someone takes. That move is basically a defense against growth and change.

God's solution for "I can't live that way anymore" is basically, "Good! Don't live that way anymore. Set firm limits against evil behavior that are designed to promote change and redemption. Get the love and support you need from other places to take the kind of stance that I do to help redeem relationship. Suffer long, but suffer in the right way." And when done God's way, chances are much better for redemption.

Even if your spouse is not growing and maturing, if you take the stances we suggest here, you can be healthy. We have seen many situations turn around when people stop ineffective behaviors, such as nagging, people pleasing and angry leaving, and take a firm stance over a process.

There are many, many unnecessary divorces. God has always intended that we do everything we can to redeem relationships, and not to leave them.

Jesus . . . acts in righteous ways. He will not participate in lies, cruelty, meanness, betrayal, addictions or irresponsibility. He will bring the boundaries of light to every situation and will live them out. Then, if people respond, they have been won over. If they do not, they go away.

In one sense, people with real boundaries could avoid many divorces. But they might have to take a strong stance; separate, not participate in the behavioral patterns against which they are setting boundaries; and demand righteousness before participating in the relationship again. If they become the light, then the other person either changes or goes away. This is why, in most cases, we say you really should not have to be the one who divorces. If you are doing the right things, and the other person is truly evil, he most likely will leave you. But you can rest in the assurance that you have done everything possible to redeem the relationship.

The problem is that sometimes a person thinks that he is setting boundaries, but in reality all he is doing is continuing to blame his spouse and demand change in her without changing himself first. Make sure that you have "gotten the log out" of your own eye before you demand that someone else take the speck out of his.

Here is a reiteration of the path we suggested in our book *Safe People* on how to repair a relationship. It is a different way of saying the same thing we said in the chapter on boundary-resistant spouses:

1. Start from a supported position so that you have the strength to deal with your spouse.
2. Solve your own problems and act righteously toward your spouse. Don't contribute to the problem with your own issues.
3. Use others to intervene (counselors, pastors, friends, family, other people with leverage).
4. Accept reality and grieve expectations. Forgive what has already happened.
5. Give your spouse a chance. After you have stopped enabling your spouse and have set good boundaries in the relationship, give it time. Your spouse may not believe you at first.
6. Longsuffering begins at this point, not earlier when you were contributing to the problem.
7. After doing the right things for a long time, separation is sometimes the only helpful option until someone in denial decides to change. In the separation, do not give your spouse the benefits of marriage if he is not pursuing change. If someone is abusive, addicted, dangerous or has other significant problems, a separation can change his life.

Boundaries in a marriage seek to change and redeem the relationship. Divorce should *never* be the first boundary. You need to set boundaries in the context of relationship, not for the purpose of ending relationship. Take a stance that you will not participate in the relationship until the destruction ends. This is a boundary that helps. But, if you take that stance, make sure that the problem is truly the other person's and that you have followed all of God's steps above.

Obviously, we want ungodly suffering in a relationship to end. But we also want redemption to happen. End your suffering and see if the boundaries you set to end your suffering can be used to bring about redemption and reconciliation as well.

We have seen it happen many times in many "hopeless" situations. When one spouse finally sets true boundaries, the other one turns around. Give it a chance.

*D*avid and Claudia Arp, a husband-and-wife team, are founders and directors of Marriage Alive International, a groundbreaking ministry dedicated to providing resources and training to empower churches to help build better marriages and families. Their Marriage Alive seminar is popular across the United States and in Europe. The Arps are popular conference speakers, columnists and authors of numerous books and video curricula, including *10 Great Dates* and the Gold Medallion Award-winning *The Second Half of Marriage*. Frequent contributors to print and broadcast media, the Arps have appeared as empty nest experts on the NBC *Today* show, *CBS This Morning* and *Focus on the Family*. Their work has been featured in publications such as *USA Today*, *The Christian Science Monitor* and Reader's Digest's *New Choices* magazine. They have been married for over thirty-five years and have three married sons and seven grandchildren.

Books

10 Great Dates Before You Say I Do
10 Great Dates to Energize Your Marriage
52 Dates for You and Your Mate
Choose to Make Your Marriage a Lighthouse
Empty Nesting
Family Moments
Fighting for Your Empty Nest Marriage
God's Words of Life on Marriage
Love Life for Parents (also seminar)
Loving Your Relatives
Marriage Devotional Bible
Marriage Moments
Quiet Whispers from God's Heart for Couples

The Second Half of Marriage (also participant's guide, seminar and video)
Where the Wild Strawberries Grow

Video (Series)
10 Great Dates

Seminars
Before You Say "I Do"
Fun in Marriage Is Serious Business
Marriage Alive
Personalized seminars

Web
www.marriagealive.org

One Great Date 31

David and Claudia Arp

*A*re you looking for a little pizzazz? Do you want your marriage to fly high? You don't have to go all the way to Alaska to add excitement, but you do need to find some time. When was the last time you talked to your spouse for thirty uninterrupted minutes? Would you like to have more fun with your spouse? Is dating something you only did before you were married?

We believe that having a healthy, growing marriage relationship requires friendship, fun and romance. And there's no better way to encourage all of these things than having dates! Great dates are more than going to see a movie and tuning out the world for a while. Great dates involve communicating with one another, reviving the spark that initially ignited your fire and developing mutual interests and goals that are not focused on your careers or your children. Great dates can revitalize your relationship. We've got the proof!

Date One: Choosing a High-Priority Marriage

Pre-date Preparation

- Make reservations at a favorite restaurant. (The one making reservations may want to let the place be a surprise.)
- If applicable, make arrangements for the children. Get a baby-sitter if needed. This could be set up on a regular weekly basis for ten weeks.
- Think about what you will wear. Choose an outfit you think your spouse would like. Remember, this is a date!

Date Night Tips

- Plan to use the whole evening. (Don't think about rushing home for your favorite TV program. If there is something you have to see, use your VCR and record it for another evening.)
- During a leisurely dinner take your own trip down memory lane. You can use the Memory Lane Exercise (Part 1) to jog your memory. Talk about your history.
- Part 2 of the date exercise will help you focus on the present and what is positive about your marriage at this stage of life. Allow enough time for each question and take turns in sharing your answers.

Chapter Summary

From our own time of crisis in the early '70s, we chose three goals to help us make our marriage a priority. By reviewing these goals from time to time, we have built a high-priority marriage, and you can too. The first goal is to look at and evaluate where your marriage is right now. The second goal is to set goals for the future. The third goal is to learn new relational skills to help your marriage grow. On this date, you'll have the opportunity to review your past and look at your marriage as it is today. We suggest also reviewing the three principles for building a successful high-priority marriage: Put your marriage first; commit to grow together; and work at staying close. You can make your marriage a high priority!

Date One Exercise

PART 1—A Trip Down Memory Lane

First time I saw my mate: _____

_____

First date: _____

_____

First kiss: _____

_____

Favorite dates: _____

_____

First time we talked about getting married: _____

_____

Wedding day: _____

_____

First home: _____

_____

First anniversary: _____

_____

Most romantic moments: _____

_____

Happiest memories: _____

_____

PART 2—What's Great About Us!

1. What are three things that are positive about our marriage relationship?

   1. _____

   2. _____

   3. _____

2. What are two things that are fine about our relationship but could be better?

   1. _____

   2. _____

3. What is one thing I personally could do to make our relationship better?

1. _____

Post-date Application

- Look for ways to compliment each other between now and the next date. Give at least one honest compliment each day.
- Do one thing to make your marriage better.

Taken from 10 Great Dates to Energize Your Marriage *by David and Claudia Arp. Copyright © 1997 by David and Claudia Arp. Used by permission of Zondervan.*

Part Ten
Marriage as Ministry

Serve wholeheartedly, as if you were serving the Lord, not men. (Ephesians 6:7)

Nancy Cobb has been the director of women's ministries at Christ Community Church, a church of 6,000, since 1997. She is also a retreat and conference speaker and a frequent radio guest. She came to a saving relationship with Christ in 1981 through the ministry of Anne Graham Lotz, daughter of Billy Graham, who was her teacher and mentor. Seven years later, Lotz, who taught a Bible-study fellowship class of 500 women in Raleigh, North Carolina, providentially chose Cobb to take her place as the teacher of the class. Lotz also selected Cobb to be a seminar leader when she began teaching women at the Billy Graham Training Center at the Cove in North Carolina. Cobb continued in these two ministries until she and her husband Ray moved to Omaha in 1992.

Cobb has coauthored three books with Connie Grigsby. The first was a finalist for the Gold Medallion Award and has just been rereleased as *The Politically Incorrect Wife*. Their second book, *How to Get Your Husband to Talk to You*, was a finalist for The Books for a Better Life Award. Their third book was released in September 2003.

The Cobbs have four children and one grandson.

Books with Nancy Cobb
The Best Thing I Ever Did for My Marriage
How to Get Your Husband to Talk to You
The Politically Incorrect Wife

Media
Lifewalk (KHBI, Omaha's Christian radio station)

*C*onnie Grigsby, a popular teacher and speaker, is coauthor of *The Politically Incorrect Wife* (formerly titled *Is There a Moose in Your Marriage?* and a finalist for the prestigious Gold Medallion Award) and *How to Get Your Husband to Talk to You* (a finalist for The Books for a Better Life Award) and has also written *How to Get Your Teen to Talk to You*. Another book, *The Best Thing I Ever Did for My Marriage*, was released by Multnomah Publishers in the fall of 2003.

With her trademark love for people and enthusiasm for life, Grigsby enjoys pointing others toward life's "bottom line." With warmth and humor, she exhorts others to refuse to be content with a "ho-hum" relationship with their Savior—which she herself was for over twenty-five years. Calling others to live beyond the casual is her passion.

Grigsby enjoys spending time with family and friends, playing tennis and eating other people's cooking. A graduate of the University of Oklahoma, she and her husband Wesley have been married for twenty-three years. They have three teenage daughters and make their home in Omaha, Nebraska.

Books
   How to Get Your Teen to Talk to You

Books with Nancy Cobb
   The Best Thing I Ever Did for My Marriage
   How to Get Your Husband to Talk to You
   The Politically Incorrect Wife

Media
   Lifewalk (KHBI, Omaha's Christian radio station)

Marriage Is a Ministry

32

Nancy Cobb and Connie Grigsby

It is an amazing thing to realize that as a woman serves her husband, Jesus Christ considers Himself the One served.

*I*t was 6:00 in the morning and I (Connie) was nearing the end of my run on the treadmill. I go regularly to my husband's place of employment and work out in the exercise room. A young woman whom I had never seen before came into the room, acknowledged me, and began walking on the treadmill beside me. She briefly looked over some note cards and then tossed them to the floor.

"Are you studying for something?" I asked.

"Yes," she replied. "I have boards coming up soon, and I'm trying to prepare for them."

After talking with her for a few minutes, I discovered that she was a fifth-year surgical resident and was six months away from completing the program. Written boards would follow, and she was beginning to review for them. She already had a job lined up in a nearby city.

She went on to say that she had just turned forty and had been married for five years. I asked her whether she thought her marriage was easier or harder than most, given the fact that she had waited until she was thirty-five to marry.

"You'd think it would be easier," she said, "but I'm not so sure. Marriage is hard. *Hard!* Far harder than medical school and residency combined."

Her bold statement piqued my interest, and I loved that she was so open and honest. "A friend and I are writing a book on marriage," I said, "so I find your comments fascinating. What do you think makes it so hard?"

"Do I have to be more specific than to simply say 'everything'?" She laughed before going on. "I guess I would say that the most difficult thing to me is how marriage seems to boil down to two people reacting to one another. We didn't react when we were dating, yet now these reactions seem to define our marriage.

"Well," she continued, "I guess we did react when we were dating, but the reactions were positive. We were drawn to one another through them. But after the wedding, the reactions took a turn. Suddenly, it's one negative reaction after another, and instead of being drawn together, we've drifted apart."

I asked for an example.

"Say my husband hurts my feelings. I express that my feelings are hurt and attempt to tell him why. He becomes defensive and says I'm too sensitive. I question his ability to gauge my sensitivity level and suggest he look into a course on sensitivity training. He responds with a remark of his own. Before you know it, we're not speaking to one another, and neither of us can even remember the original problem."

"What gets you back on track?" I asked.

"Usually, after a day or two, both of us grow weary of this behavior, and we begin to slowly treat one another with civility again. However, I can't help but believe that every time we do this, we get further and further from the marriage we had both hoped for, because now, even when things are good, they're not all that great." She sighed and shook her head.

Her honesty and vulnerability surprised me. Here was a woman who would seem to have the world at her feet. She was attractive, intelligent and pleasant. Very soon a successful medical practice would be hers as well. Yet here she was, at 6 in the morning, talking with a stranger about the pitfalls of marriage.

I then asked a penetrating question that had served as one of the turning points in my own marriage. "What is your motive for being married?"

A puzzled look crossed her face. "Motive?" she echoed. "What a strange question." With a chuckle she said, "I think of *murder* and *motive* going together, not *marriage* and *motive*. Let's see, what is my motive? Surely if I can get through a surgical residency, I can come up with a plausible sounding motive for marriage—but I can't."

She thought for a few moments more, but remained stumped. She had no idea what her motive in marriage was. *Do you?*

Motives

For years we were like the woman in the story. We had no idea that God had something to say about motive in marriage. One of us did not know the Lord, and although the other did, there was complete ignorance in this regard. We wanted to be happy in our marriages and hoped our husbands were as well, but frequently this was not the case. Once we began learning our job descriptions as wives, we quickly discovered that unless a woman's motive for her marriage lines up with God's plan, fulfillment and satisfaction will elude her.

The Apostle Paul, inspired by the Holy Spirit, told us what God said about motives when he wrote this:

> Whatever you do, work at it with all your heart, as working for the Lord, not for men, since you know that you will receive an inheritance from the Lord as a reward. It is the Lord Christ you are serving. (Colossians 3:23-24)

Do you see it? It is the *Lord Christ* you are serving. That's the motive for your marriage. As you serve your husband, you are actually serving *Him*. What an incredible opportunity!

Too often we think of marriage as a relationship between two people. More than that, though, it is about our relationship with the Lord. Perhaps this is news to you, as it was for us at one time. Is it good news or bad?

Satan attempts to make you focus on yourself and what you want, as he did with Eve in the Garden. Doing this causes you to forget the "as unto the Lord" part of your marriage.

This passage is the nuts and bolts not only of marriage, *but of life itself*. This verse illustrates a simple but powerful process, and when you choose to implement it in your marriage, you will never be the same.

Work at It with All Your Heart

Whatever you do, you are to work at it with all your heart: cleaning the house, wiping a nose, visiting a neighbor, carrying out job responsibilities, serving in church, *being a wife*.

When work is done without putting your heart into it, the outcome is compromised and the process is stagnating and unfulfilling.

When I (Connie) was a young girl, my parents went to town one morning to buy groceries. They told my sister and me to go out to the garden and pick the green beans while they were gone. It was summertime, and we wanted to watch a few programs on television we normally didn't get to see. This sounded far more fun than working in the garden. After a brief consultation, we decided that we would blitz the rows of beans, picking just enough to appease our parents. We grabbed two small sacks and filled them. We set the beans on the back porch, headed to our black-and-white television set, and eagerly turned it on. Ah, the rewards of a hard morning's work!

A few hours later our parents came home and asked if we had done our chores.

"Yes," we replied, I suspect a bit anxiously. We mentally crossed our fingers and hoped that would be the end of it.

"Where are the beans you picked?" my mother said. "I think I'll snap some for supper."

"On the back porch," I answered, suddenly wishing I had done a better job.

We heard the back door open and exchanged nervous glances as our mother went out. We then heard Mom conferring with Dad. He called us to the back porch, and, hearts dropping, we went.

"I thought you said you picked the beans," he said to us.

"Well, we kind of did," we said, trying our best to sound convincing.

" 'Kind of' isn't good enough," he said, "When you've been given a job to do, you do it the best way you know how. I don't want to hear any more about this 'kind of' stuff. Now, go get a couple of sacks and let's go pick the beans."

Is that how you're living—in a "kind of" fashion? Can you see that if that's what you're doing, you're serving the Lord in that same manner? Don't you want to be a woman who serves Him with excellence? One way you can do this is by ministering to your husband. When you do, your motive and God's Word are aligned, and that is where deep satisfaction and peace lie.

"Tell Me More"

One morning while we were working, a friend called. She asked how the writing was going. We told her we were in the middle of this chapter.

"It's about the whole idea of marriage being a ministry," we told her.

"Fascinating concept," she said, enunciating the words as only someone from England can. "I like that thought, although frankly I must say that I have no idea what you mean by ministry. You see, I was raised in a church that didn't speak about ministry, so I'm a bit confused by the whole thing. I'd love to know more, though."

Ministry simply means "to serve." When a pastor comes to minister to a church, he comes to serve the people and the needs in that church. Ultimately, though, he is serving God.

That is what is meant by ministry in your marriage. As a wife, you are to minister to, or serve, your husband. As you do so, Jesus considers Himself served.

Marriage as a ministry was a life-changing concept for us and totally revolutionized the way we interacted with and served our husbands. Jesus Christ was now a part of the picture. Certainly we already knew He was in our midst, but when we realized that the way we treated our husbands was considered by Jesus to be the way we treated Him, it forced us to take a hard look at our actions in our marriages.

Beginning to Change

Once you understand this concept, you can begin to see how the idea of ministry in marriage might bring changes to your life.

Let's say your husband has told you he'll be home at 5:30 in the evening and will be ready for dinner at 6. Uncharacteristically, he's not home, and it's now 6 o'clock. The meal is ready, and the children (and you!) are growing hungrier by the minute.

Six-thirty comes and goes and still no husband. You decide to go ahead and feed the children and are cleaning up after them at 7 o'clock, when your husband comes through the door. Normally, your first reaction might be, "Where were you? Why didn't you call? You're an hour late and dinner is cold." You want to let him know the inconvenience and irritation he's caused you.

However, if you view marriage as a ministry, your first thought would be for him. You would cheerfully greet him and ask if everything was OK. You would tell him how glad you are that he's home and graciously reheat his dinner. You might offer him compassion and warmth, letting him know how sorry you are that his day was so long. Certainly it's fine to ask him later on to please call the next time he's running late, but guard against doing so in an exasperated, judgmental fashion.

Are you beginning to get the picture? Or does it seem rather one-sided to you? Could pride be rearing its ugly head? More often than not, pride is what chokes out a ministering spirit in a marriage. Did you know that God actually resists the proud? Proverbs 3:34 says that God resists the proud but gives grace to the humble.

There have been many times when I (Connie) have wrestled with pride in my marriage. When this occurs, ministering to my husband is the last thing I feel like doing. I know what I'm called to do—but I don't want to do it.

Why would God bless an attitude like that? Be assured, He doesn't! No wonder I feel so miserable when those times occur. I'm not only missing out on God's blessing, I am experiencing His *resistance* as well.

As you begin to minister to your husband "as unto the Lord," you may need to remind yourself, especially at first, why you are choosing to do this. You're actually serving Jesus when you serve your husband.

Our model is Christ Himself:

> But whosoever will be great among you, let him be your minis-
> ter; And whosoever will be chief among you, let him be your
> servant: Even as the Son of Man came not to be ministered
> unto, but to minister, and to give his life a ransom for many.
> (Matthew 20:26-28, KJV)

Isn't it tempting to think about only wanting to be ministered
to? Yet Jesus set the example for ministry: It is to be *others focused*.
Once again you might be tempted to think that your ministry to
your husband depends on his doing his part. So many times
women tell us that things like this will work only if he does his part
and that it has to be a mutual thing. But this simply isn't true.
Your husband may *never* do his part. Does that give you permission
to disobey Jesus' command? Of course not! Why would you allow
someone else's ungodly choice to impact your own? How many
times have you told your children to do what they know to be
right, even if they're the only ones doing it? The same is true for
you!

As you live this way, you will see seemingly small, trivial things
in your life begin to change. Ministering will create great inroads
to joy and peace into your marriage. I (Nancy) remember how this
occurred in my marriage. This took place almost twenty years ago,
yet it still comes vividly to mind.

Who Will Walk the Dog?

I had been a Christian for a short time when I heard a speaker
who encouraged us to have prayer time every morning. She suggested that we pray for one hour. I thought to myself, *An hour?
How can a person pray that long?* But I wanted to try.

About the same time, a friend asked me, "What does your husband do for you?"

I thought. And thought. And thought some more. Never mind
that I was able to stay home, had a new car and lived in a lovely
home. My husband was a wonderful man, and I had a great life,
yet I could think of nothing. I finally said, "He walks our dog." My
husband had given me a dog for Christmas, and he walked him every morning.

I awoke for my prayer time that first morning and slipped out of bed. I quietly left the room and closed the door behind me. The dog began to bark and scratch at the door. My husband called out, "Where are you?" I replied, "I'm praying." So he got out of bed and dutifully took care of the dog.

The next day, the same thing happened. This time my husband asked, "What are you doing?"

"I'm *praying*," I said, this time a little more emphatically.

"For the whole world?" he asked in frustration. Again, he got out of bed and took care of the dog.

On the third day I awoke and started to slip out of the room. Once again the dog began to scratch the door and bark to be taken outside. *What is the big deal here?* I thought to myself. *I'll walk the dog before praying.*

A bit grudgingly, I took the dog outside. I still remember the beauty of that early morning. The sky was magnificent, and the moon cast shadow about me. I'm not sure I had ever seen the stars in the early morning before. The birds were chirping. It was a new day, and I was so thankful to be a part of it. The cool air stirred my soul. As I walked to the end of the driveway, I noticed the newspaper lying there.

I thought, *Why don't I take the newspaper along with a cup of coffee?* So I did. This seemingly insignificant choice was the beginning of my developing a new heart of love for my husband and receiving an overwhelming supply of love from him. I had chosen to serve him. In doing so, I had chosen to serve the Lord as well.

I felt so happy. Joy and contentment flooded my soul. I knew without a doubt that I was in a place of blessing from the Lord.

Had I not chosen to walk the dog, I never would have experienced the beauty of the morning or noticed the newspaper lying in the driveway. I wouldn't have picked it up or thought about taking my husband a cup of coffee.

Who would have thought that such a small, seemingly inconsequential thing would change my marriage so radically? Yet it did, because it began the change in me.

Change Starts with You

Is your marriage in need of change? Perhaps it has been so cold for so long that it seems hopelessly frozen. But it's not! Can you begin to see that, regardless of how you've conducted yourself in your marriage before, now it's time to conduct yourself "as unto the Lord"?

Perhaps this is disheartening news to you. You may not be ready to treat your husband in this manner, yet you can no longer justify your current treatment of him. What are you called to do in such a case? You are called to be obedient to God's Word, regardless of your feelings toward your husband.

No doubt, there are many times in your marriage when your husband has made mistakes. Perhaps he has hurt your feelings, made an error in judgment, or been unduly harsh with you or the children. When this happens, it is natural to feel that he doesn't deserve to be treated well. Your tendency might be to withdraw or to lash out at him.

But the real issue isn't how your husband deserves to be treated, *but how Jesus deserves to be treated*. This makes it so simple! And it is motivating as well.

When you treat your husband coldly, it's as if Jesus Christ is right there with you, and you are treating Him coldly, too. This puts things in a completely different perspective. The way you're serving Christ, right now—today—is a direct reflection of the way you're serving your husband. *In fact, it's been said that your present relationship with your husband is a spiritual barometer of your relationship with Christ*. The Lord notices your efforts and promises a reward for your faithful service.

An Inheritance from the Lord

One of the great promises of God is that He will reward you for the work you do as a sincere expression of your devotion to Him. *He notices what you do!* We cannot overstate this fact. Don't look to your husband to reward you for your ministry to him. God will do that!

There is a present reward—you will experience His presence and His power through the Holy Spirit. The supernatural outcome of this is fruit bearing.

There is a future reward as well as a present reward. There will be a time in eternity when you will be rewarded by Christ. He will give you crowns.

A crown that lasts forever. (1 Corinthians 9:25)

A crown of exultation. (1 Thessalonians 2:19, NASB)

A crown of righteousness. (2 Timothy 4:8)

The conqueror's crown of glory. (1 Peter 5:4, Amp.)

A crown of gold. (Revelation 4:4)

How wonderful to have crowns to lay at His nail-pierced feet. What else would we have to give Him? After all, we have nothing to boast of as we serve Him because anything done *for* Him is enabled *by* Him.

Ministering to a Difficult Husband

Perhaps you have a husband who is difficult toward you, and you are battling resignation and discouragement. Perhaps your husband is outright cold or mean-spirited and frequently puts you down. It is especially important for you to serve your husband "as unto the Lord" during those times and not slip back into believing that your husband's response determines your actions. It is helpful to remember that your will, not your feelings, determines your actions. This doesn't mean that your feelings of hurt or rejection will automatically disappear—they won't. It means, though, that you are choosing to serve God regardless of your husband's behavior. Fervently seek God during those times and ask Him to heal your wounds.

We know of a woman whose husband constantly blamed her for their poor marriage, even though it appeared she was working at it with all her heart. What did she do? She prayed even more fervently for her husband and her marriage and asked God to give her the strength to serve her husband as she would Him. And she boldly asked Him to enable her to do it in a joyful manner. "My hope is that my marriage will eventually change. But my greater hope is that I can one day stand before the Lord and have Him say to me, 'Well done, good and faithful servant. You were faithful to the end.' "

It's easy to lose focus. This is especially true if you have a husband who is not responding to your efforts. God knows what is happening. Although at times He may seem far away, He is not. He is right there, closer than the beat of your heart, waiting to comfort and encourage you. He sees every action, hears every word, notes every hurt. He sees you pushing on as the storm rages around you, *and He does not forget it*. Scripture assures us of that.

This may be all that you have to hold on to. Remember that your heavenly Father will one day look at you and reward you for your godly behavior. Your heartache and pain will be erased forever, and you will receive an inheritance like no other—a royal inheritance given to you personally by Jesus Christ.

Does your motive need to change? Doing so is just a choice away.

The Husband Paraphrase

We thought it would be fitting to end with our paraphrase of Matthew 25:35-40.

> *I was hungry for breakfast, dinner,*
> *and sometimes even lunch, snacks,*
> *a kind word, a warm hug, to talk to you, to be loved by you. . . .*
> *You gave me something to eat.*
> *I was thirsty to feel accepted by you,*
> *to take the leadership role in our home,*
> *to be admired by you, to be respected by you.*
> *I mowed the lawn and needed refreshing and . . .*
> *You gave me something to drink.*
> *I was a stranger, my mood was bad.*
> *I had been unreasonable.*
> *I had been mean, thoughtless, forgetful, unhelpful, self-centered. . . .*
> *You invited me in.*
> *I was naked, you did all my wash*
> *even when I dropped it on the floor.*
> *You sewed on my missing buttons.*
> *You ironed my wrinkled shirts.*

You let me bare my soul to you.
You saw the real me that others never see—
with all my quirks and uncovered ugliness,
and you never exposed me before our children, family or friends. . . .
You clothed me.
I was sick—you know my colds are worse than anyone else's.
Sometimes I said things to you I didn't mean.
I got depressed and . . . You cared for me.
I was in prison; my job got me some days and I withdrew from you.
When I was lonely you were there for me.
You prayed for me.
When I was consumed with a problem,
when I was unforgiving, when I didn't deserve anything
because of the way I've treated you and I was so ashamed. . . .
You came to me.
Jesus would say to you, "When you did these things for
your husband, you did them for Me."

Press on! An inheritance from the Lord awaits you.

Press on! Can't you hear the trumpets sounding? The heavens applauding? Can't you imagine the misting of your eyes as they meet the sweet soft gaze of His? Can't you sense the swelling of your heart and the joyful singing of your soul as He wraps His loving arms around you and says, "Well done"?

Press on! As you serve your husband, you serve the King of kings and the Lord of lords! Your efforts are of great worth to Him!

 Christian family and marriage counselor for twenty-two years, Steve Prokopchak earned his master of human services degree from Lincoln University. Through counseling, teaching and writing, he trains people within the Body of Christ in biblical counseling, teaching and writing. He does this work because he believes it is important to "equip the saints for the work of ministry."

As a member of the Apostolic Council of DOVE Christian Fellowship International (DCFI) in Ephrata, Pennsylvania, Prokopchak helps to provide oversight and direction for DCFI churches. He also serves on the USA Team of DCFI and the International Advisory Apostolic Group.

It is his personal vision and heart's cry to see people made whole in their personal lives, marriages and families. In his own words, he is willing to "hang in there with people" so that the life of Christ can be built in their lives. Countless individuals have been affected by his training, whether it is one-on-one or through seminars, conferences, marriage retreats and written materials. He travels regularly, ministering in churches across the nation and internationally giving people the various leadership and counseling tools they need.

The Prokopchaks have been married for twenty-eight years, have three children and reside in Elizabethtown, Pennsylvania.

Books

Called Together: A Marriage Preparation Workbook

Counseling Basics for Small Group Leaders

In Pursuit of Obedience: Deepening Our Love for God Through Obedience

Booklets

People Helping People series

Is There a Mission in Marriage?

33

─────── *Steve Prokopchak*

Scott works fifty-five hours a week in the computer field, and his wife Jan is a part-time registered nurse who logs twenty-five hours a week. They have three children and attend Crossroads Community Church as a family. Scott enjoys working with the Boys Brigade, and Jan serves on the church's hospitality committee. Every other Saturday morning, Scott participates in a men's prayer breakfast.

After considering Scott and Jan's busy schedule, I had just two simple but provocative questions for them: "For what reason(s) has God called you, as a couple, together?" and the even deeper question, "Just what do you think is the purpose of this thing we call marriage?"

I have traveled throughout the United States and into many foreign nations asking these two questions. My wife and I have conducted marriage seminars with hundreds of couples and have asked these same questions to the participants. We have served many couples in counseling and again asked them to respond. We are not surprised by the answers we hear. Often the couples have no answers. A few make a feeble attempt to answer. Rarely do we hear the responses we are looking for.

How would you and your spouse answer these two questions? Take a moment to discuss them. You may be surprised by your responses.

Marriage: God's Bright Idea

Marriage was God's idea. Marriage predates Christianity. Marriage is, in fact, an act of creation. People of all religions of the world marry, not just Christians. But what makes marriage so different for the Christian? When two persons come together as one, what is the purpose? While Scott and Jan lived a busy life, they were missing something vital to a lifelong union—walking in the purpose and mission of their call together.

I would like to share not *a* purpose, but what I've discovered to be *the* purpose of marriage after twenty-eight years of personal commitment to marriage. I have never heard this spoken at a wedding ceremony by the preacher. I have never heard it taught in a marriage seminar, and I have yet to hear it preached from the pulpit or academic broadside. I have come to believe, without a shadow of a doubt, that the purpose of marriage is *to build the life of Christ in my mate*.

In the book of Colossians, Paul the apostle reveals his love and sacrifice for the Church. He became a servant commissioned by God Himself. He presented the gospel in its fullest, and in verse 28 of chapter 1 he reveals the purpose: "We proclaim him, admonishing and teaching everyone with all wisdom, *so that we may present everyone perfect in Christ.*" What was his purpose? To present everyone perfect in Christ. Again, he shares a similar goal with the Galatian Christians in chapter 4, verse 19: " . . . until Christ is formed in you."

Here you have a scriptural mandate for what I believe to be foundational to the purpose of a Christ-centered marriage—building Christ. To Scott and to Jan, to you and to me, it means that everything I do, everything I think, every look on my face is filtered through this thought: "Is what I'm thinking, is what I'm about to say, is what I'm about to do going to build Christ in my spouse?"

"To build the life of Christ" is a phrase to commit to memory until it becomes a Holy Spirit sieve in my mind and my spirit. If my goal is to build the life of Christ in my mate, then I will not hurt my mate in thought, word or deed—it's that simple.

A Common Mission

One of the most important ways of building this life answers our first question. While Scott and Jan had their jobs and separate ministries, they lacked knowing and understanding their cooperative mission.

The Father sent His Son to the earth to fulfill a mission. Before Jesus left this earth, He revealed what we now refer to as "The Great Commission." As believers, we are in a mission with our triune God to "go" with the gospel—to the ends of the earth.

Here is the crucial question: Does your marriage have a mission? This may be the most vital missing ingredient.

What Does Couple Mission Look Like?

My wife Mary is involved in local politics. She is called to this, and I pray for her and bless her as she fulfills her calling. I am not called to the political arena. On the other hand, I am called to travel and teach more than she is. She blesses me and prays for me as I fulfill this mission. Together, however, we are called to numerous cooperative missions. We will share our personal mission statement with you:

> To love and to serve God; to love and complement one another in order to see the purposes of God fulfilled in our spouse's life; to raise our children in the truth of God's word—equipping them to live godly in a perverse generation; to be people helpers in the body of Christ—be it through counseling, nursing, teaching, pastoring, etc.; to share Christ with a dying world; to live debt-free in order to send more finances into the kingdom of God.

Adam and Eve had a mission from God: Bring increase to the earth and tend the garden. You and your spouse were called together for a purpose, a mission. Do you know what that mission is? Are you running a business together, training children, influencing grandchildren, farming, planning to do mission work or going back to school? Whatever it is, you can incorporate it into your mission statement. May I suggest the following steps to help you create this statement in order for you to better reach the purpose of your call together?

- Step 1: Begin by listing areas that you and your spouse are presently prioritizing. (This may include raising a family, jobs, ministry, etc.)
- Step 2: List any other desires you each have that you would also like to see included in your marriage mission.

- Step 3: Start building your mission statement in writing by incorporating the above areas into a marriage mission paragraph.

- Additionally, I strongly encourage you to write practical goals that will move you toward your cooperative mission statement. Begin recording these goals and commit to maintaining accountability with one another. Consider placing a time frame on each goal. For example: *We are committed to live debt-free; therefore, we will pay extra money to the principle of our thirty-year mortgage in order to complete repayment by year fifteen.* This goal is specific and has a timetable.

Consider something else that Mary and I have found to be of extraordinary value to us as a couple—an annual review/evaluation. You most likely face one of these at your workplace. The idea is not to have a negative evaluation but a life-giving overview of where you are as a couple.

Each year, Mary and I go away for an overnight trip in the month of December. The sole purpose is to review our year, assess where we are as a couple—spiritually, emotionally, financially and with our family. That means we take with us our mission statement, our schedules, our budget, our memories from the past year and our visions for the year to come.

We begin by praying and asking for God's direction through our time together. We first pray about everything we plan to cover and evaluate. It goes so much more smoothly if we commit it all in prayer first. We then practically review all the ministry we're involved in. Is God calling us to this area for the coming year, or is He wanting to change something? What committees are we serving on? Again, we review the call and the mission. What about our finances? Will there need to be cutbacks? Can we give more to missions?

When we leave the motel, we leave united and in agreement for the coming year. We review our mission statement and update it if necessary. Many cooperative mission decisions have come from this weekend together. It has always been a God-ordained time. We close with more prayer. And, if we get stuck on one issue, we stop and pray. The Lord always sees us through, even in the challenging areas.

So, for what reasons has God called you and your mate together? And what is the purpose of your marriage? We know these two questions will be a challenge to you as a couple to answer. I have come to believe they are fundamental to your marriage and your call together as a couple. If you'll take the time to answer them, you will find yourselves at a new place of commitment. Marriage is a call from God. And after twenty-eight years, I have come to realize that discovering our marriage mission can be the glue that helps to hold that call from God together.

Request of one another how you can further build the life of Christ in your spouse and take steps to do so. Provide one or two specific areas. Do not overwhelm your husband or wife with too many responses.

As you sincerely practice this simple but biblical phrase in your marriage, you will soon discover the God-ordained purpose of giving birth to children: *to build the life of Christ in my child*. And one day, your children will discover this purpose for themselves, as they build the life of Christ in your grandchildren.

*C*alled "musical ambassadors to the family" by Dr. James Dobson, Steve and Annie Chapman send straightforward messages of hope and healing to Christians as well as offer the life-changing message of the gospel to those seeking the Truth.

Originally friends who met in West Virginia, the Chapmans now reside near Nashville, Tennessee. Since their wedding day in 1975, they have worked and traveled together as a musical team as well as raised two children, Nathan and Heidi, who are now grown and married. Their stated ministry goal is, "Believing that the family is under severe attack, we want to put our efforts toward encouraging husbands and wives, mothers and fathers, and children of all ages to pursue righteousness. Like spokes in a wagon wheel, as each family member draws near the hub, Jesus Christ, they will indeed be drawn closer to each other. Putting Christ at the center of a home is the key to a healthy family!"

Books
The Family Album Songbook
The Hunter/Full Draw (Steve)
A Look at Life from a Deer Stand (also audio) (Steve)
Married Lovers, Married Friends
Putting Anger in Its Place (Annie)
Reel Time with God (Steve)
Running on Empty (Annie)
Smart Women Keep It Simple (Annie)
Wednesday's Prayer (Steve)
What Husbands & Wives Aren't Telling Each Other
With God on the Open Road (Annie)

Recordings
At the Potter's House
Chapters
Coming Home . . . For Christmas
An Evening Together
Family Favorites
For Times Like These

Kiss of Hearts
Long Enough to Know
A Mother's Touch
Never Turn Back
The Silver Bridge
This House Still Stands
Tools for the Trade
Waiting to Hear

Video
The Greatest Gift

Seminars
If Two Are Better Three Is Best
It Takes the Carpenter to Build a Good Home
Married Lovers/Married Friends
Now and Forever

Web
www.steveandanniechapman.com

Romance Starts with a Servant's Heart

Steve and Annie Chapman

A h, romance! I [Steve] remember the passionate sighs, the $400 long-distance telephone bills and roses for no reason. The feeling that life began the day _she_ walked into my dreary existence.

How I remember when those emotions first began to churn in me for Annie, the woman who would become my wife. I sent her flowers, told her she was beautiful, and even came to a complete stop at all the stop signs when she rode with me. Romance was bustin' out all over, and it was grand.

If only this delicious state of emotional intensity was as easy to maintain as it is to fall into.

Secrets Hallmark Never Told You

An engaged couple strolls down the street, hand in hand, pretty as a greeting card. Accidentally, the little lady steps on her man's foot. As he pulls her spike heel out of his arch, he gushes, "Don't worry about it, sweetheart. I've got a second foot right over here. Think nothing of it." Is he offended? Never! He seizes the opportunity to show her how incredibly tough he is in the face of pain.

Now let's fast-forward to their fifth wedding anniversary. They're walking down the same street, and she's wearing those same shoes. Yikes! She plants that spike right back into the hole in his foot she bored before. But this time as he pulls the heel out, he gives her a look that would smack King Kong into submission. "Just because you look like Bigfoot don't mean you have to walk like him, too!" he snarls. "Why don'cha watch where you're goin'?"

And he isn't the only one who's lost the romance. When she heard him say, "Wilt thou . . . ?", she wilted. The problem is, she hasn't revived since.

Unfortunately, romance seems to be a premarital condition that is cured instantly by a trip to the altar. A woman in one of our marriage seminars once gave this definition of romance: "It's the attraction during courtship that vanishes with the words 'I do.' " Most couples take "I do" to mean "Maybe I *did* when I was still trying to woo you, but I sure *don't* intend to anymore!"

Those of us who believe in Christ often don't do much better, sad to say. As I've heard a popular Christian speaker say:

> To dwell above with saints we love
> Now, won't that be glory?
> But to live below with those we know . . .
> Well, that's another story!

Where Does the Romance Go?

What happened? Why did the romance fade?

We believe it's because we've been injected with a massive overdose of soap opera syrup, and it's brainwashed us into believing romance comes from a Fourth of July fireworks of feelings, blasted into the sky by a megacharge of hormones and heavy breathing. We sigh over those fuzzy Hallmark pictures of boy and girl romping through a meadow awash with daisies, and conclude we know the elements necessary to generate romance.

The marrieds we meet often voice these "the moon shone in June while you crooned our favorite toon" explanations of where romance comes from. One man we met in a marriage seminar wrote, "Romance is walking hand in hand on a moonlit beach with the wind blowing lightly in our faces—and our walk leading up back to our cottage where there awaits a fire, roses and satin sheets whispering our names."

But are these really the essential ingredients to step up romance? If they are, what happens the next morning when our twosome begins to fuss over the wrinkles in the satin sheets as they make the bed, then haggle back and forth about who's going to take out the ashes from the fireplace or give more water to the drooping roses?

And if it takes "you and the night and the music" in order for romance to thrive, then it must be true that God has given us a mandate for marriage that's impossible for us to fulfill. He did, after all, declare in Ephesians 5 that marriage was be a picture to the world of Christ's eternal romance with His bride, the Church. If the passionate partnership He wants for a man and wife always requires crackling fires, roses and satin sheets to survive, how can we possibly keep it alive in the harsh daylight when the mortgage payment is due on the ivy-covered cottage?

Where Does Romance Come From, Anyway?

The fire of romance that keeps Hallmark in business starts with a spark of "gimme." In other words, I'm attracted to a particular woman because of what she has to give me. Maybe I believe I'll finally feel important if someone as beautiful as this lovely woman will love *me*. Perhaps it's her warmth, or when she compliments me, that gives me a feeling of worth. Possibly her willingness to follow me gives me a sense of power or control. Or else her offer to lead makes me feel secure. I may see winning her love as my chance to capture a lifetime supply of the companionship, or lovemaking, or encouragement I long for. Whatever the reason, I want her for what she can do for me. These qualities in her make me want to give myself to win her. That's when the fireworks and romance rockets explode across the sky!

Of course, there's a catch to this dynamic. If I married my wife because I wanted a 38-24-38 knockout to parade before my friends, but three pregnancies have changed the curves of her girlish figure, then I stop giving to her. And when I stop giving, our romance fades.

Or if the strong leadership she was promised during our courtship begins to look more like domineering bossiness, then *she* quits giving, and romance stops living.

What results is a story that sounds like this:

Nice night in June
Stars shone, big moon
In park with girl.
Heart pound, head swirl
Me say "Love . . ."; she coo like dove
Me smart, me fast
Me not let chance pass
"Get hitched," me say.
She say, "Okay."
Wedding bells, ring, ring
Honeymoon, everything
Settle down, married life
Happy man, happy wife.
Another night in June
Stars shine, big moon
Ain't happy no more.
Carry baby, walk floor
Wife mad, she stew
Me mad, stew too.
Life one big spat
Nagging wife, bawling brat
Realize at last Me move too fast.

But we come bringing good news—no, *wonderful* news! Romance doesn't have to be fueled by "gimme" love. It can start with "serve-you" love, or what the Bible describes as a servant's heart. Observing this giving kind of love in action is what prompted me to write:

We believe a man and wife
Would have a better married life
If they would try out-serving one another.
For deeper love is felt
When what is done is not for self
But when it's done to satisfy the other.

Marriage isn't the act of choosing the one we'll *receive* from forever. It's selecting the one we'll *give* to for a lifetime. "Serve-you" love produces acts of giving that continue to stir up romance, whether great waves of mushy feeling come washing in with it or not.

The passion that arcs between Christ and His Church has less to do with emotion than it does with a mutual decision to give ourselves in service to each other. Jesus explained to His disciples, "The Son of Man did not come to be served, but to serve" (Mark 10:45). Lasting romance begins when a husband and wife start viewing marriage as a chance to meet each other's needs. This love springs from a heart that's grateful for Christ's lavish service to us. Though it often results in the kind of electricity Hallmark would call romantic, it can continue to survive even when the rushing tides of emotion have ebbed.

Before Annie and I were married, a wise friend passed on this piece of advice: "Steve, let all that you do and say be a service to her. Pleasing *her* should be your highest priority. Take no concern for your own satisfaction. If you do this, you'll be blessed with a relationship that is not only full of joy, but also most pleasing to the Lord."

To be honest, I've not found my friend's advice the easiest to follow. But I will agree that as I've chosen to focus on Annie's needs, a servant's heart *in action* does generate romance at its best!

Maybe your marriage started on the wrong foot, like the man I heard about who pleaded with his girlfriend, "Let's get married. I'm tired of being charming!" Even with a beginning as bad as that, you and your spouse can find yourselves, after five, ten, twenty or thirty years, enjoying the same freshness, love, respect and sense of adventure that newlyweds feel for each other. How? By learning to care for each other, listening to each other and meeting each other's changing needs. The romance doesn't have to wither. As a servant's heart replaces "gimme" love, your marriage can blossom and grow anew.

So, How Do I Get a Servant's Heart?

Daily life, its responsibilities and demands, does have a way of taking the steam out of you. Most men I know come home from a hard day of work and just want to relax. Because we feel as if we've been jumping all day to the demands of our boss, customers, fellow workers or the phone, we naturally feel as if we'd rather be left *alone*. And we forget that a woman's reaction to a tough day, or even a great day, is that she wants to share it with the man she loves. Who is going to make up the difference when this gap opens up?

Annie and I aren't marriage counselors. Nor are we psychologists or ordained ministers. But we are happily married. In the middle of a world where more than half the couples marrying will later decide to split up, we're together and growing. We're facing the same money pressures and job struggles and parenting hassles as others do—but we're pressing on and (most of the time!) enjoying the journey.

Of course we've uncovered our share of what looked like irreconcilable differences. But for the most part, we've found ways to turn those differences into reasons why we need each other more.

We want to help you find what we've found and, more than that, equip you to enjoy the particular romance God designed for you and your mate. Our guide? It's certainly not the world around us, where married men sport bumper stickers on their cars with slogans like, "It used to be wine, woman and song. Now it's beer, the old lady and television."

We're not simply drawing on the examples of other Christian couples, either. The expert we've consulted is better than these. He's available 'round the clock, understands us better than we do ourselves, has all wisdom, and wants to involve Himself totally with us—all without making us feel foolish or guilty.

You've probably guessed, we're talking about Jesus.

Jesus doesn't expect us to pour out love from an empty bucket. He wants to fill our lives with His love, and from that fullness we can give. When Christ wanted to set a powerful example of service to His disciples, He drew on God's resource. The Scripture says, "Jesus, knowing that the Father had given all things into His hands, and that He had come forth from God and was going back to God," humbled Himself and washed the dirty feet of His followers (see John 13:3ff., NASB).

Jesus' needs were met by God. Therefore, He could give unselfishly. As we look to Him to meet our needs, we can then have all we require, plus the love we need to serve our mates.

It doesn't take much to acquire a servant's heart, really. First, we simply have to admit our need. Christ came to heal the diseased, not those who are already whole. We can't become eligible to receive His work in our hearts unless we admit our selfishness and inability to change ourselves into the givers we want to be.

Maybe you're not sure what a servant's heart looks like because you've never seen one in action. Perhaps your parents were not the best example of what it means to love with selfless devotion.

If that's the case, we can still look to the greatest servant of all, Jesus, for a perfect model to follow. He served us as He resisted temptation in order to live a sinless life. He served us as He allowed Himself to be brutally nailed to a cross so He could redeem us. And He now serves us in heaven as He intercedes for us with the Father. He can show us how to serve, and then empower us to do it. All we need to do is ask for His help.

If you admit your need and ask God to do surgery on your selfishness, you can expect Him to say yes! He's promised never to turn away those who seek Him. If you commit yourself to serve your spouse in *God's* strength, He will commit Himself to help you. And help you He will. You've chosen to align yourself with the design of heaven when you decide to learn to give, so heaven will align itself with you. God may reward your efforts by changing your mate in ways that please you. Or He may change *you* instead. Or both. In any case, you'll win, because when you give for Jesus' sake, He guarantees you will receive.

No matter how good—or bad—your marriage is today, you can begin at once to change for the better by learning to serve your spouse. Then you'll no longer need to ask, "Where did the romance go?"

Conclusion

Dr. Gary Chapman is a world-renowned speaker, author and seminar leader. He hosts a nationally syndicated radio program, "A Growing Marriage," and is the senior associate pastor and marriage counselor at Calvary Baptist Church in Winston-Salem, North Carolina. Chapman is the author of *The Five Love Languages*, which has topped the best-seller charts for years. His books, including *Loving Solutions* (a 1999 Gold Medallion Book Award recipient) and *The Five Love Languages of Teenagers* (a 2001 Gold Medallion Book Award recipient), have sold over 3 million copies.

Books
Covenant Marriage
The Five Love Languages (also video)
The Five Love Languages of Children
  (also video)
The Five Love Languages for Singles
The Five Love Languages of Teenagers
  (also video)
Five Signs of a Loving Family
Hope for the Separated
The Love Languages of God (also
  video)
Love Talks for Couples
Love Talks for Families
Loving Solutions
*The Other Side of Love: Handling
  Anger in a Godly Way*
Parenting Your Adult Child
Toward a Growing Marriage
*The World's Easiest Guide to Family
  Relationships*

Study Guide
Building Relationships

Video
Toward a Growing Marriage

Media
Host of *A Growing Marriage*, a
  nationally syndicated radio
  program

Web
www.fivelovelanguages.com

*K*arolyn B. Chapman is the wife of Dr. Gary Chapman, the mother of daughter Shelley and son Derek and the grandmother of Davy Grace and Elliot Isaac. She attended Temple College in Chattanooga, Tennessee, and Catawba College in Salisbury, North Carolina. She studied vocal music while at Salem College in Winston-Salem, North Carolina.

Chapman is a motivational and inspirational speaker for conferences and seminar as well as a speaker and soloist for ladies' retreats and luncheons. She has lead such seminars as Discovering Your Self-Worth, Making Every Day Count and Celebrating Life Today.

Her personal story was featured in *Challenge* magazine and *Home Life* magazine, and she was listed in "Personalities of the South." She has served as a volunteer for the Winston-Salem Contact Telephone Service and on the board of a Christian women's club. She travels abroad extensively.

A Letter of Encouragement

Conclusion

Gary and Karolyn Chapman

To the couples who read this book:

We have been married to each other for forty-two years. To be very honest, not all of them have been happy years. In fact, the first several were pretty miserable. Our personalities are very different, and we often found ourselves in conflict, sometimes over small issues and sometimes over big ones. There were times when we wondered how we could go on. Both of us were depleted emotionally and at times had little desire to work on our marriage.

Looking back, we both agree that it was our *faith in God* that kept us going. We were not very confident in our own abilities, but we did believe that He had the answers. In desperation we both sought God's help. In the process of reaching out to Him, we found our attitudes toward each other changing. We asked God to give us a spirit of understanding and a willingness to serve each other. We started listening to really hear what the other person was saying and looking for ways to help each other.

In time, warm emotions returned to our relationship, and we began to enjoy being with each other again. Eventually we discovered that the real key to building a successful marriage is *learning to serve*. For many years now, we have taken great joy in making life easier for each other. Love stimulates love.

The rewards for "sticking it out" through the hard times have been abundant. We thank God every day for His grace that taught us how to genuinely love each other. Our children are also benefactors. We remember the day our son came home from college and said to us, "I want to thank you guys for staying together. So many of my friends did not want to go home over the holidays because their parents are split and they don't feel comfortable with either parent. I know you had some hard times, but thanks for working through the problems and staying together. I love coming home." Yes, it was worth the hard work of learning to listen, understand and love.

This book contains the information you need to build a healthy marriage. Ask God for the wisdom and power to apply these principles, and you can have a successful marriage.

—Gary and Karolyn Chapman